Derbyshire Feet of Fines 1323-1546

Calendared by H. J. H. Garratt
Introduction by Carole Rawcliffe

Derbyshire Record Society
Volume XI, 1985

Published by the Derbyshire Record Society
9 Caernarvon Close, Chesterfield, Derbyshire

First published 1985

ISBN 0 946324 04 2

Produced for the Society by
Alan Sutton Publishing Ltd.
Printed in Great Britain

Typeset on a Monotype Lasercomp
at Oxford University Computing Service

CONTENTS

NOTE

Between 1885 and 1896 a calendar of 683 Derbyshire feet of fines was published in instalments in the *Journal* of the Derbyshire Archaeological and Natural History Society, Vols. VII to XVIII, extending from the beginning of the series in the twelfth century down to 1323. This volume continues the publication of the same documents to the end of the reign of Henry VIII. The Record Society hopes at a later date to issue a new edition of the earlier fines and the documents printed here have for this reason been assigned serial numbers beginning at 684. The proposed second volume will also contain Derbyshire material from among the fines filed under 'Divers Counties' in the same class at the Public Record Office.

INTRODUCTION

By the early fourteenth century, when this volume begins, the judicial process culminating in the issue of a fine had become highly formalised, as the precise legal phraseology of the documents themselves reveals.[1] Whereas the earliest fines, dating from the 1180s onwards, were usually the result of a genuine disagreement over the ownership of lands, rents or franchises, and evolved as a means of settling potentially disruptive quarrels, later models came to adopt the fiction of litigation. Thus, although couched in terms of 'querens' and 'deforciant', they were in fact the outcome of a collusive rather than a real lawsuit. This is not to deny that many fines were indeed obtained in order to terminate disputes, but the actual procedure could not be instigated until a definite agreement had been reached by the parties as to the disposal of the assets in question. To levy a fine it was first necessary for the querens (or grantee) to sue out a writ of covenant in the court of Common Pleas at Westminster, obliging the deforciant (or grantor) to adhere to the terms of a pre-arranged (but effectively fictitious) contract. The parties then obtained a *licentia concordandi*, or leave to agree, which allowed them to move into open court and reach a formal concord. The latter was drawn up by an attorney and was either read aloud before the justices, or else taken in the county where the property lay by a *dedimus potestatem*. The ordinance of the Carlisle Parliament of 1307, permitting the judges of the Common Pleas to send 'some legally experienced man' to hear concords on their behalf in the outlying regions, suggests that by this date the pressure of business in the court and the attendant delays which ensued had already become a matter of concern to the Lords and Commons alike — the members of both Houses being, indeed, the very people most likely to avail themselves of this type of transaction.[2] The bureaucratic element was considerable, for at this stage in the proceedings the chirographer, or clerk, was required to make a note of the text of the concord, preparatory to engrossing it three times in a special way on a single piece of parchment. Two of the texts were written head to head, at right-angles to the third, while the word 'cyrographum' was inscribed in large letters in the two margins between the texts. Finally, the parchment was cut in three along indented lines, this being a precaution against forgery.[3] The two facing copies were handed to the querens and deforciant respectively as deeds of title, and the third part at the bottom (hence the term *pes* or 'foot') was kept by the *custos brevium* and filed in the records of the court of Common Pleas. To expedite this process and to facilitate retrieval should it prove necessary — as was often the case — to produce the foot of fine as evidence in court, a note of the county, or counties, in which the property lay was made beneath the text in a bold, clear hand. (It is important to remember that fines concerning premises in more than one county are now arranged in a separate series known as 'divers counties' at the end of the class CP 25(1) (fines) in the Public Record Office, while the rest are filed alphabetically by county.) As a further deterrent against fraud the fine was read aloud in the court in the four law terms following the engrossment, and a record of this was endorsed at the foot.

Although they vary much as to content, final concords (which actually take their name from the opening words *'hec est finalis concordia')* always conform to the same basic pattern. Each document is dated by law term and regnal year, and gives the name of the judges before whom the agreement was read. The name(s) of the plaintiff(s) are followed by those of the defendant(s) — place of residence, *aliases*, trades, professions and social rank often being specified in the interests of clear identification. A brief description of the property or rights at issue is then given, sometimes with interesting details about life-estates held by dowagers or younger sons, and occasionally accompanied by a note of services either due to or incumbent upon the new owner. The great majority of fines end with an admission of right, whereby the defendant recognises the title of the plaintiff, releases the estate to him and grants him a warranty (thus effectively underwriting his title).[4] While engrossing this kind of fine, the chirographer would note on each copy the amount of money or 'consideration' which the grantee had, in theory, paid for the property. By our period, this sum was as much a fiction as the processs of suing out the fine itself, although in the late twelfth and early thirteenth centuries the consideration did represent a real payment. With the passage of time, however, the figure came to be calculated automatically at twenty times the maximum sworn annual value of the estate — a figure which the chirographer himself could work out on the basis of (not necessarily accurate) information already made available to him. Bearing in mind that the asking price for land during the later middle ages was usually about ten times its annual value, it will be readily appreciated that the consideration represents an unrealistically high sum in terms of the contemporary property market, although these figures are not without interest in that they give us an idea of comparative land values.[5] Somewhat less common than the fine *sur droit* is the double fine, in which an admission of right is followed by the conveyance *back* to the original grantor of all or part of the estate. This format was customarily employed to entail land upon a younger son, daughter or person other than the right heir to the property, and tended, as a result, to be used by those with fairly extensive territorial interests who could afford to hive off part of their possessions.[6]

As with so many other aspects of the medieval legal system, the Crown found ample opportunity to profit out of this complicated process. Not only was it entitled to claim one-tenth of the annual value of the land concerned as a *primer fine* before the writ of concord could be issued; but in addition half this sum again (the *post fine*, known more commonly as 'King's Silver') was demanded for a *licentia concordandi*. Since both steps were essential preliminaries to the engrossing of the fine itself, the revenues which accrued were substantial. The inevitable *douceurs* in the form of tips and gifts to court officials who expected to be rewarded at every stage increased the cost even further, and consequently placed the fine beyond the means of the less affluent.[7]

Why, we may ask, was the medieval landowner prepared to lay out a sizeable sum of money on a cumbersome and apparently outmoded legal practice? One of the great advantages of the fine to the grantee and grantor alike was the availability of incontrovertible proof of their transaction in the records of the central courts; and we, too, are fortunate that third copies were made, as most of those in private hands have now been lost or dispersed far away from the county of origin. But the final concord performed a more important function than simply providing a safeguard against loss or forgery. Not least was the fact that a party to a fine was compellable at law to perform the covenants which it contained. During the earlier period it was possible to sue out a writ *de fine tenendo* or *de tenendo fine facto*, whereby anyone who had infringed the terms of a fine by which they were bound could be forced in the courts to observe and perform them. By the mid-fourteenth century, however, this particular instrument had fallen out of use, its place having been taken by the less specific but generally more adaptable writ of *scire facias*.[8] There was, furthermore, a growing tendency as the Court of Chancery became more popular for cases regarding the implementation of fines to be heard there.[9] The solemn and binding obligation which the final concord imposed upon the grantor and grantee alike, together with the recognition accorded to it at law, meant that fines were often used to secure the titles of persons who had successfully advanced a claim to property in the courts or through arbitration. The settlement of the manor of Callow on Thomas and Elizabeth Stathum in 1386 (**963**) serves as a case in point, for the Stathums had previously been involved in litigation at the Derby assizes with the Staffordshire landowner, Sir Philip Okeover, who had himself made an enfeoffment of the manor some four years earlier, and had only relinquished his claim after a long fight. His son, Thomas, was evidently prepared to confirm the Stathums in possession through a collusive suit in 1407, but no less than thirty-six years passed before he abandoned all hope and agreed to release his title by a fine (**1095**). Since, as we shall see, this document did not necessarily prevent his next heirs from trying their luck, it was by then of limited value.[10]

The most important, and indeed the most distinctive, characteristic of the fine was that until the introduction of modifying legislation in Edward III's reign it effectively barred all claims made to the property concerned after the statutory year and a day allowed for any rival claimants to come forward and state their title. In the words of the *Modus Levandi Fines*, generally attributed to the reign of Edward I:[11]

> Fine est si haute bare et de si graunt force et de si puissaunt nature en soi qu'el forclos, nemye soulement ceux qui sount parties et prives a la fine et lour heirs, mes touz autres gentz que sount de plein age, hors du prisone, de bone memoire, et dedeinz les quatres meers le jour de le fine leve, s'ils ne mettrount lour clayme de lout accion (sur la pie) dedeinz l'an et le jour.

These sweeping powers proved rather a mixed blessing, and it was in order to establish what was effectively a preclusive bar that the Statute of Non-claim of 34 Edward III, c. 16, was introduced. Henceforward a fine could act only as an estoppel to the parties immediately concerned (or privies), and strangers possessing a reasonable title were free to contest or circumvent the terms of the final concord. An interesting example of this is to be found in the dispute between Alice Shirley and her step-mother, Isabel, the second wife of Sir John Cockayne (d. 1438) of Ashbourne. In the Michaelmas term of 1432, just after their marriage, Sir John settled upon Isabel a life-interest in the two manors of Harthill and Middleton, which he had inherited from his mother (**1085**), but had previously entailed upon his adult daughter, Alice. After his death, Isabel married the influential lawyer, Thomas Bate, and was confirmed in possession of her jointure by her son, John Cockayne the younger. Her step-daughter proved less accommodating, however, and began litigation against Isabel for the two manors, which she claimed with some justice as her rightful inheritance. The local gentlemen who gave evidence in the case based their testimony *solely* upon Sir John's will and the pronouncements made by him 'on his dethe bedde'; and when the matter was finally submitted to arbitration in 1458 a compromise solution independent of the terms of the fine had to be reached.[12]

It has been suggested that the Statute of Non-claim, which simultaneously weakened the authority of the fine and strengthened the hand of those who were powerful enough to get their own way by brute force or the maintenance of influential friends, was a contributory factor to the lawlessness of the later middle ages.[13] Certainly, far fewer people chose to employ the final concord as a means of conveying property *after* 1360 than had done so before; and it was no doubt to redress this state of affairs and check the proliferation of vexatious suits that Henry VII introduced the First Statute of Fines, 4 Henry VII, c. 24, by which the ancient bar was reintroduced, albeit in a somewhat modified form, giving married women, strangers and persons who had rights by force of an entail five years to assert their claims. As the evidence of this volume shows, the Statute of Non-claim did indeed undermine the popularity of the final concord, for whereas between 1323 and 1359 a total of 180 fines regarding property in Derbyshire alone were levied in the court of Common Pleas (that is an average of five a year), only 276 are recorded during the far longer period of 1360 to 1489 (a fall in the yearly average to just over two). The First Statute of Fines led to a noticeable improvement in this state of affairs, and during the fifty-seven years before the death of Henry VIII the yearly average rises again to almost four. These statistics should, however, be seen in the wider context of English population trends; and we must remember that the consequences of the Black Death and successive late fourteenth-century epidemics made themselves felt throughout the rest of the middle ages.

That the final concord was never entirely abandoned during the late fourteenth and fifteenth centuries was in part due to another, more permanent advantage — namely, its provision of a sound legal title to a married woman who wished to sell or otherwise dispose of land. Whereas a widow could easily repudiate an ordinary charter made during her marriage on the grounds that while her husband lived she had no will of her own, and had therefore been coerced, such an objection could not retrospectively be raised by her to the terms of a final concord.[14] Because of this, the fine offered a remarkable degree of flexibility which made it suitable for a wide range of transactions from simple enfeoffments to entails, sales, mortgages and family settlements. It could be used, on the one hand, to bestow upon her a greater share of her husband's property than that to which she was legally entitled. The partition of estates between female heirs was, likewise, often effected by means of a fine, as, for instance in 1391, when Alice and Margery, the two sisters and coheiresses of Sir John Sulny, made an enfeoffment of rents worth £12 p.a. and the advowson of Pinxton and Normanton preparatory to a division between themselves and their respective husbands, Sir Thomas Stafford and Sir Nicholas Longford (**971, 972**). The manor itself, however, was subsequently reapportioned by means of a collusive suit in the court of Common Pleas, presumably because this offered a greater security of title.[15] The death of Ralph, Lord Cromwell, without issue in 1455 was similarly followed by a settlement of his extensive estates on his two nieces and next heirs, Maud and Joan Stanhope, who shared, *inter alios*, the manor and advowson of West Hallam (**1124**).[16] For a number of reasons, therefore, women frequently appear as parties to fines;

and this adds greatly to the value of such documents for the social and economic historian, as well as the genealogist.

Scholars have long recognised the importance of the foot of fine as a means of tracing the descent of manors and smaller properties, although its usefulness extends to many other areas as well. With certain notable exceptions, the gentry and yeomanry of medieval England are not well served as regards the survival of large collections of family papers. The study of their wealth, influence, relationships and connexions must, consequently, be approached through a variety of disparate source material, both local and central, final concords being particularly informative in this respect because of the amount of personal data which they can be made to reveal. A number of Derbyshire fines provide detailed — and sometimes otherwise unrecorded — evidence about family history, especially in cases where successive remainders were settled by parents upon younger children in the event of the death without issue of the eldest son and heir presumptive (as in **700, 824, 829** and **1097**). Genealogical evidence of this kind is hard to come by outside wills, which survive in comparatively small numbers for the Derbyshire gentry, and rarely for the lower orders; and although of limited use for demographic purposes it is invaluable for the local historian. So, too, are those interesting cases where one can establish the descent of a property over three or even more generations as a result of the precise arrangements for succession made when the fine was drawn up (as in **696, 1284, 1312** and **1332**). Marriage to wealthy widows possessed of jointures and dowers from previous husbands was an accepted way for ambitious men to obtain influence in their communities; and fines often disclose information about the former marriages and assets of these ladies. We learn, for example, that Katherine, the second wife of that eminent Lancastrian retainer, Sir Roger Leche, was not only the widow of another distinguished servant of Henry IV, Sir Hugh Waterton, but also of Sir John Bromwich (a fact which comes to light in fine **1045**), who had been surveyor of the estates which Henry held as a young man in the 1380s.[17] The Staffordshire landowner, Roger Bradshaw, owed his Derbyshire property — and, implicitly, his return to parliament for the latter county in 1406 — to his marriage to Elizabeth, a daughter and co-heir of Ralph Meynell, whose previous husband, William Crawshaw, had also added appreciably to her holdings. Again, it is through a fine (**1020**) that evidence of this earlier, profitable union appears. The need to ensure a firm title at law led to the setting out of many marriage and dower settlements in the form of final concords, such as that made upon Sir Nicholas Montgomery and his wife, Anne, when they wed in 1364 (**874**). The history of the Montgomery family is in fact well documented here, as another fine, engrossed ten years later, notes some of the properties held in dower by Sir Nicholas's widowed mother; and we also have a record of the jointure settled by his son and heir, another Sir Nicholas, upon his own wife just before he died (**920** and **1086**).

Final concords do not only tell us about the arrangements following the marriages and deaths of landowners: they also help us to date these and other important events more precisely. The second marriage of Henry, Lord Grey of Codnor (d. 1496), is, for instance, generally said to have taken place in 1474,[18] but we know from a Derbyshire fine, engrossed during the Michaelmas term of 1473, that he and his new wife had already then been married for some time (**1121**). We can, likewise, establish a more accurate date for the marriage of John, Lord Audley (dead by 1558), which is otherwise only documented in an unreliable family pedigree, *and* confirm that his wife was indeed Mary, the daughter of John Griffin of Braybrooke, rather than one of the other ladies whom antiquaries have described as being married to this obscure member of the baronage (**1216**).[19] Again, whereas the death of Elizabeth, the wife of William, Lord Ferrers of Groby (d. 1445), has previously been given as occurring early in 1442, she was demonstrably still alive three years later, when the manor of Breadsall was settled by her and her husband on trustees (**1103**).[20]

Because they were so often used to convey property to feoffees chosen from among the grantor's closest and most influential friends, fines can provide an illuminating insight into the political connexions of the parties concerned; and, moreover, can enable us to trace the developments of the ties of 'good lordship' which were so important during the later middle ages. In the fourteenth century the greatest landowners in Derbyshire were the Dukes of Lancaster, who, most notably in the person of John of Gaunt, sought to enlist leading members of the local gentry into their service. That recruitment could begin at a comparatively early age is clear from a fine of 1365 (**879**), whereby John de la Pole of Hartington acquired the office of forester of Gaunt's free chase at Crowdecote. Pole, who had only just succeeded to the family estates, later went on to lease property from Gaunt, and eventually became bailiff, surveyor and steward of the Duchy lordship of the High Peak; but this document gives us our first evidence of what was to prove a mutually beneficial attachment.[21] This is also the case with regard to a settlement made in 1370 of the inheritance of Sir Thomas Wensley (**902**), who chose the Duke of Lancaster to act as his remainderman. Sir Thomas subsequently joined Gaunt's bodyguard, as well as occupying the stewardship and constableship of the High Peak. Having raised an armed force in support of Gaunt's son, Henry of Bolingbroke, in 1399, he fell at the battle of Shrewsbury four years later, fighting to uphold the Lancastrian cause. We may further note that one of Wensley's trustees in 1370 was his kinsman, Sir Godfrey Foljambe the younger, whose father was then steward of the entire Duchy of Lancaster and a leading member of Gaunt's council.[22] The Derbyshire knights and esquires who wore the Lancastrian livery formed a close-knit fellowship, constantly involved in each other's affairs. John Cockayne's enfeoffment of the manor of Bearwardcote in 1402 (**1010**) reveals a choice of trustees entirely in keeping with his position as a prominent servant of Henry IV (he was then chief baron of the Exchequer), for among those to whom he conveyed his manor were John Leventhorpe, receiver general of the Duchy of Lancaster, Sir Thomas Rempston, a former standard bearer of the king and steward of the royal household, and Sir John Leeke, Rempston's brother-in-law and a noted Lancastrian sympathiser.[23] No other noble family was able to exercise even a small proportion of the influence enjoyed in Derbyshire by the Dukes of Lancaster (who, after 1399, had the added advantage of being kings of England), simply because none possessed a sufficiently large territorial base in the county to recruit support there. Leading gentry families were, in consequence, able to build up substantial followings made up of those who, under other circumstances, might have sought the patronage of a neighbouring lord. These connexions, too, are revealed in fines such as that involving Sir Richard Vernon and the lawyer, Richard Brown of Repton, who acted together in 1436 as trustees of the manor of Willington (**1088**). Brown, who was described by his contemporaries as 'no less than a common embracer and procurer of juries', was one of Vernon's feed men, and had previously been indicted with him for illegal sales of cloth.[24]

Although, as we have seen, the fine was too costly a means of conveying property to be employed by the smallholder or peasant proprietor, its continued popularity with yeomen, gentry and nobility alike enhances our understanding of the structure and relative affluence of the middle and upper reaches of a county community. A combination of geographical and social factors made the Derbyshire gentry a self-contained and independent group, the majority of whom had fairly limited territorial interests. Unlike their neighbours in Staffordshire, they were not subject to the restraining influence of a strong, resident magnate; for the Dukes of Lancaster, although a valuable source of patronage and advancement, rarely visited the county, and neither the Lords Grey of Codnor nor the Blounts, Lords Mountjoy, who did maintain a local presence, were sufficiently powerful to dominate the community. The comparative infrequency during the fourteenth and fifteenth centuries of fines involving members of the peerage (even as trustees) underlines this fact; and even though the sixteenth century begins with a settlement of the Grey of Codnor estates upon an impressive group of feoffees (**1163**), the nobility still appear on only a few occasions. These circumstances encouraged the emergence of a ruling caste of knightly families, recently estimated to number about thirty, but clearly led by an inner group of whom such as the Vernons, Foljambes, Longfords, Cockaynes, Gresleys and Montgomerys were the richest and most powerful.[25] Their wealth and importance as landowners was, however, relative, for medieval Derbyshire was a very poor county, and, with the exception of men of the stamp of Sir Richard Vernon, few could stand comparison with their peers in, say, Lincolnshire, Yorkshire or Essex, where a landed income well in excess of £150 p.a. was by no means unusual. Moreover, whereas in the Home Counties fines involving whole groups of manors and extensive blocks of farmland are quite common — the property market being made all the more buoyant by the presence of London merchants anxious to invest their profits in land — in Derbyshire only nine fines (all after 1500) convey a title to three or more manors with their appurtenances, and of these one third (**1268, 1277** and **1278**) constitute a settlement of the Longford estates. Indeed, of the 675 fines in this volume, less than thirty name two whole manors (and, predictably, tend to concern the richer families listed above), while just over a hundred relate to the transfer of one single manor. Although quite substantial properties are conveyed in some of the other fines, the great majority deal with fairly modest holdings; and this is exactly what one would expect of a county where gentry estates were small and compact, constituting a few manors at most, and where large areas were given over to relatively unprofitable animal husbandry centred on farms and hamlets rather than larger manorial units. Several landowners did, in fact, seek to consolidate their estates by purchase, and some, like John Port and Henry Vernon, bought and sold extensively in the late fifteenth century, but on the whole the demand for land in Derbyshire was limited where agricultural holdings were concerned, and only a small proportion of the fines calendared here record ourright sales. One exception does, however, merit our attention. Derby was not only the county town but also the main economic centre of Derbyshire; and by the later middle ages it boasted a wide variety of commercial interests, trading in wool, dyestuffs and the lead produced locally in increasing quantities from the mid-fifteenth century onwards.[26] There was, evidently, a continuous demand for property in the town, and many of the richer burgesses — like John Stokkes, a merchant of the Calais Staple, who ploughed the profits of wool back into land[27] — were anxious to expand as *rentiers* into the surrounding countryside. Over seventy fines are concerned with land, tenements, shops or rents in Derby; and there seems to have been a fairly regular turn-over of assets in and around the town. To a lesser extent the same is true of Chesterfield (twenty-five fines), although it never came near to rivalling Derby's predominance.

One of the major problems encountered when using the final concord as a source of historical evidence is that of discovering the exact purpose for which the fine was made. In some cases the nature of the settlement or entail is fairly straightforward, but it is often impossible to determine the real nature of the enfeoffment, mortgage, sale or transfer without other documentation in the form of wills, inquisitions *post mortem*, deeds or legal records. The conveyance of land in Ashbourne, Offcote and Underwood in 1500 to John Kniveton and others (**1156**) is a good example of this, since without the will of Kniveton's wife, Anne, we would not know that the property in question was to be used for the endowment of a chantry, and that the parties to the fine were Anne's most trusted friends.[28] The death of Henry, Lord Grey of Codnor, in 1496 without legitimate issue led to a partition of his estates whereby the Nottinghamshire and Derbyshire manors were assigned in reversion upon the death of his widow to Sir John Zouche. The counterpart of an indenture of July 1501 reveals, however, that before he died Grey actually arranged for the property to be sold to the king for the use of his son, Henry, Duke of York; and on 18 August following the trustees (including Zouche's father-in-law, Sir Henry Willoughby) had little alternative but to release their title preparatory to an outright sale. For greater security, the text of the deed was engrossed as a final concord in the next law term (**1163**), although it is worth noting that in 1508 Sir John was graciously permitted to buy back his inheritance for £1,400, leaving King Henry with a substantial profit. The fine itself reveals nothing of these somewhat dubious transactions, the nature of which comes to light elsewhere.[29]

Medieval legal records can often admit a number of possible interpretations, and feet of fines are no exception. They must always be read with caution, and cannot necessarily be taken at face value. Even so, they still constitute a major — yet even today greatly under-used — source of information; and they are particularly valuable for a county like Derbyshire where evidence for the later medieval and Tudor period is widely scattered and often difficult of access. The fines calendared here cover a period of over two centuries which saw the outbreak and conclusion of the Hundred Years' War, the Black Death, the civil discontent between Lancaster and York and the advent of the Tudors. None of these dramatic events is directly described — or even hinted at — in the precise legal language of the final concord; but it is, nonetheless, with the help of such apparently specialist records that we are able to reconstruct a picture of English society in transition.

CAROLE RAWCLIFFE

REFERENCES

1. I am indebted to Miss M. M. Condon of the Public Record Office for her help in writing this introduction.
2. *Statutes of the Realm*, I, p. 215.
3. Examples of the layout of this tripartite indenture may be found in the frontispieces to *Feet of Fines for Essex*, ed. R. E. G. Kirk (Essex Archaeological Society, 1899-1910), Vol. I; *Final concords of the county of Lincoln, 1244-1272*, ed. C. W. Foster (Lincoln Record Society, XVII, 1920); and D. Crook, *Records of the General Eyre*, Public Record Office Handbooks, no 20 (1982).
4. There were, in fact, four types of the fine *sur droit*, which are discussed fully, along with other aspects of the history and form of the fine by C. A. F. Meekings in his valuable 'Introduction to abstracts of Surrey feet of fines, 1509-1558', in Surrey Record Society, XIX (1946), passim.
5. For typical examples of the fine *sur droit* and the formalised consideration in this volume see **713, 736, 1123** and **1236**.
6. As, for instance, **696, 724, 731, 1072** and **1257**.
7. In about 1391, Thomas, Earl of Stafford, paid out £9 in expenses sustained in suing out a fine at Westminster to secure his title to certain land in Norfolk and Suffolk which he had inherited from Lord Basset of Drayton (Staffs Record Office, D641/1/2/4 m. 4).
8. See *The Reports of Sir John Spelman*, ed. J. H. Baker, Selden Society, XCIII (1977), p. 113; XCIV (1978), p. 312.
9. As, for example, the case of William Smythe vs. William Tournoure over the terms of a fine regarding the manor of Brokenborough in Gloucestershire (Public Record Office, C 1/12/62).
10. *A Catalogue of Derbyshire Charters*, ed. I. H. Jeayes (London and Derby, 1906), no 1645; Public Record Office, JUST 1/1488 rot. 33, 64-64d, 1514 rot. 69, 70d, 71-71d; G. Wrottesley, 'Extracts from the Plea Rolls of the reigns of Edward III and Richard II', *William Salt Archaeological Society*, XIII (1892), pp. 184-5, 188-9, 195.
11. *Statutes of the Realm*, I, p. 214.
12. A. E. Cockayne, *Cockayne Memoranda* (Congleton, 1869), pt I, p. 17; *Cal. Close Rolls, 1413-19*, p. 427; *Derbyshire Charters*, no 218; *Pedigrees from the Plea Rolls*, ed. G. Wrottesley (London, 1905), p. 379; *Historical Manuscripts Commission, Rutland IV*, p. 52; Manuscripts of His Grace the Duke of Rutland at Belvoir Castle, Deeds, nos 293, 4453, 4561.
13. Meekings, op.cit., pp. xxvi-xxvii.
14. J. H. Baker, *An Introduction to English legal history* (2nd ed., 1979), p. 396.
15. *Derbyshire Charters*, nos 233, 1868, 1869; G. Wrottesley, 'Extracts from the Plea Rolls of the reigns of Richard II and Henry IV', *William Salt Archaeological Society*, XV (1894), p. 44.
16. G. E. Cockayne, *The Complete Peerage*, ed. V. Gibbs et al. (1910-59), III, pp. 552-3.
17. R. Somerville, *History of the Duchy of Lancaster* (1953, 1970), I, pp. 417, 419.
18. *The Complete Peerage*, VI, p. 131.
19. Ibid., I, p. 342.
20. Ibid., V, p. 356.
21. Somerville, op.cit., I, p. 382; *John of Gaunt's Register, 1379-1383*, ed. R. Somerville and E. Lodge (Camden Society, 3rd series (1937), LVI, LVII), I, nos 112-3, II, nos 946, 1060.
22. Somerville, op.cit., I, pp. 366, 382, 550; *John of Gaunt's Register*, I, p. 9 and no 590; N. B. Lewis, 'Indentures of retinue with John of Gaunt, Duke of Lancaster', *Camden Miscellany*, XXII (1964), p. 92; Public Record Office, DL 42/15, f. 70d.
23. *Expeditions to Prussia and the Holy Land made by Henry, Earl of Derby*, ed. L. Toulmin Smith (Camden Society, new series (1894), LII), pp. 106, 131, 304; *Rotuli Parliamentorum*, III, p. 553; R. L. Storey, 'English officers of state, 1399-1485', *Bulletin of the Institute of Historical Research*, XXI (1958), p. 87; *Plumpton Correspondence*, ed. T. Stapleton (Camden Society, 1st series (1839), IV), p. xxviii.

24. Public Record Office, KB 9/11 m. 15; *Cal. Fine Rolls, 1437-45*, p. 175; S. M. Wright, *The Derbyshire gentry in the fifteenth century* (Derbyshire Record Society, VIII, 1983), pp. 129-33.
25. Wright, op.cit., pp. 3-6 and Appendix I.
26. In 1380, the parliamentary burgesses of Derby (the only town in the shire to return members to the House of Commons in the middle ages) asserted that it was *'la meilloure ville du dite countee'* (*Rotuli Parliamentorum*, III, p. 95).
27. As fines **1029**, **1053**, **1069** and **1078** reveal. For Stokkes's involvement in the Calais Staple see *Cal. Pat. Rolls, 1422-9*, pp. 348, 432.
28. Wright, op.cit., pp. 205, 236.
29. *The Complete Peerage*, VI, p. 132; *Cal. Ancient Deeds*, V, nos A10747-8, A13484.

ACKNOWLEDGEMENTS

I would like to express my thanks to all those whose help has enabled me to prepare a much fuller and more useful calendar than I could otherwise have done. In particular, to Carole Rawcliffe for many hours spent in the Public Record Office peering at MSS by ultra-violet light and subsequently suggesting additions and corrections. To Miss Sinar and her staff at the Derbyshire Record Office for considerable help in identifying and pin-pointing place-names. To the staff of numerous other record offices and libraries similar help. To my sister for the many hours spent helping to prepare index cards and checking the typescript for spelling errors, and not least to Mrs Sylvia Thomas, archivist to the Yorkshire Archaeological Society, for her help in enabling me to achieve sufficient ability in reading medieval Latin to make this project possible in the first place. To all these people, my very sincere thanks.

H.J.H.G.

ABBREVIATIONS

a.	acre(s)
bov.	bovate(s)
chiv.	chivaler
cit.	citizen
esq.	esquire
ext.p.	extra-parochial
gent.	gentleman
h.w.	his wife
jun.	junior
kt	knight
mess.	messuage(s)
p.	parish
r.	rood(s)
sen.	senior
virg.	virgate(s)

For an explanation of 'P' (Plaintiff) and 'D' (Deforciant) see above, p. v.

DERBYSHIRE FEET OF FINES

EDWARD II

CP 25/1/38/29

684. York. Quindene of Michaelmas 1323. P: Roger de Somervill and Margery h.w. D: Master Robert de Wydmerpol. Concerning the manor of Blakwell. Robert had the manor of the gift of Roger and he granted and rendered it to Roger and Margery to hold to themselves and Roger's heirs of the chief lord etc forever. (151)

685. York. Quindene of Michaelmas 1323. P: Richard son of Benedict de Shakilcros. D: Adam son of William de Fernileygh. Concerning 1 mess., 30a. land, 30a. pasture, 8½d rent and a rent of 1 arrowhead in Overfarnileygh. Adam remised, quitclaimed and warranted these of himself and his heirs to Richard and his heirs forever. Richard gave 20 marks of silver. (152)

686. Westminster. Quindene of Hilary 1325. P: John son of Stephen le Eyre of Chestrefeld by Roger de Bakewell his attorney. D: William son of John de Kynwaldmersh and Maude h.w. Concerning 1 mess. and 1 bov. land in Barlebrugh. John had these of the gift of William and Maude to hold to himself and his heirs of the chief lord etc forever. William and Maude warranted for themselves and the heirs of Maude. John gave 20 marks of silver. (153)

687. Westminster. Octave of Hilary 1325. P: Ralph de Frechevill and Margaret h.w. by Robert de Whitewell attorney for Margaret by brief of the king. D: John de Herdeby, chaplain. Concerning the manor of Alwoston. John had the manor of the gift of Ralph and he granted and rendered it to Ralph and Margaret and the heirs of their bodies to hold of the chief lord etc forever. Remainder to the right heirs of Ralph. (154)

688. Westminster. Octave of Trinity 1325. P: Robert de Ingwardeby. D: William de Ingwardeby. Concerning the manor of Wyvelesleye. Robert had the manor of the gift of William and he granted and rendered it to William to hold of Robert and his heirs for the life of William paying therefor 1 rose each year at the feast of the Nativity of St John the Baptist for all services, customs and dues pertaining to Robert and his heirs and doing to the chief lord of that fee on behalf of Robert and his heirs all those other services pertaining to the manor for William's life. After William's death, the manor to revert to Robert and his heirs to hold of the chief lord etc forever. (155)

689. Westminster. Michaelmas 3 weeks 1324. P: Ralph de Frechevvill and Margaret h.w. by Robert de Whitewell attorney for Margaret. D: Peter de Retherby, chaplain. Concerning 2 parts of the manor of Staveleye and the advowson of the church of the same manor. Peter had these of the gift of Ralph and granted and rendered them to Ralph and Margaret and the male heirs of their bodies to hold of the king and his heirs etc forever. Remainder to the right heirs of Ralph. The agreement was made by order of the king. (156)

690. Westminster. Octave of Michaelmas 1324. P: Roger Beler. D: Ralph de Freschevvill. Concerning the manor of Cruche. Ralph rendered the manor to Roger (with the exception of the homage and services of the 30 people listed below) to hold to himself and his heirs of the king and his heirs etc forever. He also granted to Roger the homage and services aforesaid to hold to himself and his heirs etc and warranted the manor on behalf of himself and his heirs to Roger and his heirs forever. Roger gave £200. The agreement was made by order of the king. The 30 people whose homage and services were excepted were: the Abbot of [D]erleye, Nicholas de Longeford, kt, John de Herts, kt, Thomas de Chaworth, kt, John de Annesleye, kt, Adam de Reresby, kt, Geoffrey de Dethek, Peter de Wakebrugg, Robert de Codyngton, Ralph de Reresby, Henry de Musters, Richard le Heyward, Geoffrey de Plaghstowe, Alan le Thacker, William Bythewater, William Hamond, Simon son of Henry, Geoffrey le Coupere, Robert son of Henry, William vicar of the church of Cruche, Robert Kibble, John le Savage, William de Lyndale, Robert de Codyngton, Thomas le Mower, John le Clerk, John Kebble, John son of Nicholas, Robert son of Henry, and John Bythewater. Endorsed: Ralph son of Ralph de Frechevill lays his claim. (157)

691. Westminster. The morrow of the Purification 1326. P: John le Catour of Smalleye. Impedients: Nicholas de Caumnill of Amynton and Sarah h.w. Concerning 2 mess. and 28a. land in Smalleye. John had these of the gift of Nicholas and Sarah to hold to himself and his heirs of the chief lord etc forever. Nicholas warranted for himself and his heirs. John gave 10 marks of silver. (158)

692. Westminster. Octave of Hilary 1326. P: John Mareys, clerk. D: Nicholas Mareys and Joan h.w. Concerning 1 mess. and a moiety of 1 virgate of land in Ednynghale. Nicholas and Joan rendered these to John to hold to himself and his heirs of the chief lord etc forever, and warranted for themselves and the heirs of Joan. John gave 100 shillings of silver. (159)

693. Westminster. Quindene of Hilary 1326. P: Walter Waldeshef and Joan h.w. D: Robert Burdet and Elizabeth h.w. Concerning the manor of Howen (excepting 9 mess. and 5 virgates and 8a. land in the same manor). Robert and Elizabeth acknowledged the manor to be the right of Walter and remised and quitclaimed it of themselves and the heirs of Elizabeth to Walter, Joan and Walter's heirs. Walter and Joan gave £60. (160)

694. Westminster. Quindene of Easter 1326. P: Nicholas son of Simon de Cromford by Peter de Querndon, his attorney by brief of the king. Impedients: Henry son of William de Cromford and Joan h.w. Concerning 4 tofts, 2 bov. 22a. land and 14a. meadow in Cromford. Nicholas had these of the gift of Henry and Joan to hold to himself and heirs of the chief lord etc forever. Henry warranted for himself and his heirs. Nicholas gave 40 marks of silver. (161)

695. Westminster. The morrow of Ascension 1326. P: William de Hopton, junior and Joan h.w. by Reginald de Ingwardby attorney for Joan. D: Roger de Baukwell. Concerning 4 mess., 8 bov. land and 40s rent in Hopton, Kersinton, Allerwasshelegh, Knyveton and Wynster. Roger had these of the gift of William and he granted and rendered them to William and Joan to hold to themselves and the heirs of their bodies of the chief lord etc forever. Remainder to the right heirs of William. (162)

696. Westminster. Octave of Trinity 1326. P: John de Heritz. D: Thomas de la Forche, clerk, and Robert de Senland. Concerning the manors of Tybesshelf and Wynefeld. John acknowledged the manors to be the right of Thomas who, with Robert, had them of the gift of John. Thomas and Robert granted and rendered them to John to hold for his life, the manor of Tybesshelf of the king and his heirs and of the honour of Peverill, and the manor of Wynefeld of the chief lord etc. Remainder to Roger Beler for life. Remainder to Roger son of Roger Beler and Margaret, daughter of Richard de la Ryvere, kt, senior and the heirs of their bodies. Remainder to Thomas son of Roger Beler and Margaret, junior, daughter of the same Richard de la Ryvere and the heirs of their bodies. Remainder to the right heirs of Thomas. The agreement relating to the manor of Tybesshelf was made by order of the king. (163)

697. Westminster. The morrow of All Souls 1326. P: Walter Caym of Derby. Impedients: Herbert Wyn of Risley and Maude h.w. Concerning a

3

toft in Derby. Walter had the toft of the gift of Herbert and Maude to hold to himself and his heirs of the chief lord etc forever. Herbert and Maude warranted for themselves and the heirs of Maude. Walter gave 100 shillings of silver. (164)

EDWARD III

CP 25/1/38/30

698. Westminster. Easter one month 1327. P: Robert, vicar of the church of St Peter, Derby, and Robert de Alastre, chaplain by Robert de Makworth their attorney by brief of the king. D: Richard del...ustes and Margaret h.w. Concerning 3 mess., 3 tofts, 120a. land, 15a. meadow, 40a. pasture, 60a. woodland 10s rent and a rent of 1 clove in Burleye. Richard and Margaret acknowledged these to be the right of Robert the vicar and they remised and quitclaimed them of themselves and their heirs of Margaret to Robert the vicar, his heirs and Robert de Alastre. The two Roberts gave 100 marks of silver. Endorsed: Henry son of William de Burleye, senior, lays his claim. (1)

699. Westminster. Easter one month 1327. P: Richard Curzoun and Joan h.w. D: William, parson of the church of Ketelston. Concerning the manor of Keteleston, 2 mess., 2 carucates of land and £10 rent in Parva Weston. William had these of the gift of Richard and he granted and rendered them to Richard and Joan to hold to themselves and the heirs of the body of Richard of the chief lord etc forever. Remainder to the right heirs of Richard. (2)

700. Westminster. Octave of Trinity 1327. P: Agnes Selveyn. D: William son of Henry de Knyveton. Concerning the manor of Knyveton. William granted and rendered the manor to Agnes to hold of William and his heirs for the life of Agnes paying therefor 1 rose each year at the feast of the Nativity of St John the Baptist for all services etc due to William and his heirs and doing to the chief lord etc. Succesive remainders to Agnes's children John, Edmund, Eleanor and Margery and the heirs of their bodies. Reversion to William and his heirs. (3)

701. York. The morrow of All Souls ... P: William ...houses and Margaret h.w. D: Thomas de Mackeleye and Emma h.w. Concerning 1 mess., 1 carucate ... in Mackeleye and Saperton. William acknowledged these to be

4

the right of Thomas who, with Emma, had them of the gift of William. Thomas and Emma granted and rendered them to William and Margaret to hold to themselves and the heirs of their bodies of Thomas and Emma and Thomas's heirs forever, paying therefor 6 marks of silver each year (3m. at the feast of the Nativity of St John the Baptist and 3m. at the feast of St Martin) during the life of Thomas and Emma and 1 rose each year at the feast of the Nativity of St John the Baptist to Thomas's heirs for all services etc due to Thomas, Emma and Thomas's heirs and doing to the chief lord etc. Remainder to Roger de Milton and the heirs of his body. Thomas warranted for himself and his heirs. Reversion to Thomas, Emma and Thomas's heirs. (4)

702. York. Octave of Hilary 1328. P: Roger le Savvage and Isabel h.w. by Roger de Shirburn attorney for Isabel by brief of the king. D: Geoffrey de Langeholt, chaplain. Concerning the manor of Steynesby. Geoffrey had the manor of the gift of Roger and he granted and rendered it to Roger and Isabel to hold to themselves and the heirs of their bodies of the king and his heirs forever. Remainder to the right heirs of Roger. The agreement was made by order of the king. (5)

703. York. Octave of Hilary 1328. P: John son of Roger Bythebrok. D: William le Horsknave and Agnes h.w. Concerning 1 mess. and 6a. 1 rood land in Tyddeswelle. John had these of the gift of William and Agnes to hold to himself and his heirs of the chief lord etc forever. William and Agnes warranted for themselves and the heirs of Agnes. John gave 20 marks of silver. (6)

704. York. The morrow of the Purification 1328. P: John de Shepeye. D: John de Touk. Concerning the manor of Smythesby. John de Touk had the manor of the gift of John de Shepeye and he granted and rendered it to him to hold of the chief lord etc for the life of John de Shepeye. Remainder to Alice, daughter of Robert de Touk, for her life. Remainder to the right heirs of John de Shepeye. (7)

705. York. The morrow of the Purification 1328. P: Henry de Meignill of Kyrkelongeley. Impedients: Henry de Aston and Maude h.w. and Simon le Spenser and Agnes h.w. Concerning 1 mess., 2 bov. land and 12d rent in Kyrkelongeley. Henry de Meignill had these of the gift of Henry de Aston, Maude, Simon and Agnes to hold to himself and his heirs of the chief lord etc forever. Henry, Maude, Simon and Agnes warranted for themselves and the heirs of Maude and Agnes. Henry de Meignill gave 20 marks of silver. (8)

706. York. The morrow of the Purification 1328. P: Robert de Touk. D: John de Touk. Concerning the manor of Potlok. John had the manor of the gift of Robert and he granted and rendered it to him to hold of the chief lord etc for the life of Robert. Remainder to Robert's son, John, and Catherine, daughter of William Curteys and the heirs of their bodies. Remainder to the right heirs of Robert. (9)

707. York. Easter three weeks 1328. P: John de Wiggeleye. D: John son of Walter de Bildeswath and Alice h.w. Concerning 1 mess. and 1 bov. 2a. land in Wiggeleye and Brampton. John de Wiggeleye had these of the gift of John and Alice to hold to himself and his heirs of the chief lord etc forever. John and Alice warranted for themselves and the heirs of Alice. John de Wiggeleye gave 100 shillings of silver. (10)

708. York. Octave of Trinity 1328. P: Ralph the Smyth of Bradewell. Impedients: Geoffrey son of Jordan de Aston and Alice h.w. Concerning 1 mess., 8a. land, 2a. meadow and one third part of a toft in Overofferton. Ralph had these of the gift of Geoffrey and Alice to hold to himself and his heirs of the chief lord etc forever. Geoffrey and Alice warranted for themselves and the heirs of Alice. Ralph gave 40 marks of silver. (11)

709. York. Quindene of Michaelmas 1328. P: Ralph de Cungesdon. D: John son of Ives de Tadinton and Agnes h. w. Concerning 1 mess. and 4½a. land in Moniash. Ralph had these of the gift of John and Agnes to hold to himself and his heirs of the chief lord etc forever. John and Agnes warranted for themselves and the heirs of Agnes. Ralph gave 20 marks of silver. (12)

710. York. Octave of Martinmas 1328. P: Hugh Alotessone of Gresele and Agnes h.w. D: Richard Walkeleyn. Concerning 1 mess. and 7a. land in Gresele. Richard granted and rendered these to Hugh and Agnes to hold of the chief lord etc for their lives. Remainder to their son Robert and his heirs. (13)

711. York. Quindene of Michaelmas 1328. P: Peter de Querundon of Stephull. D: Robert de Colleye and Agnes h.w. Concerning 1 mess. and 7a. 1r. land in Wirkesworth. Peter acknowledged these to be the right of Agnes. Robert and Agnes granted and rendered them to Peter to hold to himself and his heirs of the chief lord etc forever and they warranted for themselves and the heirs of Agnes. (14)

712. Westminster. Octave of Hilary 1329. P: William de Ingewardeby. D: Thomas Barbry, chaplain. Concerning the manor of Wyvellesleye and 5 mess. and 5 virgates land in Pakynton next Wyvellesleye. Thomas had these of the gift of William and he granted and rendered them to him to hold of the chief lord etc for the life of William. Remainder to William's son Nicholas for his life. Successive remainders to Nicholas's sons William, John, Nicholas, Philip and Thomas and the heirs of their bodies. Remainder to the right heirs of William de Ingwardeby. (15)

6

713. York. Octave of the Purification 1329. P: Hugh de Gunston D: John de Covene and Lettice h. w. Concerning 2 mess. and 3 shops in Bauquell. Hugh had these of the gift of John and Lettice to hold to himself and his heirs of the chief lord etc forever. John and Lettice warranted for themselves and the heirs of Lettice. Hugh gave 20 marks of silver. (16)

714. York. Quindene of Hilary 1329. P: Alan de Denston. D: Henry de Beek. Concerning the manor of Westbrocton. Henry had the manor of the gift of Alan and he granted and rendered it to him to hold of the chief lord etc for the life of Alan. Remainder to Nicholas de Denston and Agnes h.w. and the heirs of their bodies. Remainder to the right heirs of Alan. Endorsed: Robert prior of Tuttebury lays his claim. (17)

715. Westminster. Quindene of Trinity 1329. P: Henry de Caumbes and Agnes h.w. D: John de Walton. Concerning 7 tofts and 100a. land in Kyrkelangeleye. John had these of the gift of Henry and he granted and rendered them to Henry and Agnes to hold of the chief lord etc for their lives. Remainder to Richard de Wodeford and Joan h.w. and the heirs of the body of Joan. Remainder to John de Twyford and his heirs. (18)

716. Westminster. Quindene of Michaelmas 1329. P: Joan, widow of John de la Launde. D: Richard son of Richard Foleiaumbe and Elizabeth h.w. Concerning the manor of Caldelowe and a mill in Hedricheshay. Joan acknowledged these to be the right of Elizabeth. Richard and Elizabeth granted and rendered them to Joan to hold of themselves and the heirs of Elizabeth for the life of Joan paying therefor 1 rose each year at the feast of the Nativity of St John the Baptist for all services etc due to Richard, Elizabeth and Elizabeth's heirs and doing to the chief lord etc. Reversion to Richard, Elizabeth and Elizabeth's heirs. (19)

717. Westminster. Octave of Hilary 1330. P: Richard de Wylughby and Isabel h. w. by William de Colewyke attorney for Isabel. D: Hugh son of Hugh Ponger of Riselegh and Beatrice h.w. Concerning 1 mess., 1 toft, 2 bov. 5a. land and 3a. meadow in Riselegh. Hugh and Beatrice acknowledged these to be the right of Richard and they rendered them to Richard and Isabel to hold to themselves and the heirs of Richard of the chief lord etc forever. Hugh warranted for himself and his heirs. Richard and Isabel gave 100 marks of silver. (20)

718. Derby. 2 July 1330. P: John de Rocheford. D: Ralph de Shepeye and Alice h.w. Concerning 1 mess., 1 carucate of land and 16s rent in Berwardecote, Brunaldeston and Hatton. Ralph and Alice remised and quitclaimed these of themselves and the heirs of Alice to John and his heirs to hold of the chief lord etc forever. John gave one unmewed sparrowhawk. (21)

7

719. Derby. 2 July 1330. P: Robert de Mogynton and Isabel h.w. D: Walter de Mogynton. Concerning 2 mess., 2 virgates 48a. land and 20s rent in Mogynton and Murcaston. Walter had these of the gift of Robert and he granted and rendered them to Robert and Isabel to hold to themselves and the heirs of their bodies of the chief lord etc forever. Remainder to the right heirs of Robert. (22)

720. Derby. 2 July 1330. P: Henry de Hambury and Isabel h.w. Impedients: John de Rocheford and Joan h.w. Concerning 5 mess., 6½ bov. land and 1a. meadow in Howen. John and Joan acknowledged these to be the right of Henry, who, with Isabel, had them of the gift of John and Joan to hold to themselves and the heirs of Henry of the chief lord etc forever. John and Joan warranted for themselves and the heirs of John. Henry and Isabel gave one unmewed sparrowhawk. (23)

721. Derby. 2 July 1330. P: John son of Gervase de Castelton. D: Thomas de Wormhull and Joan h.w., Henry de Clifton and Agnes h.w. and John Martyn and Emma h.w. Concerning 1 mess. and 1 bov. land in Fernileye. The deforciants rendered these to John son of Gervase to hold to himself and his heirs of the chief lord etc forever. They warranted for themselves and the heirs of Joan, Agnes and Emma. John gave one unmewed sparrowhawk. (24)

722. Derby. 2 July 1330. P: Adam de Gonshull and Alice h.w. D: Robert de Neubold of Haversegge, chaplain. Concerning a moiety of the manor of Haversegge. Robert had the moiety of the gift of Adam and he granted and rendered it to Adam and Alice to hold to themselves and the heirs of their bodies of the chief lord etc forever. Remainder to the right heirs of Adam. (25)

CP 25/1/38/31

723. Derby. 2 July 1330. P: Emma, widow of Robert de Barneby. D: John de Okebrok, chaplain. Concerning 1 mess. in Derby. John had the messuage of the gift of Emma and he granted and rendered it to her to hold of the chief lord etc for her life. Remainder to Emma's daughter Margaret for life. Remainder to the right heirs of Emma. (26)

724. Derby. 2 July 1330. P: Robert de Masey and Maude h.w. D: Ralph de Marchinton and Elizabeth h.w., Reginald de Marchinton and Catherine h.w. and John de Turville and Joan h.w. Concerning 2 mess., 60a. land and 32s 9d rent in Tiddeswell. Robert acknowledged these to be the right of Elizabeth, Catherine and Joan. The deforciants granted and rendered them to Robert and Maude to hold of themselves and the heirs of Elizabeth,

Catherine and Joan for the life of Maude paying therefor 1 rose each year at the feast of St John the Baptist for all services etc due to the deforciants and the heirs of Elizabeth, Catherine and Joan and doing to the chief lord etc. Reversion to the deforciants and the heirs of Elizabeth, Catherine and Joan. (27)

725. Derby. 2 July 1330. P: Thomas de Chaworth, senior. D: John Erle, chaplain. Concerning the manor of Alferton. John had the manor of the gift of Thomas and he granted and rendered it to him to hold of the chief lord etc for the life of Thomas. Remainder to Thomas, son of Thomas de Chaworth, and Joan h.w. and the heirs of their bodies. Remainder to the right heirs of Thomas the son. (28)

726. Derby. 2 July 1330. P: William son of Henry de Lokynton of Braydeston. D: Thomas de Sandiacre of Braydeston, chaplain. Concerning 2 mess. and 4½ bov. land in Braydeston. Thomas had these of the gift of William and he granted and rendered them to him to hold of the chief lord etc for the life of William. Remainder to William's son William and the heirs of his body. Remainder to the right heirs of William son of Henry. (29)

727. Derby. 2 July 1330. P: John son of John Wychard and Alice h.w. D: John son of Henry Wychard of Osbasston. Concerning 1 mess, 1 carucate of land and 2s 3d rent in Chaddesden which Simon de Parva Cestre held for life of the inheritance of John son of Henry and which ought to revert to John son of Henry on Simon's death. John son of Henry granted for himself and his heirs that these should remain, instead, to John son of John and Alice and the heirs of their bodies to hold of John son of Henry and his heirs forever paying therefor 1 rose each year at the feast of the Nativity of St John the Baptist for all services etc due to John and his heirs and doing to the chief lord etc. Reversion to John son of Henry and his heirs. Endorsed: Afterwards the aforesaid Simon came into this court and agreed etc. (30) *[There is a note at the beginning of CP 25/1/38/31 that No 30 is not a foot of fine but a note from the Derbyshire eyre of 1330-31; cf. E 101/33/8.]*

728. Derby. 2 July 1330. (1) P: Roger de Eyncourt and Maude h.w. and Robert de Panely and Agnes h.w. Tenens: Henry, earl of Lancaster, whom Nichola, wife of Philip de Strelley, who, through the default of Philip, was admitted to defend her right, called to warrant and who warranted her of 8 bov. land and 60a. woodland in Repyndon. (2) P: as above. Tenens: the same Henry, earl of Lancaster whom Robert, son of Robert de Beeke, who, through the default of the same Robert de Beeke, was admitted to defend his right, called to warrant and who warranted him of 8 bov. land and 60a. woodland also in Repyndon. (3) P: as above. Tenens: the same Henry, earl of Lancaster, whom Robert de Beeke and Robert his son without whom the same Robert de Beeke was not able to reply and who attached himself to the

9

same Robert de Beeke in order to reply, and whom Robert de Beeke and Philip de Strelley and Nicholas his wife called to warrant and who warranted them of 4 bov. land in Repyndon. The plaintiffs acknowledged the tenements to be the right of the earl and they remised and quitclaimed of themselves and the heirs of Maude and Agnes to the earl and his heirs. The earl gave 120 marks of silver. (31)

729. Derby. 2 July 1330. P: Robert de Sallowe. D: Robert son of Robert de Spondon, chaplain. Concerning 8 mess., 12 tofts, 1 mill, 28 bov. 109a. land, 8a. meadow and 67s 8d rent in Sanndyacre, Breydeston, Ryseleye, Kyrkehalum, Spondon, Lochagh, Longa Eyton, Boleton, Alwoston, Derby, Chadesden, Ilkeston, Parva Halum, Stanton next Sanndyacre and Langeleye next Henovere. Robert son of Robert had these of the gift of Robert de Sallowe and he granted and rendered them to him to hold of the chief lord etc for the life of Robert de Sallowe. Remainder to Robert de Sallowe's son, Robert, and the heirs of his body. Remainder to the right heirs of Robert de Sallowe. (32)

730. Derby. 2 July 1330. P: Richard de Draicote of Eyton and Gillian h.w. D: John le Lorimer of Eyton. Concerning 1 mess. and 1 bov. land in Eyton. John had these of the gift of Richard and Gillian and he granted and rendered them to them to hold of the chief lord etc for their lives. Remainder to Gillian, daugher of Robert Trunket for life. Successive remainders to her children, Richard and Catherine, and the respective heirs of their bodies. Remainder to the right heirs of Gillian, daughter of Robert. (33)

731. Derby. 2 July 1330. P: Henry son of William de Knyveton and Isabel h.w. D: Roger de Deynecourt, parson of the church of Asshovre and Robert de Channdos, parson of the church of Rodburn. Concerning (i) 60a. land in Underwode which Agnes Selveyne held for her life of the inheritance of Roger; (ii) a third part of the manor of Bradeleye, 4 mess., 100a. land and 10a. meadow in Underwode all of which Isabel, widow of William de Knyveton, held as dowry of the inheritance of Roger; and (iii) the other 2 parts of the manor and 60s rent in Assheburn, Underwode and Holonde. Henry acknowledged all of these tenements to be the right of Roger whereof Roger and Robert had the rent, 2 parts of the manor, the messuages, 100a. land and the meadow of the gift of Henry. Roger and Robert granted them to Henry and Isabel and rendered the 2 parts and the rents to them to hold to themselves and the male heirs of their bodies of the chief lord etc forever. Remainder to the right heirs of Henry. Roger and Robert also granted that the remaining tenements (i.e. (i) and (ii)), which ought to revert to Roger and Robert and the heirs of Roger on the deaths of Agnes Selveyne and Isabel widow of William de Knyveton, should remain instead to Henry and

Isabel and the male heirs of their bodies. Remainder to the right heirs of Henry. Endorsed: John de Knyveton, Edmund de Knyveton, Eleanor de Knyveton and Margery de Knyveton lay their claims. (34)

732. Derby. 2 July 1330. P: Richard son of Thomas de Shakelcros. D: Thomas son of Alan de Wormehull and Joan h.w., John Martyn and Emma h.w. and Henry de Clyfton and Agnes h.w. Concerning 12a. land in Horwych. The defendants rendered the land to Richard to hold to himself and his heirs of the chief lord etc forever. They warranted for themselves and the heirs of Joan, Emma and Agnes. Richard gave one unmewed sparrowhawk. (35)

733. Derby. 2 July 1330. P: Henry de Hambury and Isabel h.w. Impedients: Henry de Shanynton and Joan h.w. Concerning 40a. land in Snelleston. Henry de Shanynton and Joan acknowledged the land to be the right of Henry de Hambury who, with Isabel, had it of the gift of Henry and Joan to hold to themselves and the heirs of Henry of the chief lord etc forever. Henry and Joan warranted for themselves and the heirs of Joan. Henry and Isabel gave one unmewed sparrowhawk. Endorsed: Roger de Okoume lays his claim etc. (36)

734. Derby. 2 July 1330. P: Robert de Irlond and Isote h.w. D: Nicholas de Grendon. Concerning the manor of Yildresleye (excepting 1 mess. and 100a. land within the manor) one third part of which Margery, widow of Serle de Munioye, holds as dowry of the inheritance of Nicholas. Robert and Isote acknowledged the manor, with exceptions, to be the right of Nicholas whereof Nicholas had 2 parts of the gift of Robert and Isote. He granted the manor to them and rendered the 2 parts to them to hold of the chief lord etc for their lives. Successive remainders to Robert's sons, Robert and John, and the heirs of their bodies. Remainder to the right heirs of Isote. Nicholas also granted that the remaining third part which ought to revert to himself and his heirs on the death of Margery should remain, instead, to Robert and Isote for their lives. Remainders as for the 2 parts. The agreement was made in Margery's presence, she agreeing, and she did fealty to Robert and Isote. (37)

735. Westminster. Quindene of Easter 1331. P: Roger de Bradeburn and Maude h.w. by Henry de la Pole attorney for Maude by brief of the king. D: John de Brerton. Concerning (i) 2 mess. and 1 carucate and 30a. land in Knyveton and Peverwych which William son of Roger de Bradeburn held for life; (ii) 30a. land in Oftecote and Underwode which John de Bradeburn, senior, held for life; (iii) 4a. land in Longeleye which Henry de Meynill held for life; (iv) 4a. land in Longeleye which Emma, widow of Robert del Burghes held as dowry; (v) a moiety of a mill in Wyrkesworth which Richard son of Roger de Bradeburn held for life; (vi) the other moiety of the

11

same mill which John, Richard's brother held for life of the inheritance of John de Brerton; and (vii) the manor of Bradeburn, 2 mess., 2 mills, 1 carucate 32a. land, 10a. meadow, 3a. woodland and £6 3s 3d rent in Assheburne, Oftecote, Underwode, Clyfton, Knyveton, Peverwyche, Fennybenteleye, Holand, Stretton, Wyrkesworth, Wyardeston, Holynton, Yeveleye, Braylesford, Longeleye and Parva Ireton. Roger acknowledged all these tenements to be the right of John who had those listed in (vii) of the gift of Roger. John granted and rendered them to Roger and Maude to hold to themselves and the heirs of their bodies of the chief lord etc forever. Remainder to the right heirs of Roger. John also granted that the remaining tenements (i.e. (i) to (vi)), which ought to revert to him and his heirs on the deaths of William, John de Bradeburn, senior, Henry, Emma, Richard and his brother John, should remain instead to Roger and Maude and the heirs of their bodies. Remainder to the right heirs of Roger. Endorsed: Thomas son of Roger de Bradebourn lays his claim (38)

736. Westminster. Octave of Michaelmas 1331. P: John de Leycestre. D: Adam le Taillour of Tharlesthorp and Alice h.w. Concerning 20a. land in Tharlesthorp. Adam and Alice rendered the land to John to hold to himself and his heirs of the chief lord etc forever and they warranted for themselves and the heirs of Alice. John gave 20 marks of silver. (39)

737. Westminster. The morrow of Martinmas 1331. P: Thomas de Gonshull, chivaler. D: Nicholas de Langeford, chivaler. Concerning the advowson of the church of Whitewell. Nicholas rendered the advowson to Thomas to hold to himself and his heirs of the chief lord etc forever and he warranted it for himself and his heirs. Thomas gave 100 marks of silver. (40)

738. Westminster. Quindene of Martinmas 1331. P: William de Cardoyle of Spondon, chaplain, by Robert de Macworth his attorney by brief of the king. D: Laurence de Braylesford and Maude h.w. Concerning 3 mess., 160a. land and 3a. meadow in Spondon, Chaddesden and Lokhawe. Laurence and Maude remised and quitclaimed these of, and warranted for, themselves and the heirs of Maude to William and his heirs forever. William gave 20 marks of silver. (41)

739. Westminster. Quindene of Hilary 1332. P: Henry de Cobynton, chaplain. D: John de Tymmor and Joan h.w. by Roger de Elynton attorney for Joan by brief of the king. Concerning the manor of Hurst and 18 mess., 7 virgates, 12½a. land and 38s 5d rent in Egynton. John acknowledged these to be the right of Henry who had them of the gift of John. Henry granted and rendered them to John and Joan to hold to themselves and the heirs of their bodies of the chief lord etc forever. Remainder to the right heirs of John. (42)

740. Westminster. Octave of the Purification 1332. Easter one month 1332. P: William le Herberiour of Chaddesden, chivaler, and Isabel h.w. by John de Luton their attorney by brief of the king. D: Robert, vicar of the church of Magna Overe. Concerning 36 mess., 2 mills, 24 bov. 330a. land, [24]a. meadow, 40a. pasture, 7a. woodland and 60s rent in Spondon, Chaddesden, Lochawe, Lutchirch, and Twyford. Robert granted and rendered these to William and Isabel to hold of the chief lord etc for their lives. Successive remainders to William's sons William, Thomas, Henry, Chad and Edmund and the heirs of their bodies. Remainder to the right heirs of William le Herberiour. Endorsed: Robert Molde of Twyford lays his claim. (43)

741. Westminster. Octave of Hilary 1332. Quindene of Easter 1332. P: Robert de Bilburgh, chaplain, by John de Shirwode his attorney by brief of the king. D: Richard son of Richard de Riboef. Concerning the manor of Etewell which Hugh de Gonshill, Robert Ingram, chivaler, and Orframina, Robert's wife, held by a surrender of Richard for the lives of Robert and Orframina. Richard granted for himself and his heirs that the manor, which ought to revert to himself and his heirs on the deaths of Robert and Orframina, should remain instead to Robert de Bilburgh to hold for his life of Richard and his heirs paying therefor 1 rose each year at the feast of the Nativity of St John the Baptist for all services, customs, and taxes. Remainder to Richard's son, Walter, and Margery, daughter of Robert Ingram, and the heirs of their bodies to hold as above forever. Richard warranted and quit the manor for himself and his heirs to Robert de Bilburgh for Robert's life and to Walter and Margery and their heirs forever, for the services as above. Reversion to Richard and his heirs to hold of the chief lord etc forever. Robert de Bilburgh gave £10. The agreement was made in the presence of Hugh, Robert Ingram and Orframina who agreed and did fealty to Robert de Bilburgh. Endorsed: Robert de Foucher of Osmundeston lays his claim. (44)

742. Westminster. Octave of Hilary 1332. Quindene of Easter 1332. P: Richard son of Richard de Riboef. D: William de Cossale, clerk. Concerning the manor of Magna Stretton in Scarvesdale. William had the manor of the gift of Richard and he granted and rendered it to him to hold of the chief lord etc for the life of Richard. Remainder to Richard's son, Walter, and Margery, daughter of Robert Ingram, and the heirs of their bodies. Remainder to the right heirs of Richard. (45)

743. Westminster. Octave of Trinity 1332. Octave of Michaelmas 1332. P: John, parson of the church of St Gregory, London and Richard de la Pole. D: John Gernonn. Concerning the manor of Baukwell. John the parson and Richard had the manor of the gift of John Gernonn and they granted a nd rendered it to him to hold of the king and his heirs etc for the life of John Gernonn. Remainder to John Gernonn's son John and Alice, his wife, and the heirs of their bodies. Remainder to the right heirs of John Gernonn. The agreement was made by order of the king. (46)

744. Westminster. Michaelmas three weeks 1332. The morrow of Martinmas 1332. P: Robert de Fyndern by John de Fyndern his attorney. D: Simon Cundi of Wylugton and Alice h.w. Concerning 1 mess., 14a. land and a moiety of 1a. meadow in Wylugton. Robert had these of the gift of Simon and Alice to hold to himself and his heirs of the chief lord etc forever. Simon and Alice warranted for themselves and the heirs of Alice. Robert gave 20 marks of silver. (47)

745. Westminster. Octave of Martinmas 1332. Easter one month 1333. P: John son of Walter de Longedon. D: William Vyncent of Stapenhull. Concerning (i) 1 mess., 17½a. land and a moiety of 1a. meadow which William son of John le Bone of Stapenhull and Agnes h.w. held as Agnes's dowry; (ii) 1 mess. and 1½a. land which Agnes Fidecok held for life; (iii) 3a. land which Roger Vyncent held for life of the inheritance of William; and (iv) 1 mess., 1½a. meadow, 2a. woodland and 1 carucate less 22a. land, all of which tenements lay in Stapenhull. William acknowledged all these tenements to be the right of John and he rendered to him the items in (iv) to hold to himself and his heirs of the chief lord etc forever. William also granted for himself and his heirs that the remaining tenements (i.e. (i) to (iii)), which ought to revert to him and his heirs on the deaths of Agnes, wife of William de Stapenhull, Agnes Fidecok and Roger, should remain instead to John and his heirs. William warranted for himself and his heirs. John gave 100 marks of silver. (48)

746. Westminster. Quindene of Trinity 1333. P: Robert de Touk and Edith h.w. D: Richard de Ireton. Concerning the manor of Sidenfen. Richard had the manor of the gift of Robert and he granted and rendered it to Robert and Edith to hold of the chief lord etc for their lives. Remainder to the right heirs of Robert. (49)

747. Westminster. Quindene of Trinity 1333. York. Quindene of Michaelmas 1333. P: Richard son of Nicholas del Hull of Hertindon by Henry de la Pole his attorney. D: Maude Basset. Concerning (i) 1 mess. and 3. bov land which Ralph Basset of Netherhaddon held for life; and (ii) 1 mess. and 1 bov. land which Deonise Basset held for life of the inheritance of Maude. Maude granted for herself and her heirs that these tenements, which ought to revert to her and her heirs on the deaths of Ralph and Deonise, should remain instead to Richard and his heirs to hold of the chief lord etc forever. Maude warranted for herself and her heirs. Richard gave 100 marks of silver. (50)

14

748. Westminster. Octave of Trinity 1333. York. Octave of Michaelmas 1333. P: William son of Thomas de Fennybenteleye. D: Gilbert de Cruch and Joan h.w. Concerning 3 tofts, 2½a. land, 5a. meadow and 7s 11d rent in Assheburn, Underwode, Benteleye and Bradeleye. William had these of the gift of Gilbert and Joan to hold to himself and his heirs of the chief lord etc forever. Gilbert and Joan warranted for themselves and the heirs of Joan. William gave 20 marks of silver. (51)

749. York. Quindene of Michaelmas 1333. William le Clerk of Longeley and Alice h.w. D: Henry Moyse of Knyveton, chaplain. Concerning 1 mess. and 24a. land in Kyrkelongeley. Henry had these of the gift of William and he granted and rendered them to William and Alice to hold to themselves and the male heirs of their bodies of the chief lord etc forever. Remainder to the right heirs of William. (52)

750. Westminster. Octave of Trinity 1333. York. Octave of Michaelmas 1333. P: Robert son of Richard del Clogh. D: Henry le Cok and Alice h.w. Concerning 8a. 1 rood land in Boudon. Robert acknowldeged the land to be the right of Alice. Henry and Alice granted and rendered it to Robert to hold of the chief lord etc for his life. Successive remainders to Robert's children Robert, John, Maude and Alice and the heirs of their bodies. Remainder to the right heirs of John. (53)

751. York. Easter three weeks 1334. P: John de Shepeye and Agnes h.w. D: Roger de Shepeye. Concerning the manor of Smythesby. Roger had the manor of the gift of John and he granted and rendered it to John and Agnes to hold to themselves and the heirs of John of the chief lord etc forever. (54)

752. York. Quindene of Midsummer 1334. Michaelmas one month 1334. P: John son of Thomas de Fennybenteleye by John de Assheburne his attorney by brief of the king. D: Thomas de Dunston and Emma h.w. Concerning 1 toft, 4a. land and 1½a. meadow in Fennybenteleye. John had these of the gift of Thomas and Emma to hold to himself and his heirs of the chief lord etc forever. Thomas and Emma warranted for themselves and the heirs of Emma. John gave 100 shillings of silver. (55)

753. York. Octave of Midsummer 1334. Quindene of Michaelmas 1334. P: Richard de Stafford, parson of the church of Birtton by Peter de Querndon, his attorney by brief of the king. Impedients: Richard son of John le Porter of Caldelowe and Alice h.w. Concerning 22a. land in Caldelowe. Richard and Alice remised and quitclaimed the land of themselves and the heirs of Richard to Richard de Stafford and his heirs. Richard son of John warranted for himself and his heirs. Richard de Stafford gave 20 marks of silver. (56)

754. York. Easter three weeks 1334. Quindene of Michaelmas 1334. P: John de Lymestre by John de Assheburn his attorney. D: Richard Pikard of Mapelton and Riquera h.w. Concerning 1 mess., 1 toft, 16a. land and 5s rent in Eyton next Alsop. John had these of the gift of Richard and Riquera to hold to himself and his heirs of the chief lord etc forever. Richard and Riquera warranted for themselves and the heirs of Riquera. John gave 20 marks of silver (57)

755. York. Easter three weeks 1334. Quindene of Hilary 1335. P: William son of William Trussel of Cublesdon, kt, by Henry de la Pole, his attorney. D: John son of Urian de Sancto Petro, chivaler. Concerning the manor of Eyton and a fourth part of the manor of Walton which Isote, widow of Urian de Sancto Petro, held as dowry of the inheritance of John. John granted for himself and his heirs that the manor and fourth part which ought to revert to him and his heirs on the death of Isote, should remain instead to William and his heirs to hold of the chief lord etc forever. William gave 100 marks of silver. The agreement was made in the presence of Isote who agreed and did fealty to William. (58)

756. York. The morrow of All Souls 1334. Quindene of Hilary 1335. P: Robert de la Forde. D: William Stalworth, junior, and Emma h.w. Concerning 1 mess. and 12a. land in Eyum. Robert had these of the gift of William and Emma to hold to himself and his heirs of the chief lord etc forever. William and Emma warranted for themselves and the heirs of Emma. Robert gave 20 marks of silver (59)

757. York. Octave of the Purification 1335. Easter three weeks 1335. P: Robert de Yildreslegh, chaplain. D: Robert de Irlaunde and Isote h.w. Concerning the manor of Lokhaye. Robert de Yildreslegh granted and rendered the manor to Robert and Isote to hold of the chief lord etc for their lives. Successive remainders to Robert de Irlaunde's son, John, and John's wife Hawis and the heirs of their bodies, and then to John's brother, Robert, and the heirs of his body. Remainder to the right heirs of Isote. (60)

758. York. Quindene of Easter 1335. P: Edmund de Britannia. D: William Argent and Maude h.w. Concerning 1 mess., 7a. 1 rood land and 1a. 3 roods meadow in Stonystannton. Edmund had these of the gift of William and Maude to hold to himself and his heirs of the chief lord etc forever. William and Maude warranted for themselves and the heirs of Maude. Edmund gave 20 marks of silver. (61)

759. York. Easter three weeks 1335. Quindene of Trinity 1335. P: Richard de Longeford of Derby and Sarah h.w. by Henry de Pole attorney for Sarah. D: John son of William son of Peter de Normonton and Margery h.w. Concerning 1 mess. and 3a. land and a moiety of 1a. meadow in

Normonton. John and Margery acknowledged these to be the right of Richard who, with Sarah, had them of the gift of John and Margery to hold to themselves and the heirs of Richard of the chief lord etc forever. John and Margery warranted for themselves and the heirs of Margery. Richard and Sarah gave 20 marks of silver. (62)

760. York. Easter one month 1335. The morrow of Midsummer 1335. P: Thomas son of Henry Randolf. D: Henry Randulf of Longeyton and Alice h.w. Concerning (i) 1a. land which Richard de Draycote held for life by a surrender of Alice; and (ii) 1 toft and 3a. 3 roods land, all in Longeyton. Thomas had the toft and the land in (ii) of the gift of Henry and Alice and he granted and rendered them to Henry and Alice to hold for their lives of himself and his heirs, paying therefor 1 rose each year at the feast of the Nativity of St John the Baptist for all services etc due to Thomas and his heirs and doing to the chief lord etc. Reversion to Thomas and his heirs. Henry and Alice granted for themselves and the heirs of Alice that the 1a. land in (i), which ought to revert to Henry and Alice and Alice's heirs on the death of Richard, should remain instead to Thomas and his heirs to hold of the chief lord etc forever. Henry and Alice warranted for themselves and Alice's heirs. (63)

761. York. The morrow of Midsummer 1335. P: Margaret Abel by Thomas de Assheburn her attorney by brief of the king. D: Henry de Barwe. Concerning 7a. 1 rood land, a fifth part of 1 mess. and a third part of 1 mess. in Caldewell and a sixth part of the manor of Caldewell. Henry granted and rendered these to Margaret to hold for her life, of Henry and his heirs paying therefor one penny each year at the feast of St Michael for all services etc due to Henry and his heirs and doing to the chief lord etc. Remainder to Thomas Abel, junior, and the heirs of his body. Reversion to Henry and his heirs. Margaret gave £20. Endorsed: John, son and heir of Thomas Abel, lays his claim. (64)

762. York. Octave of Trinity 1335. Octave of Michaelmas 1335. P: Roger son of Gilbert de Somerby. D: Gilbert de Somerby and Maude h.w. Concerning 1 mess., 42a. land, 16a. meadow and 1a. woodland in Beghton. Roger had these of the gift of Gilbert and Maude to hold to himself and his heirs of the chief lord etc forever. Gilbert and Maude warranted for themselves and the heirs of Maude. Roger gave 100 marks of silver. (65)

763. York. Octave of Trinity 1335. Octave of Michaelmas 1335. P: Robert son of Robert del Sclak. D: Henry le Ku and Alice h.w. Concerning 5a. 3 roods land in Boudon. Henry and Alice granted and rendered the land to Robert to hold of the chief lord etc for his life. Remainder to Robert's son, Thomas, and his heirs. (66)

17

764. York. Octave of Trinity 1335. Octave of Michaelmas 1335. P: John son of Robert del Clogh. D: Robert son of Hugh del Clogh and Deonise h.w. Concerning 11a. 3 roods land in Boudon. Robert and Deonise granted and rendered the land to John to hold to himself and the heirs of his body of the chief lord etc forever. Successive remainders to John's brother, Robert, and his sisters, Maude, Alice and Agnes and the heirs of their bodies. Remainder to the right heirs of John. (67)

765. York. Quindene of Michaelmas 1335. The morrow of All Souls 1335. P: William Moton and Joan h.w. D: Philip la Zouche. Concerning 4 mess. and 4 virgates land in Octhorp which William la Zouche of Okthorp held for life of the inheritance of Philip and which ought to revert to Philip and his heirs on the death of William la Zouche. Philip granted for himself and his heirs that these should remain instead to William Moton and Joan and the heirs of their bodies to hold of the chief lord etc forever. Remainder to the right heirs of William Moton. Philip warranted for himself and his heirs. William and Joan gave 20 marks of silver. The agreement was made in the presence of William la Zouche who agreed and did fealty to William and Joan. (68)

766. York. The morrow of the Purification 1336 Quindene of Easter 1336. P:. Hugh de Meynill, chivaler. D: Richard son of Richard le Foun. Concerning 1 mess. and 1 carucate land in Yeveleye. Hugh had these of the gift of Richard to hold to himself and his heirs of the chief lord etc forever. Richard warranted for himself and his heirs. Hugh gave 20 marks of silver. (69)

767. Westminster. Quindene of Hilary 1335. York. Easter one month 1336. P: Thomas de Rolleston. D: William son of William de Egynton. Concerning 2 mess., 30a. land and 3a. meadow in Egynton which Maude, widow of William de Egynton, held as dowry of the inheritance of William and which ought to revert to William and his heirs on the death of Maude. William acknowledged these to be the right of Thomas and granted for himself and his heirs that they should remain instead to Thomas and his heirs to hold of the chief lord etc forever. William warranted for himself and his heirs. Thomas gave £20. (70)

768. York. Easter one month 1336. Quindene of Michaelmas 1336. P: James Coterell. D: John le Webbester and Cecily h.w. Concerning 1 mess. and 1 bov. land in Thornesete. James had these of the gift of John and Cecily to hold to himself and his heirs of the chief lord etc forever. John and Cecily warranted for themselves and the heirs of Cecily. James gave £20. (71)

18

769. York. Quindene of Midsummer 1336. The morrow of All Souls 1336. P: Thomas de Miners and Amice h.w. D: John de Miners and Isabel h.w. Concerning 1 mess., 2 carucates land and 10 marks rent in Willardesleye, Croumford and Holynton. John and Isabel granted and rendered these to Thomas and Amice to hold to themselves and the heirs of their bodies of John and Isabel and John's heirs paying therefor 1 rose each year at the feast of the Nativity of St John the Baptist for all services etc due to John and Isabel and John's heirs and doing to the chief lord etc. Reversion to John and Isabel and John's heirs. Thomas and Amice gave 100 marks of silver. (72)

770. York. Quindene of Trinity 1336. Quindene of Michaelmas 1336. P: Roger de Bradeborne and Maude h.w. D: Henry de la Pole and Peter de Brereton. Concerning 2 mess. and 1 carucate land in Bradeborne. Roger and Maude acknowledged these to be the right of Henry who, with Peter, had them of the gift of Roger and Maude. Henry and Peter granted and rendered them to Roger and Maude to hold of the chief lord etc for their lives. Successive remainders to Roger's sons, John and William, and their heirs of their bodies. Remainder to the heirs of the bodies of Roger and Maude. Remainder to the right heirs of Maude. (73)

771. York. Octave of Trinity 1336. Octave of Michaelmas 1336. P: Gilbert Henry of Yoxhale. D: Nicholas Marreys and Joan h.w. Concerning 1 mess. and 8a. 2½ virgates land in Ednynghale. Gilbert acknowledged these to be the right of Joan. Nicholas and Joan granted and rendered them to Gilbert to hold of the chief lord etc for his life. Remainder to Richard, son of Nicholas and Joan, and Maude, Gilbert's daughter, and the heirs of their bodies. Remainder, as to a moiety of the messuage situated towards the east and 4a. 1¼ virgates of land lying in 'The Middelfeld', to the right heirs of Richard and, as to the other half of the tenements, to the right heirs of Gilbert. (74)

772. York. Quindene of Trinity 1336. Octave of Michaelmas 1336. P: Robert de Greseleye, chivaler, by Nicholas de Greseleye his attorney. D: Nicholas le Mareys of Ednynghale and Joan h.w. Concerning 12a. land in Ednynghale. Nicholas and Joan rendered the land to Robert to hold to himself and his heirs of the chief lord etc forever. They warranted for themselves and the heirs of Joan. Robert gave 20 marks of silver. (75)

CP 25/1/38/33

773. York. Octave of Midsummer 1336. The morrow of All Souls 1336. P: John son of Henry son of Robert de Fennybenteleye and Sibyl h.w. D: Henry son of Robert de Fennybenteleye and Joan h.w. Concerning (i) 6a.

19

land, 1a. meadow and a third part of a messuage in Fennybenteleye which Agnes, widow of Robert son of Thomas de Fennybenteleye, held as dowry; (ii) 16a. land, 2a. meadow, 16d rent and a third part of a moiety of 2 mess. which Henry son of Geoffrey de Mapulton held for his life of the inheritance of Joan, in Fennybenteleye; and (iii) 32a. land, 6a. meadow, 14½d rent, 2 parts of the mess. and a moiety of 2 mess. in Fennybenteleye, Assheburn, Offidecote, Underwode and Thorp. Henry and Joan granted and rendered the tenements in (iii) to John and Sibyl to hold to themselves and the heirs of their bodies of Henry and Joan and the heirs of Joan paying therefor 1 rose each year at the feast of the Nativity of St John the Baptist for all services etc due to Henry and Joan and Joan's heirs and doing to the chief lord etc. Henry and Joan also granted for themselves and the heirs of Joan that the tenements in (i) and (ii), which ought to revert to them and Joan's heirs on the deaths of Agnes and Henry son of Geoffrey, should remain instead to John and Sibyl and the heirs of their bodies. Henry and Joan warranted for themselves and Joan's heirs. Reversion to Henry and Joan and Joan's heirs. John and Sibyl gave 100 marks of silver. (76)

774. York. Quindene of Trinity 1336. The morrow of All Souls 1336. P: Payne le Draper of Derby and Avis h.w. D: John de la Corner of Derby and Joan h.w. Concerning 1 mess., 1 toft, 1 shop, 15a. land and 1½a. meadow in Derby. John and Joan granted and rendered these to Payne and Avis to hold to themselves and their heirs of their bodies of John and Joan and Joan's heirs paying therefor 1 rose each year at the feast of the Nativity of St John the Baptist for all services etc due to John and Joan and Joan's heirs and doing to the chief lord etc. Reversion to John and Joan and Joan's heirs. Payne and Avis gave 20 marks of silver. (77)

775. York. Quindene of Martinmas 1336. Quindene of Hilary 1336. P: Roger son of Robert de Wynfeld of Esshover. D: John de Musters of Tirswell and Alice h.w. Concerning a fourth part of the manor of Esshover. John and Alice acknowledged this to be the right of Roger and they rendered it to him with the exception of 10s rents. They granted the rents to him together with the homage and services of Roger Deyncourt, Ralph de Reresby and Richard le Hunt and their heirs of all the tenements that they formerly held of John and Alice, to hold to Roger son of Robert and his heirs of the chief lord etc forever. John and Alice warranted for themselves and the heirs of Alice. Roger gave £20. (78)

776. York. Quindene of Michaelmas 1336. The morrow of Martinmas 1336. P: Roger Deyncourt, chivaler. D: William de Russhyndene and Alice h.w. Concerning 1 bov. land, 6a. meadow, 6d rent and a fourth part of a toft in Dokemonton. William and Alice rendered these to Roger to hold to himself and his heirs of the chief lord etc forever. They warranted for themselves and the heirs of Alice. Roger gave 20 marks of silver. (79)

777. York. Quindene of Michaelmas 1336. The morrow of Martinmas 1336. Roger Deyncourt, chivaler. D: Thomas de Ryther of Netherlangwath and Edene h.w. Concerning 1 bov. land, 6a. meadow, 8d rent and a fourth part of a toft in Dokemonton. Thomas and Edene rendered these to Roger to hold to himself and his heirs of the chief lord etc forever. They warranted for themselves and the heirs of Edene. Roger gave 10 marks of silver. (80)

778. York. Octave of Michaelmas 1336. The morrow of All Souls 1336. P: Richard de la Pole of Hertindon. D: Gratian le Palmere of London and Gillian h.w. Concerning 2 mess., 1 mill, 122a. land, 5a. meadow and a fifth part of 15 mess., 3 furlongs 2 bov. 50a. land, 10a. meadow and 5s rent in Bucstones, Wormhulle, Castelton, Peverwych, Asshebourne, Bradeleye and Lee next Bradebourne. Richard had 1 mess., the mill and 100a. land of the gift of Gratian and Gillian who rendered the remaining tenements to Richard to hold to himself and his heirs of the chief lord etc forever. They also warranted these same tenements for themselves and the heirs of Gillian. Richard gave £100. (81)

779. York. Quindene of Martinmas 1336. The morrow of the Purification 1337. P: William son of William Bateson of Parva Hokelowe. D: Thomas son of Thomas de Weston and Isabel h.w. Concerning 1 mess. and 8½a. land in Tyddeswelle. William had these of the gift of Thomas and Isabel to hold to himself and his heirs of the chief lord etc forever. Thomas and Isabel warranted for themselves and the heirs of Isabel. William gave 20 marks of silver. (82)

780. York. Quindene of Michaelmas 1336. Quindene of Hilary 1337. P: Thomas de Alsop of Peverwych by John de Caldon his attorney. D: Ralph son of Richard de Wardelowe del Tounstedes and Maude h.w. Concerning 1 mess. and a moiety of 1 furlong of land in Peverwych. Thomas had these of the gift of Ralph and Maude to hold to himself and his heirs of the chief lord etc forever. Ralph and Maude warranted for themselves and the heirs of Maude. Thomas gave 10 marks of silver. (83)

781. York. Octave of Hilary 1337. P: Margery widow of William atte Barre of Derby. D: Peter le Syvekere of Derby, chaplain. Concerning 2 mess., 54a. land and 2a. meadow in Chaddesden. Peter had these of the gift of Margery and he granted and rendered them to her to hold of the chief lord etc for her life. Remainders to William, son of William atte Barre, for life and then the abbot and convent of Derleye and the abbot's successors. The agreement was made by order of the king. (84)

782. York. Octave of the Purification 1337. Easter three weeks 1337. P: Ralph de Braylesford and Margaret h.w. by Thomas de Baggeley attorney for Margaret by brief of the king. D: Thomas de Braylesford, parson of the church of Braylesford, and Philip de Baryngton. Concerning 8 mess., 228½a. land, 4a. meadow, 64a. pasture, 52a. woodland, 40s rent and a moiety of a mill in Chesterfeld, Derby, Dronfeld, and Barley and the manor of Wyngirworth except the advowson of Dronfeld church. Ralph acknowledged these to be the right of Thomas who, with Philip, had them of the gift of Ralph. Thomas and Philip granted and rendered them to Ralph and Margaret to hold (a) 4 mess. in Chesterfeld and Derby and the manor less the advowson to themselves and the heirs of Ralph; (b) all the remaining tenements in Dronfeld and Barley to themselves and the heirs of their bodies of the chief lord etc forever. As concerns the tenements in (b), remainder to the right heirs of Ralph. (85)

783. York. Octave of Midsummer 1337. P: John de Bakepuiz and Margery h.w. by Nicholas de Rossynton attorney for Margery by brief of the king. D: Ralph de Bakepuiz, parson of the church of Barton Bakepuiz and William de Saperton, chaplain. Concerning 20 mess., 1 toft, 17 bov. 126a. and a moiety of 1a. 1 rood land, 13a. 1 rood meadow, 11½a. pasture, 25a. woodland, 14s 3d rent and a third part of 1 mess. in Barton Bakepuiz and Boilleston. John acknowledged these to be the right of Ralph who, with William, had them of the gift of John. Ralph and William granted and rendered them to John and Margery to hold to themselves and the heirs of John of the chief lord etc forever. (86)

784. York. Quindene of Michaelmas 1336. Octave of Midsummer 1337. P: John de Musters and Alice h.w. D: John son of Richard de Sutton of Duerham and Joan h.w. Concerning a moiety of a fourth part of the manor of Esshovre. John son of Richard and Joan acknowledged the moiety to be the right of Alice and they remised and quitclaimed it of themselves and the heirs of Joan to John de Musters, Alice and Alice's heirs. John and Alice gave £20. (87)

785. York. The morrow of All Souls 1337. P: Roger le Eyr of Cestrefeld D: John son of Adam son of Hugh de Neubolt and Alice h.w. Concerning 1 toft and 4½a. land in Cestrefeld. John and Alice remised and quitclaimed these of, and warranted for, themselves and the heirs of Alice. Roger gave 20 marks of silver. (88)

786. York. Quindene of Hilary 1338. P: Margery widow of William atte Barre of Derby. D: Peter le Sivekere of Derby, chaplain. Concerning 1 mess., 1 shop and 9½a. land in Derby. Peter had these of the gift of Margery and he granted and rendered them to her to hold of the chief lord etc for her life. Remainder to Robert, Margery's brother, for his life. Remainder to the abbot and convent of Burton on Trent and the abbot's successors. The agreement was made by order of the king. (89)

22

787. York. Octave of the Purification 1338. P: John de Spondon, vicar of the church of Lokynton and William de Aston. D: John son of John Russel and Joan h.w. Concerning 3 mess., 6 virgates land, 2a. meadow, 8a. woodland and 3s 4d rent in Herteshorn. John son of John and Joan acknowledged these to be the right of William and they remised and quitclaimed of, and warranted for, themselves and the heirs of Joan to John de Spondon and William and William's heirs. John and William gave 100 marks of silver. (90)

788. York. Quindene of Easter 1338. Quindene of Trinity 1338. P: Adam Strygil of Denby. D: Thomas Rosel and Alice h.w. Concerning 1 mess., 3a. land and a moiety of 2 mills in Denby. Adam had these of the gift of Thomas and Alice and he granted and rendered them to them to hold of himself and his heirs for the lives of Thomas and Alice, paying therefor 1 rose each year at the feast of the Nativity of St John the Baptist for all services etc due to Adam and his heirs and doing to the chief lord etc. Reversion to Adam and his heirs. (91)

789. York. The morrow of All Souls 1338. Westminster. Octave of Hilary 1339. P: Henry de Coventre, chaplain. D: Henry de Thurleston of Derby and Joan h.w. Concerning 5 mess., 12a. land and 2a. meadow in Derby. Henry de Coventre had these of the gift of Henry and Joan and he granted and rendered them to them to hold to themselves and the heirs of Henry de Thurleston of the chief lord etc forever. (92)

790. York. Michaelmas three weeks 1338. Westminster. The morrow of the Purification 1339. P: Gilbert del Leghs. D: Peter Spark of Derleye and Beatrice h.w. Concerning 1 mess., 2a. land, 1a. meadow and 1a. woodland in Yelgreve. Peter and Beatrice rendered these to Gilbert to hold to himself and his heirs of the chief lord etc forever. They warranted for themselves and the heirs of Beatrice. Gilbert gave 100 shillings of silver. (93)

791. York. Quindene of Martinmas 1338. Westminster. Quindene of Hilary 1339. P: Robert son of John de Wyggeley. D: Richard son of Nicholas de Thwathweyt and Edusa h.w. Concerning 1 mess. and 1 bov. land in Brampton. Richard and Edusa rendered these to Robert to hold to himself and his heirs of the chief lord etc forever. They warranted for themselves and the heirs of Edusa. Robert gave 20 marks of silver. (94)

792. Westminster. Quindene of Easter 1339. P: Roger son of Roger de Rossyngton and Joan h.w. by Nicholas de Rossyngton attorney for Joan. D: Roger Chasteleyn. Concerning 3 mess., 90a. land and 12a. meadow in Howene. Roger Chasteleyn acknowledged these to be the right of Roger son of Roger who, with Joan, had them of the gift of Roger Chasteleyn to hold to themselves and the heirs of Roger of the chief lord etc forever. Roger

Chasteleyn warranted for himself and his heirs. Roger and Joan gave 100 marks of silver. (95)

793. Westminster. Easter three weeks 1339. P: Robert de Hampton of Chastirfeld and Ellen h.w. by William de Wakebrugge their attorney. D: Ralph son of Henry Muryman of Baukwell and Margery h.w. Concerning 1 mess. in Baukwell. Ralph and Margery granted and rendered this messuage to Robert and Ellen to hold to themselves and the heirs of their bodies of the chief lord etc forever. Remainder to the right heirs of Robert. Ralph and Margery warranted for themselves and the heirs of Margery. Robert and Ellen gave 100 shillings of silver. (96)

794. Westminster. Quindene of Michaelmas 1339. P: William son of Nicholas Creuker and Margery h.w. by Henry de Barewe, guardian of Margery. D: Robert de Usflet. Concerning the manor of Twyford. William acknowledged the manor to be the right of Robert who had it of the gift of William. Robert granted and rendered it to William and Margery to hold to themselves and the heirs of their bodies of the chief lord etc forever. Remainder to the right heirs of William. (97)

795. Westminster. Quindene of Michaelmas 1339. P: Robert Burdet. D: Roger son of Roger de Rossynton and Joan h.w. Concerning 3 mess., 90a. land and 12a. meadow in Howene. Robert had these of the gift of Roger and Joan to hold to himself and his heirs of the chief lord etc forever. Roger and Joan warranted for themselves and the heirs of Roger. Robert gave 100 marks of silver. (98)

796. Westminster. Quindene of Michaelmas 1339. P: William Sparwe of Tyddeswell D: Robert le Taillour of Tyddeswell and Margery h.w. Concerning 3a. land in Tyddeswell. William had this land of the gift of Robert and Margery to hold to himself and his heirs of the chief lord etc forever. Robert and Margery warranted for themselves and the heirs of Margery. William gave 10 marks of silver. (99)

797. Westminster. Octave of Michaelmas 1339. P: John de Neuport and Sarah h.w. and Nicholas their son. D: John de Caldecote, parson of the church of Lecheworth. Concerning 1 mess., 91a. land, 8a meadow, 5a. woodland and 6s 5d rent in Algerthorp, Brampton, Hulm, Lynacre and Cestrefeld. John de Neuport and Sarah acknowledged these to be the right of John de Caldecote who had them of their gift. John de Caldecote granted and rendered them to John, Sarah and Nicholas to hold of the chief lord etc for their lives. Remainder to Cecily, daughter of Adam de Neubold of Cestrefeld, and John, son of Nicholas de Hulm, and the heirs of his body. Remainder to the right heirs of Nicholas, son of John de Neuport and Sarah. (100)

798. Westminster. Octave of Michaelmas 1339. P: Thomas le Porter of Pershovere and Emma h.w. D: Thomas de Rolleston and Reyna h.w. Concerning 2 mills and 6a. land in Alrewaslegh. Thomas le Porter acknowledged these to be the right of Reyna. Thomas de Rolleston and Reyna granted and rendered them to Thomas and Emma to hold to themselves and the heirs of their bodies of the chief lord etc forever. Remainder to the right heirs of Thomas le Porter. Thomas and Reyna warranted for themselves and the heirs of Reyna. (101)

799. Westminster. Quindene of Easter 1340. P: Hugh de Bassyngbourn. D: Humphrey de Bassyngbourn and Olive h.w. Concerning the manor of Wynle. Hugh had the manor of the gift of Humphrey and Olive to hold to himself and his heirs of the chief lord etc forever. Humphrey and Olive warranted for themselves and the heirs of Olive. Hugh gave 100 marks of silver. (102)

800. Westminster. Octave of Trinity 1340. P: William de Byngham, kt. D: Ralph de Caldewell and Cecily h.w. Concerning the manor of Caldewell. Ralph and Cecily remised and quitclaimed of, and warranted for, themselves and the heirs of Ralph to William and his heirs. William gave 100 marks of silver. (103)

801. Westminster. Michaelmas one month 1340. P: Roger de Somervill and Margery h.w. D: John de Steynesby of Walley. Concerning the manor of Blacwell. John had the manor of the gift of Roger and Margery and he granted and rendered it to them to hold of the chief lord etc for their lives. Remainder to William Trussebut, chivaler, and Joan h.w. and William's heirs. (104)

802. Westminster. Octave of the Purification 1329. P: John Bosonn and Isabel h.w. by Robert de Macworth attorney for Isabel. D: John de Steynesby and Richard de Edenesoure, chaplain. Concerning the manor of Edensoure. Later, *[venue not stated]* Michaelmas one month 1340, after the death of John Bosonn, P: Isabel. D: John and Richard. John Bosonn acknowledged the manor to be the right of Richard who, with John de Steynesby, had it of the gift of John Bosonn. John and Richard granted and rendered it to John and Isabel to hold to themselves and the heirs of their bodies of the chief lord etc forever. Remainder to the right heirs of John Bosonn. (105)

803. Westminster. Quindene of Michaelmas 1339. Quindene of Easter 1340. P: John Cokayn of Assheburn. D: Walter de Rydeware, chivaler, and Joan h.w. Concerning 2 mess., 21a. land, 5a. meadow, a moiety of 1 toft and a fifth part of 12 mess., 2 furlongs 2 bov. 40a. land and 12s rent in Hope, Peverwyche, Knyveton, Assheburn, Bradeburn, Castelton in Pecco and la Lee next Bradeburn. Walter and Joan rendered all these tenements, with the exception of those listed in (i) and (ii) below, to John to hold to himself and his heirs of the chief lord etc forever. They also granted for themselves and the heirs of Joan that (i) the fifth part of 1 mess. in Peverwyche which Robert de la Dale and Agnes h.w. held for their lives; and (ii) the fifth part of 2s 4d rent and a third of the fifth part of 2 mess. and 2 furlongs land also in Peverwyche which Agnes, widow of Robert de Huncyndon, held as dowry of the inheritance of John, which tenements ought to revert to Walter and Joan on the deaths of Robert and Agnes and of Agnes, widow of Robert de Huncyndon, should remain instead to John and his heirs. Walter and Joan warranted for themselves and the heirs of Joan. John gave 40 marks of silver. (106)

804. Westminster. Octave of Michaelmas 1340. Quindene of Hilary 1341. P: Thomas Adam of Assheburn. D: Henry Rosel and Emma h.w. Concerning 1 toft, 8a. land and 1a. 1 rood meadow in Marketon and Macworth. Thomas had these of the gift of Henry and Emma who remised and quitclaimed of, and warranted for, themselves and the heirs of Emma to Thomas and his heirs. Thomas gave £10. (107)

805. Westminster. Quindene of Michaelmas 1341. P: John Touyot of Chestrefeld. D: William Trussebut, chivaler, and Joan h.w. Concerning 1 mess., 1 toft, 74a. land, 4a. meadow and 5a. woodland in Heghegge and Duffeldfryth. William and Joan remised and quitclaimed of, and warranted for, themselves and the heirs of William to John and his heirs. John gave £20. (108)

806. Westminster. Quindene of Trinity 1342. P: William son of Richard de Wyrthorp and Agnes h.w. by John de Clapton, attorney for Agnes. D: Gervase de Wilford and John de Clifton. Concerning a moiety of the manor of Ailwaston. William acknowledged the moiety to be the right of Gervase who, with John, had it of the gift of William. Gervase and John granted and rendered it to William and Agnes to hold to themselves and the heirs of their bodies of the chief lord etc forever. Remainder to the right heirs of William (109)

807. Westminster. The morrow of All Souls. 1342. Octave of Hilary 1343. P: Henry de Hambury, chivaler. D: Richard Foliambe of Caldelowe, junior, and Elizabeth h.w. Concerning 4 mess., 120a. land and 20a. meadow in Snelleston, Rossynton and Northbury. Henry had these of the gift of Richard and Elizabeth to hold to himself and his heirs of the chief lord etc forever. Richard and Elizabeth warranted for themselves and the heirs of Richard. Henry gave £100. Endorsed: William de Moston and Lucy h.w.,

26

Robert del Grene and Joan h.w. and Alice Tuchet laid their claims. (110)

808. Westminster. Quindene of Hilary 1343. P: Walter de Monte Gomeri, chivaler, and Alice h.w. D: William de Saperton, chaplain, and John Roger. Concerning the manors of Sudbury and Cobeleye. Walter acknowledged the manors to be the right of John who, with William, had the manor of Cobleye (with exceptions) and two parts of the manor of Sudbury (with exceptions) of the gift of Walter. William and John granted and rendered these to Walter and Alice to hold to themselves and the heirs of the body of Walter of the chief lord etc forever. Morever, William and John granted for themselves and the heirs of John that the tenements listed below with the life tenants, which ought to revert to them and the heirs of John on the deaths of the respective life tenants should remain instead to Walter and Alice and the heirs of the body of Walter to hold as above. Remainder to the right heirs of Walter. William and John warranted for themselves and the heirs of John. Tenements and life tenants: (i) 1 mess. and 20a. land in the manor of Cobeleye — William Fraunkeleyn. (ii) 40a. land — Walter, son of Walter de Monte Gomeri, and Margaret h.w. (iii) 1 mess. and 20a. land — Richard de Longeford and Joan h.w. (iv) 1 mess. and 6a. land — Adam de Scoleye and Annabell h.w. (v) 1 mess. — Robert le Wodeward. (vi) 1 mess. and 18a. land — Thomas le Souter and Avis h.w. (vii) 2 mess. and 15a. land — Agnes Balle. (viii) 1 mess. and 36a. land — Richard Broun and Joan h.w. (ix) 1 mess. and 15a. land — William le Mareschal. (x) 1 mess. and 6a. land — Richard Tirry. (xi) 1 mess. and 6a. land — Agnes del Hermitage. (xii) 2 mess. and 16a. land — William le Cook. (xiii) 1 mess. and 9a. land — John Daukyn. (xiv) 5a. land — William del Hull. (xv) 4 mess. and 4 bov. land — Robert le Breton and Philippa h.w. (her dowry). All the above tenements in the manor of Cobeleye. All the following tenements in the two parts of the manor of Sudbury: (xvi) 1 mess. and 1 bov. land — Walter Geneson and Margery h.w. (xvii) 1 mess. and 2 bov. 3a. land — Thomas Margerieson and Thomas his son. (xviii) 1 mess. and 40a. land — Henry Matheu and Lettice h.w. and Henry their son. (xix) 1 mess. and 4 bov. land — Roger atte Yate and Avis h.w. (xx) 1 mess. and 2 bov. land — Richard de Creyghton. (xxi) 4a. land — John Wildegos. (xxii) 1 mess. — Robert le Souter and Agnes h.w. (xxiii) 1 mess. and 2 bov. land — John de Monte Gomeri. (xxiv) 2 mess. and 2 bov. land — John le Parker and Margery h.w. (xxv) 10a. land — Edward de Monte Gomeri and Catherine h.w. (xxvi) 1 mess. and 9a. land — Walter de Yerdeleye and Hawis h.w. (xxvii) 3 bov. 10a. land — John Prine, Thomas the clerk and William his son. (xxviii) 1 mess. and 4 bov. land — Walter, son of Walter de Monte Gomeri, and Margaret h.w. (xxix) 1 mess. and 4a. land — John le Smyth. (xxx) 1 mess. and 1 bov. 3a. land — John de Brotton. (xxxi) 12a. land — Nicholas Fitz Herberd and Alice h.w. (xxxii) 1 mess. and 2 bov. land — William de Saperton. (xxxiii) the third part of the manor of Sudbury — Robert le Breton and Philippa h.w. (her dowry of the inheritance of John Roger). (111)

809. Westminster. Quindene of Easter 1343. Octave of Trinity 1343. P: Thomas le Chapman. D: William de Staynton and Agnes h.w. Concerning 1 mess., 34a. land, 7a. meadow and 8d rent in Ekynton. William and Agnes remised and quitclaimed of, and warranted for, themselves and the heirs of Agnes to Thomas and his heirs. Thomas gave 20 marks of silver. (112)

810. Westminster. Octave of Trinity 1343. P: John de Sneyth and Alice h.w. by John de Chelaston attorney for Alice. D: William le Pryker of Derby and Eleanor h.w. Concerning 1 mess. in Derby. John acknowledged the messuage to be the right of Eleanor. William and Eleanor granted and rendered it to John and Alice to hold to themselves and the heirs of their bodies of the chief lord etc forever. Remainder to the right heirs of John. (113)

811. Westminster. Octave of Trinity 1343. Octave of Michaelmas 1343. P: Martin del Halle and Isabel h.w. and John their son by William de Haddon, John's guardian. D: Nicholas de Thornhull. Concerning the manor of Berde. Martin and Isabel acknowledged the manor to be the right of Nicholas who granted and rendered it to Martin and Isabel to hold to themselves and John and the heirs of the body of John, of the chief lord etc forever. Remainder to the right heirs of Martin. (114)

812. Westminster. The morrow of Ascension 1343. Quindene of Michaelmas 1343. Hugh de Stredeleye by John de Caldon his attorney. D: William Hert of Netherhaddon and Margery h.w. Concerning 1 mess. and 8a. land in Calton. Hugh had these of the gift of William and Margery to hold to himself and his heirs of the chief lord etc forever. William and Margery warranted for themselves and the heirs of Margery. Hugh gave 20 marks of silver. (115)

813. Westminster. Octave of Hilary 1344. P: William de Gray of Sandiacre. D: Robert Hillary, parson of the church of Sutton in Colefeld and Richard de Grey, parson of the church of Sutton en le Dale. Concerning the manors of Sutton en le Dale and Halom and the advowson of the church of Sutton en le Dale. William acknowledged these to be the right of Richard. Richard and Robert had the manor and advowson of Sutton of the gift of William and they granted and rendered them to him to hold to himself and the male heirs of his body of the chief lord etc forever. Furthermore, Richard and Robert granted for themselves and the heirs of Richard that the manor of Halom, which Hugh Burdet held for life of the inheritance of Richard and which ought to revert to Robert and Richard on the death of Hugh, should remain instead to William and his heirs as above.

28

Remainder to Edward, son of Henry Hillary, and Alice h.w. and the heirs of their bodies. Remainder to the right heirs of William. (116)

814. Westminster. Quindene of Easter 1343. P: John Touyot of Chestrefeld, clerk. D: William de Enefeld and Cecily h.w. Concerning 1 mess., 1 toft, 74a. land, 4a. meadow and 5a. woodland in Heghegge and Duffeldfrith. William and Cecily remised and quitclaimed of, and warranted for, themselves and the heirs of Cecily to John and his heirs. John gave 100 marks of silver. (117)

815. Westminster. Easter three weeks 1343. P: John le Wyne, chivaler, and Elizabeth h.w. by Roger de Padelay, Elizabeth's guardian. D: Thomas Dobyn, parson of the church of Westbury and Richard Pygot, parson of the church of Penkeston. Concerning the manors of Penkeston and Normanton and the advowsons of the churches of both manors. John acknowledged these to be the right of Thomas who, with Richard, had them of the gift of John. Thomas and Richard granted and rendered them to John and Elizabeth to hold to themselves and the heirs of their bodies of the chief lord etc forever. Remainder to Margery, wife of Ede de Hodinet for her life. Remainder to the right heirs of John. (118)

816. Westminster. Quindene of Michaelmas 1343. P: John son of Richard Foleiaumbe of Longesdon. D: Roger Foleiaumbe of Parva Longesdon. Concerning 1 mess., 1 carucate land and 30s rent in Parva Longesdon, Menesale and Brytrychefeld. John had these of the gift of Roger and he granted and rendered them to Roger to hold to himself and the male heirs of his body of John and his heirs paying therefor 1 rose each year at the feast of the Nativity of St John the Baptist for all services etc due to John and his heirs and doing to the chief lord etc. Reversion to John and his heirs. (119)

817. Westminster. Quindene of Hilary 1344. P: William de Gray of Sandiacre. D: Robert Hillary, parson of the church of Sutton in Colfeld and Richard de Gray of Sandiacre, parson of the church of Sutton in Dal. Concerning the manor of Sandiacre. Robert and Richard had the manor of the gift of William and they granted and rendered it to him to hold to himself and the male heirs of his body of the king and his heirs etc forever. Remainder to Edward, son of Henry Hillary, and Alice h.w. and the heirs of their bodies. Remainder to the right heirs of William. The agreement was made by order of the king. (120)

818. York. Octave of Michaelmas 1337. Westminster. Quindene of Easter 1344. P: Richard de la Pole of Hertyndon. D: Gratian le Palmere of London and Gillian h.w. Concerning a fifth part of 1 mess., 60a. land, 10s rent and a third part of 1 mess. and 2 furlongs of land in Hope, Assheburn, Bradburn,

Knyveton and Peverwych. Richard had the fifth part of the land and rent of the gift of Gratian and Gillian to hold to himself and his heirs of the chief lord etc forever. Gratian and Gillian granted for themselves and the heirs of Gillian that (i) the fifth part of the messuage in Peverwych which Robert de la Dale and Agnes h.w. held for their lives; and (ii) the fifth part of the third part, also in Peverwych, which Margery, widow of Robert de Huncyndon held as dowry of the inheritance of Gillian, which tenements ought to revert to Gratian, Gillian and Gillan's heirs on the deaths of Robert, Agnes and Margery, should remain instead to Richard and his heirs. Gratian and Gillian warranted for themselves and the heirs of Gillian. Richard gave 40 marks of silver. (121)

819. Westminster. Octave of the Purification 1339. Quindene of Easter 1344. P: Richard de la Pole of Hertyngdon. D: William Pygot of London and Isabel h.w. Concerning 1 mess., 1 toft, 21a. land, 5a. meadow and a moiety of 4 mess., 12a. land, 2s 6d rent and a fifth part of 12 mess, 2 furlongs 2 bov. 40a. land and 12s rent in Castelton in Pecco, Hope, Peverwyche, Knyveton, Assheburn, Bradeley, Bradeburn and la Lee next Bradeburn. William and Isabel rendered all these tenements, with the exception of those listed in (i) and (ii) below, to Richard to hold to himself and his heirs of the chief lord etc forever. They also granted for themselves and the heirs of Isabel that (i) the fifth part of 1 messuage in Peverwyche which Robert de la Dale and Agnes h.w. held for their lives; and (ii) the fifth part of 2s 4d rent and third part of 1 messuage and 2 furlongs land in Peverwyche which Margery, widow of Robert de Huncyndon, held as dowry of the inheritance of Isabel, which tenements ought to revert to William and Isabel and Isabel's heirs on the deaths of Robert, Agnes and Margery, should remain instead to Richard and his heirs. William and Isabel warranted for themselves and the heirs of Isabel. Richard gave £100. (122)

820. Westminster. Easter three weeks 1344. Quindene of Trinity 1344. P: Henry de la Pole of Hertyndon. D: Richard del Hull, parson of the church of Wolvardynton. Concerning 2 mess., 50a. land, 8a. meadow and pasture for 6 animals in Netherhaddon. Richard rendered to Henry 1 mess., 40a. land, 4a. meadow and the pasturage to hold to himself and his heirs of the chief lord etc forever and he granted that the remainder of the tenements, which Deonise Bassett held for life of the inheritance of Richard and which ought to revert to Richard and his heirs on the death of Deonise, should remain instead to Henry and his heirs. Richard warranted for himself and his heirs. Henry gave £40. (123)

821. Westminster. Easter three weeks 1340. Quindene of Easter 1344. P: Richard de la Pole of Hertyndon. D: Thomas de Swanlond and Elizabeth h.w. Concerning 1 mess., 21a. land, 4½a. meadow and a moiety of 1 mess. and a fifth part of 4 mess., 2 furlongs land and 12s rent in Assheburne, Peverwych, Knyveton and la Lee next Bradburne. Thomas and Elizabeth rendered all these tenements, with the exception of those listed in (i) and (ii) below, to Richard to hold to himself and his heirs of the chief lord etc forever. They also granted for themselves and the heirs of Elizabeth that (i) the fifth part of 1 messuage which Robert de la Dale and Agnes h.w. held for their lives; and (ii) the fifth part of 3s 4d rent and the third part of 1 messuage and 2 furlongs land which Margery, widow of Robert de Huncyndon held as dowry of the inheritance of Elizabeth, in Peverwych, which tenements ought to revert to Thomas, Elizabeth and Elizabeth's heirs on the deaths of Robert, Agnes and Margery, should remain instead to Richard and his heirs. Thomas and Elizabeth warranted for themselves and the heirs of Elizabeth. Richard gave 40 marks of silver. (124)

822. York. Octave of Michaelmas 1338. Westminster. Quindene of Easter 1344. P: Richard de la Pole of Hertyndon. D: Ralph de Shirley and Margaret h.w. Concerning 3 mess., 1 toft, 20a. 3 roods land, 4a. 1 rood meadow, 3s 6d rent and a fifth part of 3 mess., 2 furlongs land and 10s rent in Assheburn, Knyveton, Peverwiche, Bradburn and la Lee next Bradburn. Richard had 3 mess., 20a. 3 roods land, the toft, the meadow and 3s 6d rent in Assheburn, Knyveton, Bradburn and la Lee next Bradburn of the gift of Ralph and Margaret. Ralph and Margaret rendered to Richard a fifth part of 1 mess., two parts of 1 mess. and 2 furlongs land in Peverwiche. They also granted to him a fifth part of 7s 8d rent together with the homage and services of Nicholas de Ingwardby, Geoffrey del Stones, Margery, widow of Ralph de Peverwiche, Roger son of Nicholas de Peverwiche, Roger le Bernreve, Richard le Bernreve and Henry de Garton and their heirs, of all the tenements that they formerly held of Ralph and Margaret, to hold to Richard and his heirs of the chief lord etc forever. Ralph and Margaret also granted for themselves and the heirs of Margaret that (i) the fifth part of 1 messuage in Peverwiche which Robert de la Dale of Peverwiche and Agnes h.w. held for life; and (ii) the fifth part of 2s 4d rent and third part of 1 messuage and 2 furlongs land also in Peverwiche which Margery, widow of Robert de Hunsyndon, held as dowry of the inheritance of Margaret, which tenements ought to revert to Ralph and Margaret and Margaret's heirs on the deaths of Robert, Agnes and Margery, should remain instead to Richard and his heirs. Ralph and Margaret warranted for themselves and the heirs of Margaret. Richard gave £100. (125)

823. Westminster. Quindene of Hilary 1345. P: John son of Robert de Fynderne. D: Robert le Hunte of Uttoxhather and Felise h.w. Concerning 1 mess. and 1 carucate land in Walton upon Trent. Robert and Felise remised and quitclaimed of, and warranted for, themselves and the heirs of Felise to John and his heirs. John gave 40 marks of silver. (126)

824. Westminster. Quindene of Hilary 1345. P: Isabel daughter of William de Brassyngton. D: Giles de Meygnyll, chivaler. Concerning 4 mess. and 54a. land in Derby, Kyrkelongeleye and Stapenhull. Giles granted and rendered to Isabel 3 mess. and 20a. land in Derby and Kyrkelongeleye to hold to herself and her heirs of the chief lord etc forever. Giles warranted for himself and his heirs. He also granted and rendered to Isabel [1] mess. and 34a. land to hold of himself and his heirs paying therefor 1 rose each year at the feast of the Nativity of St John the Baptist for all services etc due to Giles and his heirs and doing to the chief lord etc for her life. Successive remainders to Isabel's children, Hugh and Isabel, and Giles's brothers, Robert and John, and the heirs of their bodies. Reversion to Giles and his heirs. (127)

825. Westminster. Quindene of Easter 1345. P: John Roger and Roger de Murcaston. D: Walter de Monte Gomeri, chivaler. Concerning the manor of Marchynton. Walter acknowledged the manor to be the right of John. John and Roger had 2 parts of it (except 7 mess. and 100a. land) of the gift of Walter and they granted and rendered this to him to hold of the chief lord etc for his life. They also granted for themselves and the heirs of John that (i) 1 mess. and 24a. land which Edward de Monte Gomeri and Catherine h.w. held for their lives; (ii) 20a. land which Edward also held for life; (iii) 1 mess. and 3a. land which Richard le Prest held for life; (iv) 1 mess. and 3a. land which John son of Thomas held for life; (v) 1 mess. and 24a. land which Henry le Shepehird held for life; (vi) 6a. land which Thomas le Clerk and John his son held for life; (vii) 1 mess. and 15a. land which Thomas atte Brok held for life; (viii) 1 mess. and 1a. land which Richard de Beverley and Margery h.w. held for the life of Margery; (ix) 1 mess. 24a. land which William Thomson and Joan h.w. held for life; and (x) the third part of the manor which Richard le Breton and Philippa h.w. held as Phillipa's dowry of the inheritance of John Roger, which tenements ought to revert to John and Roger and the heirs of John on the deaths of the respective life tenants, should remain instead to Walter for his life. Remainder to Walter's son, William, and Margaret, daughter of Richard de Stafford, chivaler, and the heirs of their bodies. Remainder to the right heirs of Walter. (128)

826. Westminster. The morrow of Midsummer 1345. P: Walter Aust and Mabel h.w. D: Thomas de Smythisby, chaplain. Concerning 25a. land and 2½a. meadow in Drakelowe. Thomas had these of the gift of Walter and Mabel and he granted and rendered them to them to hold to themselves and the heirs of their bodies of the chief lord etc forever. Remainder to the right heirs of Mabel. (129)

827. Westminster. Easter three weeks 1345. Quindene of Trinity 1345. P: John son of Richard de Chalencheswod and William son of John Child of Caldewell. D: John Child of Caldewell. Concerning 1 mess., 6a. 2½ virgates land and 3a. meadow in Caldewell. John Child acknowledged these to be the right of John son of Richard who, with William, had them of the gift of John. John and William granted and rendered them to John Child to hold of the chief lord etc for his life. Remainder to Henry, son of Richard de Chalencheswod, and Alice, daughter of John Child, and the heirs of their bodies. Remainder to the right heirs of John Child. (130)

828. Westminster. Quindene of Midsummer 1345. P: Hugh de Muskham. D: Robert de Sallowe. Concerning 5 mess., 3 virgates land, 20a. pasture and 2s rent in Stanton next Sandiacre. Robert had these of the gift of Hugh and he granted and rendered them to him to hold of the chief lord etc for his life. Successive remainders to Hugh's wife, Felise, for her life, to the heirs of their bodies, to Hugh son of William Danvers of Stannton and the heirs of his body and lastly to the right heirs of Hugh de Muskham. (131)

829. Westminster. Quindene of Easter 1346. P: Nicholas de Ingwardeby and Isabel h.w. D: Richard de Ingwardeby, parson of the church of Stonystannton, and Roger le Botyler of Shurstoke. Concerning 2 mess., 50a. land, 8a. meadow, 20a. pasture, 30a. moorland and 11 marks rent in Peverwych and Chattesworth. Nicholas and Isabel acknowledged these to be the right of Richard who, with Roger, had them of the gift of Nicholas and Isabel. Richard and Roger granted and rendered them to them to hold of the chief lord etc for their lives. Remainder to Nicholas's children, Philip, Aubrey (daughter) and Thomas for their lives. Remainder to the right heirs of Nicholas. (132)

830. Westminster. Easter three weeks 1346. P: William son of Roger de Bradburne, junior, and Margaret h.w. D: John Dounville and Maude h.w. Concerning 1 mess., 1 carucate 5 bov. 30a. land, 10 marks rent and a moiety of a mill in Bradburne, Assheburne, Wircusworthe, Perwyche, Benteleye and Kneveton. John and Maude granted and rendered the messuage, carucate of land and rent to William and Margaret to hold to themselves and the heirs of their bodies of the chief lord etc forever. They also granted for themselves and the heirs of Maude that (i) the 5 bov. 35a. land in Kneveton and Perwyche which William de Bradburne, senior, held for life;

33

and (ii) the moiety of the mill in Wircusworth which Richard de Bradburne and John de Bradburne held for life of the inheritance of Maude, which tenements ought to revert to John Dounville, Maude and Maude's heirs on the deaths of William, Richard and John, should remain instead to William, son of Roger, and Margaret and the heirs of their bodies. Remainder to the right heirs of William, son of Roger. William and Margaret gave 40 marks of silver. (133)

831. Westminster. The morrow of Ascension 1346. P: Edward de Monte Gomeri and Catherine h.w. D: William Honbel of Sudbury. Concerning 4 messuage, 1 mill, 1 carucate 1 bov. land, 30a. meadow and 13s rent in Derby, Brailesford, Bolton, Witton, Thurvaston and Longeford. Edward acknowledged these to be the right of William who had them of the gift of Edward and Catherine. William granted and rendered them to Edward and Catherine to hold of the chief lord etc for their lives. Successive remainders to William, son of William de Hyntes, Thomas, Walter and John, the three sons of Edward, and the male heirs of their bodies in each case. Remainder to the heirs of the bodies of Edward and Catherine. Remainder to the right heirs of Catherine. (134)

832. Westminster. Quindene of Michaelmas 1346. P: Thomas Fasmon of Derby and Agnes h.w. D: Robert son of William de Spondon of Derby and Emma h.w. and William del Heye and Avis h.w. Concerning 1 mess. in Derby. The deforciants acknowledged the messuage to be the right of Thomas who, with Agnes, had it of their gift to hold to themselves and the heirs of Thomas of the chief lord etc forever. The deforciants warranted for themselves and the heirs of Avis. Thomas and Agnes gave 100 shillings of silver. (135)

833. Westminster. The morrow of All Souls 1346. P: William de Byngham, chivaler. D: Geoffrey de Leicestre of Tharlesthorp and Joan h.w. Concerning the manor of Tharlesthorp. William had the manor of the gift of Geoffrey and Joan to hold to himself and his heirs of the chief lord etc forever. Geoffrey and Joan warranted for themselves and the heirs of Geoffrey. William gave 100 marks of silver. (136)

834. Westminster. Easter one month 1347. The morrow of Midsummer 1347. P: Roger de Eyncourt, chivaler, and Maude h.w. D: Walter, parson of the church of Hallewynnefeld and John, parson of the church of Morton. Concerning a moiety of 14 mess., 12½ bov. land and 4a. meadow in Rouseleye, Derleye, Edenesoure, Baukewelle and Yelgreve and a moiety of the manor of Boythorp. Roger and Maude acknowledged these to be the right of John who, with Walter, had the moiety of the tenements of their gift. They granted for themselves and the heirs of Maude that the moiety of the manor, which Richard de Bynham held for life of the inheritance of

34

Maude and which ought to revert to Roger and Maude on the death of Richard, should remain instead to Walter and John and the heirs of John to hold of the chief lord etc forever. Walter and John granted and rendered the moiety of the tenements to Roger and Maude to hold to themselves and the heirs of their bodies of the chief lord etc forever. Remainder to the right heirs of Maude. (137)

835. Westminster. Quindene of Easter 1347. Octave of Trinity 1347. P: Thomas de Gunston. D: Philip son of Philip de Stredleye and Alice h.w. Concerning 3 mess., 2 carucates 10a. land, 1a. meadow and 16s rent in Baukewell, Birchulles, Hassop, Parva Longesdon and Magna Longesdon and an eighth part of the manor of Yolgreve. Philip and Alice rendered these to Thomas to hold to himself and his heirs of the chief lord etc forever and they warranted for themselves and the heirs of Alice. Thomas gave 100 marks of silver. (138)

836. Westminster. Easter three weeks 1347. Quindene of Trinity 1347. P: John de Dronfeld, chaplain. D: Richard Foliambe and Elizabeth h.w. Concerning 1 mess., 1 mill, 120a. land and 20a. meadow in Alsop and Idrichehay. Richard and Elizabeth rendered these to John to hold to himself and his heirs of the chief lord etc forever and they warranted for themselves and the heirs of Elizabeth. John gave 100 marks of silver. Endorsed: Lucy de Morleye and Simon Trichet, clerk, laid their claims. (139)

837. Westminster. Octave of Hilary 1348. P: Richard le Clerk of Lee. D: Robert de Bateleye and Agnes h.w. Concerning 5a. land in Lee. Robert and Agnes remised and quitclaimed of themselves and the heirs of Agnes to Richard and his heirs. They warranted for themselves and Agnes's heirs to Richard and his heirs, a moiety of the land lying in a certain croft called Wlrychecroft towards the east. Richard gave 100 shillings of silver. (140)

838. Westminster. Quindene of Hilary 1348. P: Hugh de Meignyll, chivaler, and Alice h.w. D: Peter de Stepell of Wirkesworth and Margery h.w. Concerning 1 mess., 80a. land, 2a. meadow, 10a. pasture and 10a. woodland in Wirkesworth and Cromnford. Hugh acknowledged these to be the right of Margery who, with Peter, had them of the gift of Hugh. Peter and Margery granted and rendered them to Hugh and Alice to hold of the chief lord etc for their lives. Successive remainders to Thomas, son of Hugh, John, brother of Thomas, and Robert, son of Hugh, and the heirs of their bodies. Remainder to the right heirs of Hugh. Peter and Margery warranted for themselves anf Margery's heirs. (141)

839. Westminster. The morrow of Ascension 1348. P: John de Bereford son of Edmund de Bereford and Eleanor d'Arundel, daughter of Richard, earl of Arundel. D: Edmund de Bereford, clerk. Concerning the manor of Sutton except 3 knights' fees. Edmund granted and rendered the manor to

John and Eleanor to hold to themselves and the heirs of their bodies of Edmund and his heirs forever paying 1 rose each year at the feast of the Nativity of St John the Baptist for all services etc due to Edmund and his heirs and doing to the chief lord etc. Successive remainders to the heirs of the body of John, and to Baldwin, John's brother, and the male heirs of his body. Reversion to Edmund and his heirs. John and Eleanor gave 100 marks of silver. (142)

840. Westminster. Quindene of Michaelmas 1348. P: Nicholas Bek, chivaler. D: John de Draycote, chivaler, and Alice h.w. Concerning a moiety of the manor of Dore next Norton. John and Alice granted the moiety to Nicholas and remised and quitclaimed to him and his heirs whatsoever interest they had in it for their lifetime, forever. Nicholas gave 20 marks of silver. (143)

841. Westminster. Quindene of Easter 1349. Alfred son of Alfred de Sulny. D: Edmund de Appelby, junior, and Agnes h.w. Concerning a moiety of the manor of Neutonsulny. Edmund and Agnes remised and quitclaimed of themselves and the heirs of Agnes to Alfred and his heirs. Alfred gave 100 marks of silver. (144)

842. Westminster. Quindene of Easter 1349. P: John Bele, chaplain. D: John de Aston and Maude h.w. Concerning 3a. land and a moiety of 1 mess. in Makworth. John Bele had these of the gift of John and Maude and granted and rendered them to them to hold of the chief lord etc for their lives. Successive remainders to Walter de Folvyll, William Tochet, William's brother Thomas and Thomas's brother Edmund, each for his life. Remainder to Thomas Tochet, chivaler, and Joan h.w. and the heirs of their bodies. Remainder to the right heirs of Thomas Tochet. (145)

843. Westminster. Quindene of Easter 1349. P: John Bele, chaplain. D: William Blount and Emma h.w. Concerning 9½a. land and a moiety of 1 mess. and 1a. meadow in Makworth. John had these of the gift of William and Emma and granted and rendered them to them to hold of the chief lord etc for their lives. Successive remainders to Walter de Folvyll, William Tochet, William's brother Thomas and Thomas's brother Edmund, each for his life. Remainder to Thomas Tochet, chivaler, and Joan h.w. and the heirs of their bodies. Remainder to the right heirs of Thomas Tochet. (146)

844. Westminster. Octave of Trinity 1350. P: Henry de Walton, archdeacon of Richemund and John Bulneys, clerk. D: Guy de Upton and Margaret h.w. Concerning 4 mess., 3 carucates 10 virgates 10 bov. 43a. land, 86a. meadow and £39 rent in Overhaddon, Netherhaddon, Baukwell, Cheilmerdon, Cordeburgh, Assheford, Roulesleye, Ednesoure, Hulm, Wardelowe, Moniasshe and Burton next Baukwell and a moiety of the manor of Moniasshe. Guy and Margaret acknowledged these to be the right of Henry who, with John, had them of the gift of Guy and Margaret to hold to themselves and the heirs of Henry of the chief lord etc forever. Guy and Margaret warranted for themselves and the heirs of Margaret. Henry and John gave 300 marks of silver. (147)

845. Westminster. Easter three weeks 1348. Quindene of Michaelmas 1350. P: Richard de la Pole of Hertyndon. D: John son of John del Halle of Castelton. Concerning 1 mess. and 2 bov. 9a. land in Castelton. John granted for himself and his heirs that (i) 1 mess. and 2 bov. $3\frac{1}{2}$a. land which Felise, widow of Gervase del Halle, held for life; and (ii) $4\frac{1}{2}$a. land which Henry, son of Gervase, held for the life of Felise of the inheritance of John, which tenements ought to revert to John and his heirs on the death of Felise, should remain instead to Richard and his heirs to hold of the chief lord etc forever. John warranted for himself and his heirs. Richard gave 20 marks of silver. (148)

846. Westminster. The morrow of the Purification. 1352. P: Thomas de Bernhull and Isabel h.w. D: Robert de Clifton and Margery h.w. Concerning the manor of Etewell. Robert and Margery granted and rendered the manor to Thomas and Isabel to hold to themselves and the heirs of Isabel of the chief lord etc forever. Robert and Margery warranted for the life of Margery. Thomas and Isabel gave 100 marks of silver. (149)

847. Westminster. The morrow of Ascension 1352. Octave of Trinity 1352. P: Edmund Savage and Margery h.w. by the same Edmund, attorney for Margery. D: Walter Rabbe. Concerning 1 mess., 140a. land, 12a. meadow, 8a. woodland and 100s rent in Staveley. Edmund acknowledged these to be the right of Walter who granted and rendered them to Edmund and Margery to hold to themselves and the heirs of their bodies of Walter and his heirs paying therefor to Walter for his life 4 marks each year at Pentecost and 4 marks each year at the feast of St Martin and to Walter's heirs 1 rose each year at the feast of the Nativity of St John the Baptist, for all services etc due to Walter and his heirs and doing to the chief lord etc. Remainder to Walter's son, Henry and the heirs of his body. Reversion to Walter and his heirs. Walter warranted for himself and his heirs. Edmund and Margery gave 100 marks of silver. (150)

CP 25/1/38/36

848. Westminster. Quindene of Michaelmas 1352. P: William Cursonn, parson of the church of Churchelangele. D: Richard de Wodeford and Joan h.w. Concerning 1 mess. and 1 carucate land in Churchelangele. Richard and Joan remised and quitclaimed of themselves and the heirs of Joan to William and his heirs. William gave 100 marks of silver. (151)

37

849. Westminster. Octave of Trinity 1353. Octave of Michaelmas 1353. P: Thomas de Birchovere and Cecily h.w. D: Robert de Aldeport, parson of the church of Neuton, and Robert de Wirkesworth, chaplain. Concerning 6 mess., 1 mill, 12 bov. land, 10a. meadow, 10a. pasture, 8a. woodland, 75s rent and a rent of 1 peppercorn in Birchovere, Wynstre and Stanton. Thomas acknowledged these to be the right of Robert de Aldeport who, with Robert de Wirkesworth, had them of the gift of Thomas. Robert and Robert granted and rendered them to Thomas and Cecily to hold to themselves and the male heirs of their bodies of the chief lord etc forever. Successive remainders to their daughters, Elizabeth and Catherine and the male heirs of their bodies, and Alice and her heirs. (152)

850. Westminster. Octave of Michaelmas 1353. Octave of Hilary 1354. P: Richard Foliaumbe, parson of the church of Normanton. D: William Overlynton, vicar of the church of Baukewell, and James de Normanton, chaplain. Concerning 1 mess., 4 bov. land, 10a. meadow and 30s rent in Birchilles. Richard acknowledged these to be the right of William who, with James, had them of the gift of Richard. William and James granted and rendered them to Richard to hold of the chief lord etc for his life. Successive remainders to John the son and Beatrice the daughter of Isabel de Crest, and the heirs of their bodies. Remainder to the right heirs of Richard. (153)

851. Westminster. Quindene of Easter 1354. P: Walter de Elmeton and Joan h.w. D: Bertram de Bolyngbrok and Joan h.w. Concerning 2 mess., 2 tofts, 60a. land and 2s rent in Cestrefeld, Brymyngton, Tapton, Calale, Haseland, Boythorp, Walton, Brampton, Hulm, Dunston, Langeleye, Neubold and Whityngton. Bertram and Joan acknowledged these to be the right of Walter and they remised and quitclaimed of, and warranted for, themselves and the heirs of Joan to Walter and Joan and Walter's heirs. Walter and Joan gave 100 marks of silver. (154)

852. Westminster. Octave of Hilary 1355. P: Richard de Barwe, vicar of the church of Duffeld. D: Thomas de Tyssynton and Agnes h.w. Concerning 6½a. meadow in Duffeld. Richard had the meadow of the gift of Thomas and Agnes to hold to himself and his heirs of the chief lord etc forever. Thomas and Agnes warranted for themselves and the heirs of Agnes. Richard gave 10 marks of silver. (155)

853. Westminster. Quindene of Michaelmas 1355. P: Master Nicholas de Chaddesdene, clerk, Geoffrey de Chaddesdene, parson of the church of Longa Whatton, and William de Duffeld, clerk. D: Henry de Sheldford and Alice h.w. Concerning 2 mess., 30a. land, 6a. meadow and 10s rent in Chaddesdene, Horseleye and Denby. Henry and Alice acknowledged these to be the right of Nicholas who, with Geoffrey and William, had them of their gift. Henry and Alice remised and quitclaimed of, and warranted for, themselves and the heirs of Alice to Nicholas, Geoffrey and William and the heirs of Nicholas. The plaintiffs gave 100 marks of silver. (156)

854. Westminster. Quindene of Hilary 1356. P: Robert del Shypen of Derby and Lettice h.w. by Hugh Adam their attorney. D: Thomas Beauchamp and Joan h.w. Concerning 1 mess. in Derby. Thomas and Joan acknowledged the messuage to be the right of Robert who, with Lettice, had it of their gift to hold to themselves and the heirs of Robert of the chief lord etc forever. Thomas and Joan warranted for themselves and Joan's heirs. Robert and Lettice gave 10 marks of silver. (157)

855. Westminster. Quindene of Hilary 1356. P: John de Bredon of Derby by William de Derby, his attorney. D: Thomas de Beauchamp and Joan h.w. Concerning 2 tofts and 6a. land in Derby. John had these of the gift of Thomas and Joan to hold to himself and his heirs of the chief lord etc forever. Thomas and Joan warranted for themselves and Joan's heirs. John gave 10 marks of silver. (158)

856. Westminster. Quindene of Hilary 1356. P: William del Marche of Derby and Alice h.w. by Hugh Adam, their attorney. D: Thomas Beauchamp and Joan h.w. Concerning 1 mess. in Derby. Thomas and Joan acknowledged the messuage to be the right of William who, with Alice, had it of their gift to hold to themselves and the heirs of William of the chief lord etc forever. Thomas and Joan warranted for themselves and Joan's heirs. William and Alice gave 10 marks of silver. (159)

857. Westminster. Easter three weeks 1356. P: Henry de la Pole of Hertyngdon. D: William de Patteshull and Joan h.w. Concerning 20s rent in Hertyngdon. Henry had the rent of the gift of William and Joan to hold to himself and his heirs of the chief lord etc forever. William and Joan warranted for themselves and William's heirs. Henry gave 20 marks of silver. (160)

858. Westminster. Quindene of Easter 1356. P: William de Northwell, clerk. D: Thomas de Bernhull and Isabel h.w. Concerning the manors of Etewell and Strecton in Scarvesdale. Thomas and Isabel rendered the manors to William to hold to himself and his heirs of the chief lord etc forever and they warranted for themselves and Isabel's heirs. William gave 200 marks of silver. (161)

859. Westminster. Quindene of Michaelmas 1356. P: Otes de Holand, chivaler. D: Thomas de Holand, chivaler, and Joan h.w. Concerning the manors of Chesterfeld and Assheford and the advowson of the hospice of St Leonard in Chesterfeld. Thomas and Joan granted and rendered these to Otes to hold of the king and his heirs etc for his life. Reversion to Thomas and Joan and Joan's heirs. Otes gave 200 marks of silver. The agreement was made by order of the king. (162)

860. Westminster. Octave of the Purification 1357. Octave of Trinity 1357. P: Hugh de Meignyll, chivaler, by William Derby, his attorney. D: Robert le Cook and Margaret h.w. and Andrew Cray and Joan h.w. Concerning 1 mess. and 1 carucate land in Holynton. The deforciants rendered these to Hugh to hold to himself and his heirs of the chief lord etc forever and they warranted for themselves and the heirs of Margaret and Joan. Hugh gave 20 marks of silver. (163)

861. Westminster. Quindene of Michaelmas 1356. Quindene of Michaelmas 1357. P: Alfred de Sulny, chivaler, by Roger de Greseley, his attorney. D: William le Wyn, chivaler. Concerning the manors of Penkeston and Normanton next Blacwell and the advowsons of the churches of the same manors. William granted for himself and his heirs that these manors and advowsons, which Eudes de Hodynet and Margery h.w. held for the life of Margery of the inheritance of William and which ought to revert to William and his heirs on the death of Margery, should remain instead to Alfred and his heirs to hold of the chief lord etc forever. William warranted for himself and his heirs. Alfred gave 200 marks of silver. (164)

862. Westminster. Quindene of Michaelmas 1358. P: John Chaundos, chivaler. D: John de Beleye of Brampcote and Elizabeth h.w. Concerning 1½ bov. land and a moiety of 1 mess. in Rodeburne and a moiety of a fourth part of the manor of Rodeburne and a moiety of the advowsons of the churches of Mogynton and Egynton. John and Elizabeth rendered these to John Chaundos to hold to himself and his heirs of the chief lord etc forever and they warranted for themselves and the heirs of Elizabeth. John Chaundos gave 200 marks of silver. (165)

863. Westminster. Quindene of Michaelmas 1358. Quindene of Hilary 1359. P: Robert de Hethcote and Emma h.w. D: Nicholas de Stafford, chivaler, and Elizabeth h.w. Concerning 1 mess. in Tiddeswell. Nicholas and Elizabeth granted and rendered the messuage to Robert and Emma to hold of themselves and the heirs of Elizabeth for the lives of Robert and Emma paying therefor to Nicholas and Elizabeth during their lifetime 3s 4d each year at the feast of the Nativity of St John the Baptist and 3s 4d each year at the feast of St Michael, and to the heirs of Elizabeth 1 rose each year at the feast of the Nativity of St John the Baptist, for all services etc due to Nicholas, Elizabeth and Elizabeth's heirs and doing to the chief lord etc. Reversion to Nicholas, Elizabeth and Elizabeth's heirs. Robert and Emma gave 20 marks of silver. (166)

864. Westminster. Quindene of Michaelmas 1359. P: William de Lynton, parson of the church of Ilkeston, and Robert Mold, vicar of the church of Spondon. D: Ralph de Stathum and Goditha h.w. Concerning the manor of Morleye. Ralph and Goditha acknowledged the manor to be the right of

William who, with Robert, had it of their gift. William and Robert granted and rendered it to Ralph and Goditha to hold to themselves and the male heirs of their bodies of the chief lord etc forever. Successive remainders to the male heirs of the body of Goditha, the heirs of the body of Goditha, Thomas de Stathum, Ralph's brother, and the male heirs of his body, and the right heirs of Goditha. (167)

865. Westminster. Easter three weeks 1360. P: Henry de Stanydelf. D: Henry son of William son of Roger de Meysham and Maude h.w. Concerning 1 mess. and 50a. land in Meysham. Henry son of William and Maude granted these to Henry de Stanydelf and remised and quitclaimed whatsoever they had in the tenements for the life of Maude to Henry and his heirs. Henry de Stanydelf gave 20 marks of silver. (168)

866. Westminster. Octave of Michaelmas 1360. P: William de Hokelowe. D: William Note and Alice h.w. Concerning 1 mess. and 1 bov. land in Eyum. William had these of the gift of William Note and Alice to hold to himself and his heirs of the chief lord etc forever. William and Alice warranted for themselves and the heirs of Alice. William de Hokelowe gave 10 marks of silver. (169)

867. Westminster. The morrow of All Souls 1362. P: William de Roldeston of the Lee. D: Walter son of Robert del Grene of Asshovre and Elizabeth h.w. Concerning 1 mess. and 6 bov. land in Ogaston, Brakynthwayt and Wyssyngton. William had these, except 2a. land, of the gift of Walter and Elizabeth to hold to himself and his heirs of the chief lord etc forever. Walter and Elizabeth granted for themselves and Walter's heirs that the 2a. land which Edene de Ogaston held for her life of the inheritance of Walter and which ought to revert to Walter, Elizabeth and Walter's heirs on the death of Edene, should remain instead to William and his heirs. Walter and Elizabeth warranted for themselves and Walter's heirs. William gave 100 marks of silver. (170)

868. Westminster. The morrow of All Saints 1362. P: Godfrey Foliaumbe and Avina h.w. and Richard their son. D: William atte Wode, sergeant at arms of the king. Concerning a moiety of the manor of Derleye in le Peek. William acknowledged the moiety to be the right of Godfrey and he rendered it to Godfrey, Avina and Richard to hold to themselves and the heirs of Godfrey of the king and his heirs etc forever. William warranted for himself and his heirs. Godfrey and Avina and Richard gave 200 marks of silver. The agreement was made by order of the king. (171)

869. Westminster. Michaelmas three weeks 1362. P: Oliver de Barton. D: John son of Nicholas de Onecote of Grendon and Maude h.w. Concerning the manor of Trusseley. John and Maude granted the manor to Oliver and remised and quitclaimed whatsoever they had in the manor for the life of

41

Maude. Oliver granted for himself and his heirs that he would pay John and Maude 7 marks each year at the feast of the Annunciation of the Blessed Mary and 7 marks each year at the feast of St Michael during Maude's lifetime and if he or his heirs default in these payments at any term it will be lawful for John and Maude to distrain him and his heirs or those who hold thereafter by all the goods and chattels in the manor and retain them until the arrears have been paid. After Maude's death Oliver and his heirs will be quit of the annual payments. (172)

870. Westminster. Octave of Hilary 1363. P: William del Lee of Weryngton and Agnes h.w. D: William Gybon of Derby and Aline h.w. Concerning 1 mess. in Derby. William and Aline acknowledged the messuage to be the right of William del Lee who, with Agnes, had it of their gift to hold to themselves and the heirs of William of the chief lord etc forever. William and Aline warranted for themselves and the heirs of William. William del Lee and Agnes gave 10 marks of silver. (173)

871. Westminster. Quindene of Easter 1363. Quindene of Trinity 1363. P: John Hilberd, parson of the church of Thornford and John Dene, chaplain. D: Bertram de Bolyngbrok and Joan h.w. Concerning 2 mess., 2 carucates land, 12a. meadow and 20a. woodland in Barleburgh and Whitewell. Bertram and Joan acknowledged these to be the right of John Hilberd who, with John Dene had them of their gift to hold to themselves and the heirs of John Hilberd of the chief lord etc forever. Bertram and Joan warranted for themselves and the heirs of Joan. John and John gave 100 marks of silver. (174)

872. Westminster. Michaelmas one month 1363. P: John Cokayn. D: William de Stapenhull and Margery h.w. Concerning 3 mess., 2 tofts, 4 furlongs 10a. land 10a. meadow and 6d rent in Peverwyche. William and Margery remised and quitclaimed of themselves and their heirs and warranted for themselves and the heirs of Margery to John and his heirs. John gave 20 marks of silver. (175)

CP 25/1/39/37

873. Westminster. Quindene of Hilary 1364. P: William son of Richard de Matlok. D: William Drewe of Matlock, tailor, and Alice h.w. Concerning 1 mess., 16a. land and 2a. meadow in Matlok. William son of Richard had these of the gift of William and Alice who remised and quitclaimed them of, and warranted them for, themselves and the heirs of Alice to William son of Richard and his heirs. He then gave 10 marks of silver. (176)

874. Westminster. Quindene of Easter 1364. P: Nicholas son of Walter de Moungomery, kt, and Ann h.w. D: Walter de Moungomery, kt and Maude h.w. Concerning £6 rent in Cubleye and a moiety of the manor of Snelleston. Walter and Maude granted and rendered these to Nicholas and Ann to hold to themselves and the heirs of the body of Nicholas of Walter and Maude and Walter's heirs forever paying therefor 1 rose each year at the feast of the Nativity of St John the Baptist for all services etc due to Walter, Maude and Walter's heirs and doing to the chief lord etc. Walter and Maude warranted for themselves and Walter's heirs. Reversion to them. Nicholas and Ann gave 100 marks of silver. (177)

875. Westminster. Easter one month 1364. P: William de Macworth, parson of the church of Shenleye. D: William Pakemon of Derby and Margery h.w. Concerning 1 mess. in Derby. William de Macworth had the messuage of the gift of William and Margery and he granted and rendered it to them to hold to themselves and the heirs of William of the chief lord etc forever. (178)

876. Westminster. Quindene of Michaelmas 1362. Easter three weeks 1364. P: Alfred de Sulny, chivaler. D: Guy de Upton and Margaret h.w. Concerning the manors of Penkeston and Normanton and the advowsons of the churches of the manors. Guy and Margaret granted for themselves and the heirs of Margaret that these tenements, which Margery, widow of Eudes de Hodynet, held for life of the inheritance of Margaret and which ought to revert to Guy and Margaret and Margaret's heirs on the death of Margery, should remain instead to Alfred and his heirs to hold of the chief lord etc forever. Guy and Margaret warranted for themselves and Margaret's heirs. Alfred gave 200 marks of silver. (179)

877. Westminster. Quindene of Michaelmas 1364. P: Roger de Shirleye. D: Roger de Wynstre and Annabel h.w. and Richard son of Philip de Rollesleye and Mary h.w. Concerning 1 mess. 2a. land in Baukewell. The deforciants remised and quitclaimed of, and warranted for, themselves and the heirs of Annabel and Mary to Roger de Shirleye and his heirs. He then gave 10 marks of silver. (180)

878. Westminster. Quindene of Michaelmas. 1364. P: Thomas son of Thomas de Berkleye of Cobberleye, chivaler, and Gillian h.w. D: Edmund de Brugge, Walter de Pircton, John Philips, parson of the church of Cobberleye and William de Herdewyk, parson of the church of Adreston. Concerning the manor of Childecote. The deforciants granted and rendered the manor to Thomas and Gillian to hold to themselves and the heirs of the body of Thomas of the chief lord etc forever. Remainder to Thomas de Berkleye of Cobberleye for life. Successive remainders to the plaintiff's brothers, John, Nicholas and Walter, and the heirs of their bodies. Remainder to the right heirs of Thomas de Berkleye. Thomas and Gillian gave 200 marks of silver. (181)

879. Westminster. Octave of Hilary 1365. P: John son of John de la Pole of Hertyngdon. D: John de Honford and Emma h.w. Concerning 4 mess., 3 tofts, 1 carucate land and the bailiwick of the office of forester in the free chase of John, duke of Lancaster, and Blanch h.w. of Croudecote, in Hertyngdon, Kyngesbucstones and Coudale. John de Honford and Emma granted these to John son of John and remised and quitclaimed whatsoever they had in the tenements and bailliwick for the life of Emma to John who gave 100 marks of silver. (182)

880. Westminster. Easter three weeks 1361. Quindene of Hilary 1365. P: Henry de Tiddeswell. D: Thomas del Burghes and Agnes h.w. Concerning a third part of 1 mess. in Tiddeswell. Thomas and Agnes rendered the third part to Henry to hold to himself and his heirs of the chief lord etc forever. They also warranted for themselves and the heirs of Agnes. Henry gave 10 marks of silver. (183)

881. Westminster. Quindene of Easter 1365. P: John de Longesdon, clerk. D: John de Penyston and Felise h.w. Concerning 7 tofts, 68a. land and 2a. meadow in Rolond. John and Felise rendered these to John de Longesdon to hold to himself and his heirs of the chief lord etc forever. They also warranted for themselves and the heirs of Felise. John de Longesdon gave 100 marks of silver. (184)

882. Westminster. Quindene of Michaelmas 1365. P: Henry atte Touneshende of Luton. D: Richard son of Thomas le Dicher and Joan h.w. Concerning 5a. 1 rood land in Luton. Henry had the land of the gift of Richard and Joan who remised and quitclaimed it of, and warranted for, themselves and the heirs of Joan to Henry and his heirs. Henry gave 10 marks of silver. (185)

883. Westminster. Quindene of Easter 1366. P: John son of Thomas del Tunstedes. D: William Ragge and Maude h.w. Concerning 1 mess. and 21a. land in Fowelowe and Eyum. William and Maude remised and quitclaimed of, and warranted for, themselves and the heirs of Maude to John and his heirs. John gave 20 marks of silver. (186)

884. Westminster. Quindene of Easter 1366. P: John Fitzherbert of Somursale and Alice h.w. D: John Knolles and Constance h.w. Concerning 2 mess., 54a. land and a moiety of 1a. meadow in Churchesomursale and Marchynton Mountgomery. John and Constance acknowledged these to be the right of John Fitzherbert who, with Alice, had them of their gift to hold to themselves and the heirs of John of the chief lord etc forever. John and Constance also warranted for themselves and the heirs of Constance. John Fitzherbert and Alice gave 100 marks of silver. (187)

885. Westminster. Quindene of Easter 1366. P: John Foliaumbe of Longesdon. D: William Meter, chaplain and Henry son of John de Lokhaie, chaplain. Concerning 1 mess., 1 carucate land and 12s rent in Mornesale, Wrightrichefeld and Parva Longusdon. John acknowledged these to be the right of William who, with Henry, had them of the gift of John and they granted and rendered them to John to hold of the chief lord etc for his life. Successive remainders to Robert de Derby and Isabel h.w., to Catherine, John's daughter and Isabel's sister and to Margaret, John's daughter and Catherine's sister, and the heirs of their bodies. Remainder to John, son of Robert de Shalcrosse and his heirs. (188)

886. Westminster. Quindene of Michaelmas 1366. P: John son of Henry de Monyasshe. D: John son of Nicholas Coterell and Emma h.w. Concerning 1 mess., 1 carucate land and 1 mill in Bobenhull and Basselowe. John and Emma rendered these to John son of Henry to hold to himself and his heirs of the chief lord etc forever. John and Emma warranted for themselves and Emma's heirs. John son of Henry gave 100 marks of silver. (189)

887. Westminster. Quindene of Michaelmas 1366. P: John de Spondon and William le Meter, chaplain. D: Robert le Breton and Joan h.w. Concerning 1 mess., 1 toft, 1 carucate 1 bov. 4a. land, 5a. meadow, 6s rent and a moiety of a mill in Parva Longusdon, Yolgreve and Byrchelis. Robert and Joan acknowledged these to be the right of Joan who, with William, had them of their gift to hold all except the bovate of land and the moiety of the mill to themselves and the heirs of John of the chief lord etc forever. They also warranted for themselves and Joan's heirs. John and William then granted and rendered the bovate and moiety to Robert and Joan to hold of the chief lord etc for their lives. Remainder to Robert, son of Robert, and Catherine h.w. and the heirs of their bodies. Remainder to the right heirs of Joan. (190)

888. Westminster. Quindene of Hilary 1367. Quindene of Easter 1367. P: William Hauberk and Christian h.w. D: Henry de Codyngton, parson of the church of Botelesford and Lawrence Hauberk. Concerning 3 mess., 4 tofts, 4 carucates 4 bov. land, 20a. meadow and 12s rent in Ufton, Alfreton, Birchewode, Routhorn and Batele. William and Christian acknowledged these to be the right of Lawrence who, with Henry, had them of their gift. Lawrence and Henry then granted and rendered them to William and Christian to hold to themselves and the heirs of their bodies of the chief lord etc forever. Successive remainders to the heirs of the body of Christian and the right heirs of William. (191)

889. Westminster. The morrow of All Souls 1366. Quindene of Easter 1367. P: Godfrey Foliaumbe, kt. D: John Lorwenche and Margery h.w.

Concerning an eighth part of the manor of Chadesden and an eighth part of 3 mess. and 2 carucates 1 virgate land in Broghton, Twyford, and Cortelay next Duffeld. John and Margery rendered to Godfrey an eighth part of 1 mess. and 1 carucate in Cortelay to hold to himself and his heirs of the chief lord etc forever. They also granted for themselves and the heirs of Margery that (i) the eighth part of the manor, 1 mess. and 1 virgate in Twyford which Isabel, widow of William Herberio, chivaler, held for life; and (ii) the eighth part of 1 mess. and 1 carucate in Broghton which Joan, widow of William de Chaddesden, held for life of the inheritance of Margery, which tenements ought to revert to John, Margery and Margery's heirs on the deaths of Isabel and Joan, should remain instead to Godfrey and his heirs. John and Margery warranted for themselves and Margery's heirs. Godfrey gave 100 marks of silver. (192)

890. Westminster. Quindene of Michaelmas 1367. P: Robert Mold, parson of the church of Breydesale, and Henry de Adderleye. D: Ralph de Stathum and Godiva h.w. Concerning 1 mess. 2 tofts, 60a. land 12a. meadow 6s rent, a rent of 1 cock and 6 hens and an eighth part of a mill in Derby. Ralph and Godiva acknowledged these to be the right of Robert who, with Henry, had them of their gift. They remised and quitclaimed of, and warranted for themselves and the heirs of Godiva to Robert and Henry and the heirs of Robert. Robert and Henry gave 100 marks of silver. (193)

891. Westminster. Quindene of Michaelmas 1367. P: John de Herleston, chaplain, and John de Haddon, chaplain. D: John atte Wode and Deonise h.w. and John Penyston and Felise h.w. Concerning 2 mess., 12½a. land, 1a. meadow, 1a. woodland and 1a. pasture in Bobenhull and Basselowe. The deforciants acknowledged these to be the right of John de Herleston who, with John de Haddon, had them of their gift to hold to themselves and the heirs of John de Herleston of the chief lord etc forever. The deforciants warranted for themselves and the heirs of Deonise and Felise. The plaintiffs gave 100 marks of silver. (194)

892. Westminster. Quindene of Hilary 1367. Quindene of Michaelmas 1367. P: Richard de Chestrefeld, clerk, Richard de Tyssynton, clerk, and William de Wakebrugge and Elizabeth h.w. D: Thomas de Gonshull, kt. Concerning 1 carucate land, 20a. meadow, 40a. woodland, 60a. pasture and £8 rent in Matlok. Thomas acknowledged these to be the right of William and he rendered them to the plaintiffs. He also granted to them the rent, together with the homage and all services of William de Dethek and his heirs, of all the tenements that he, Thomas, previously held in Matlok to hold to themselves and the heirs of William of the chief lord etc forever. Thomas warranted for himself and his heirs. The plaintiffs gave 100 marks of silver. (195)

893. Westminster. Quindene of Easter 1368. P: John Warde. D: William Everard and Elizabeth h.w. Concerning 1 mess., 1 bov. land and 6a. meadow in Glossop and Hatfeld. William and Elizabeth rendered these to John to hold to himself and his heirs of the chief lord etc forever and they warranted for themselves and Elizabeth's heirs. John gave 20 marks of silver. (196)

894. Westminster. Easter three weeks 1368. P: John Jolyf of Tuttebury. D: John Pentrye and Alice h.w. Concerning 1 mess., 50a. land, 10a. meadow and 17d rent in Dovvebrugge and Uttoxheter. John and Alice rendered these to John Jolyf to hold to himself and his heirs of the chief lord etc forever and they warranted for themselves and the heirs of Alice. John Jolyf gave 20 marks of silver. (197)

895. Westminster. The morrow of All Souls 1368. P: Godfrey Foliaumbe, kt. D: Alice daughter of Ralph de Makleye. Concerning an eighth part of the manor of Chaddesden and of 4 mess., 4 carucates land and 50s rent in Twyford, Benteleye, Broghton and Corteley. Godfrey had these of the gift of Alice who remised and quitclaimed of, and warranted for, herself and her heirs to Godfrey and his heirs. Godfrey gave 100 marks of silver. (198)

896. Westminster. Quindene of Easter 1368. Quindene of Michaelmas 1368. P: Edmund Savage and Margery h.w. D: Richard Savage and Agnes h.w. Concerning 1 mess., and 6 bov. land in Shirbrok. Richard and Agnes granted these to Edmund and Margery and remised and quitclaimed whatsoever they had in the tenements for the life of Agnes. Edmund and Margery granted for themselves and the heirs of Edmund that they would pay Richard and Agnes 5s each year at Pentecost and 5s each year at the feast of St Martin during Agnes's lifetime and if they or Edmund's heirs should default in these payments at any term it will be lawful to distrain *[by the same terms as in 869]*. After Agnes's death Edmund, Margery and Edmund's heirs will be quit of the annual payments. (199)

897. Westminster. Quindene of Easter 1369. P: Richard le Sower of Ambaston and John his brother. D: William de Braylesford of Thurleston and Alice h.w. Concerning 7a. land in Ambaston. William and Alice acknowledged the land to be the right of John and they rendered it to John and Richard to hold to themselves and the heirs of John of the chief lord etc forever. William and Alice warranted for themselves and the heirs of Alice. Richard and John gave 10 marks of silver. (200)

CP 25/1/39/38

898. Westminster. The morrow of Ascension. 1368. Quindene of Trinity 1369. P: John Cokeyn of Assheburn, William de Burleye, chaplain, and

Nicholas de Sheile. D: Thomas de Rideware and Agnes h.w. Concerning 1 mess. and 21a. 1 rood land in Lutchirch. Thomas and Agnes acknowledged these to be the right of John Cokeyn and they granted for themselves and the heirs of Agnes that these tenements, which John de Covere and Margery h.w. and John their son held for their lives of the inheritance of Agnes and which ought to revert to Thomas, Agnes and Agnes's heirs on the death of John, Margery and John, should remain instead to John, William and Nicholas and the heirs of John Cokeyn to hold of the chief lord etc forever. The deforciants warranted for themselves and the heirs of Agnes. The plaintiffs gave 20 marks of silver. (201)

899. Westminster. Easter three weeks 1370. P: John de Trowelle of Derby and Richard his brother. D: William de Shethesby of Coventre and Margery h.w. Concerning 1 mess. and 16a. land in Derby. William and Margery acknowledged these to be the right of John who, with Richard, had them of their gift. They remised and quitclaimed of, and warranted for, themselves and the heirs of Margery to John and Richard and John's heirs. John and Richard gave 20 marks of silver. (202)

900. Westminster. Quindene of Easter 1370. P: Thomas Robardson of Thurleston. D: Richard de Smalleye and Alice h.w. Concerning 1 mess., 4a. land and a moiety of 1a. meadow in Aylwaston and Thurleston. Thomas had these of the gift of Richard and Alice who remised and quitclaimed of, and warranted for, themselves and the heirs of Alice to Thomas and his heirs. Thomas gave 10 marks of silver. (203)

901. Westminster. Michaelmas one month 1369. Quindene of Easter 1370. P: Henry de Bakewell, chaplain, John de Milton, chaplain, William de Bretteby, chaplain, William le Botiller and William de Balsham. D: John de Verdon of Derlaston, kt. Concerning a third part of the manor of Potlok. John de Verdon acknowledged the third part to be the right of Henry and he granted that this part which John le Foucher held for the life of Catherine, wife of Walter son of Walter de Monte Gomery, of the inheritance of John de Verdon and which ought to revert to John and his heirs on the death of Catherine, should remain instead to the plaintiffs and the heirs of Henry to hold of the chief lord etc forever. John de Verdon warranted for himself and his heirs. The plaintiffs gave 100 marks of silver. (204)

902. Westminster. Octave of Midsummer 1370. P: Roger Touper and Godfrey Foliammbe, junior. D: Thomas son of Roger de Wenesley. Concerning 8 mess., 10 shops, 3 carucates 5 bov. and a moiety of 1a. land and 6s rent in Baukewell, Assheford, Netherhaddon, Cordeburgh and Magna Roulesley and 2 parts of the manor of Overhaddon and a moiety of the manors of Wardelowe, Monyassh and Chelmerdon. Thomas

48

acknowledged these to be the right of Roger who, with Godfrey, had them of the gift of Thomas. Roger and Godfrey granted and rendered them to Thomas to hold of the chief lord etc for his life. Remainder to John, Duke of Lancaster, and his heirs. (205)

903. Westminster. Octave of Michaelmas 1370. P: John Coteler. D: Robert Hervy and Cecily h.w. Concerning 2 tofts, 3 bov. land and 6a. pasture in Leghes. John had these of the gift of Robert and Cecily who remised and quitclaimed of, and warranted for, themselves and the heirs of Cecily to John and his heirs. John gave 20 marks of silver. (206)

904. Westminster. Michaelmas one month 1370. P: John de Pare, parson of the church of Rolleston, Robert de Assewell, parson of the church of Makworth and Nicholas del Weld, parson of a third part of the church of Derley. D: Robert son of Robert de Irlond, kt. Concerning the manor of Lokhagh. Robert acknowledged the manor to be the right of John who, with Robert de Assewell and Nicholas, had it of the gift of Robert. Robert remised and quitclaimed the manor of, and warranted for, himself and his heirs to the plaintiffs and the heirs of John who gave 200 marks of silver. (207)

905. Westminster. Quindene of Michaelmas 1370. P: John Saucheverell. D: Robert de Strelleye of Hopowell and Agnes h.w. Concerning 2 mess. and 2 bov. 3a. 1 rood land in Hopowell. John had these of the gift of Robert and Agnes who remised and quitclaimed of, and warranted for, themselves and the heirs of Agnes to John and his heirs. John gave 10 marks of silver. (208)

906. Westminster. Quindene of Michaelmas 1370. P: Richard de Tissynton, clerk. D: William del Blakwalle of Tissynton and Maude h.w. Concerning a moiety of 1 mess. and a fourth part of 1 bov. 6a. land and 6a. meadow in Tissynton and Fennybenteleye. Richard had these of the gift of William and Maude who remised and quitclaimed of, and warranted for, themselves and the heirs of Maude to Richard and his heirs. Richard gave 10 marks of silver. (209)

907. Westminster. The morrow of All Souls 1371. P: Godfrey Foliaumbe, kt. D: Thomas de Nedham and Joan h.w. Concerning 5 mess. and 30a. land in Cheylmardun. Thomas and Joan rendered these to Godfrey to hold to himself and his heirs of the chief lord etc forever and they warranted for themselves and the heirs of Joan. Godfrey gave 20 marks of silver. (210)

908. Westminster. Octave of Hilary 1371. P: Walter de Cokeseye, chivaler. D: Fulk de Penbruge, chivaler, and Margaret h.w. Concerning the manor of Eyton in Dovedale. Fulk and Margaret remised and quitclaimed the manor of themselves and the heirs of Margaret to Walter and his heirs. Walter gave 100 marks of silver. (211)

909. Westminster. Octave of Michaelmas 1370. Quindene of Michaelmas 1371. P: Henry de Bakewell, chaplain, John de Milton, chaplain, William de Bretteby, chaplain, William le Botyler and William de Balsham. D: William Bakepus, chivaler, and Joan h.w. Concerning a third part of the manor of Potlok. William Bakepus and Joan acknowledged the third part to be the right of Henry and they granted for themselves and the heirs of Joan that this third part, which John Foucher held for the life of Catherine, wife of Walter son of Walter de Mountgomery, of the inheritance of Joan and which ought to revert to William Bakepus, Joan and Joan's heirs on the death of Catherine, should remain instead to the plaintiffs and the heirs of Henry to hold of the chief lord etc forever. William Bakepus and Joan warranted for themselves and the heirs of Joan. The plaintiffs gave 100 marks of silver. (212)

910. Westminster. Quindene of Easter. 1372. P: John Thomasson of Staveley. D: Robert de Norton of Staveley and Agnes h.w. Concerning 1 mess. in Staveley. Robert and Agnes rendered the messuage to John to hold to himself and his heirs of the chief lord etc forever and they warranted for themselves and the heirs of Agnes. John gave 10 marks of silver. (213)

911. Westminster. Quindene of Trinity 1372. P: Aymer de Lichefeld and Margery h.w. D: Nicholas de Lichefeld, parson of the church of Chesterton, Henry de Tymmore, parson of the church of Elford and Thomas de Walton, chaplain. Concerning the manor of Stretton. Aymer and Margery acknowledged the manor to be the right of Nicholas who, with Henry and Thomas, had it of their gift. Nicholas, Henry and Thomas granted and rendered it to Aymer and Margery to hold to themselves and the heirs of their bodies of the chief lord etc forever. Remainder to the heirs of the body of Margery. Remainder to the right heirs of Aymer. (214)

912. Westminster. Quindene of Michaelmas 1372. P: Geoffrey de Chaddesden, parson of the church of Longa Whatton, William de Sudbiry and Ralph de Boveye. D: Thomas de Hele of Stanton next Sandeacre and Agnes h.w. Concerning 1 mess. and 1 bov. land in Kirkhalum. Thomas and Agnes acknowledged these to be the right of Geoffrey who, with William and Ralph, had them of their gift and they remised and quitclaimed of, and warranted for, themselves and the heirs of Agnes to Geoffrey, William and Ralph and the heirs of Geoffrey. The plaintiffs gave 20 marks of silver. (215)

913. Westminster. Quindene of Easter 1373. P: Godfrey Foliambe, chivaler, and Avina h.w. D: John de Hokeneston and Isabel h.w. Concerning an eighth part of the manor of Chaddesden. John and Isabel acknowledged this to be the right of Godfrey who, with Avina, had it of their gift. They remised and quitclaimed it of, and warranted for, themselves and the heirs of Isabel to Godfrey, Avina and the heirs of Godfrey. Godfrey and Avina gave 100 marks of silver. (216)

914. Westminster. Easter three weeks 1373. P: The abbot of Basyngwerk. D: Richard de Woleye and Joan h.w. and William Andreu and Agnes h.w. Concerning 1 mess. and 3 bov. land in Chisseworth. The deforciants acknowledged these to be the right of the abbot and his church of the Blessed Mary in Basynwerk and they remised and quitclaimed of, and warranted for, themselves and the heirs of Joan and Agnes to the abbot, his successors and his church. The abbot gave 20 marks of silver. (217)

915. Westminster. Quindene of Easter 1373. P: John de Hukelowe. D: William Lemyng and Nichola h.w. Concerning 1 mess. and 6a. land in Wheston. John had these of the gift of William and Nichola who remised and quitclaimed of, and warranted for, themselves and the heirs of Nichola to John and his heirs. John gave 10 marks of silver. (218)

916. Westminster. The morrow of Ascension 1373. Octave of Trinity 1373. P: Robert de Spondon and Alice h.w. D: John Park by William de Helpryngham, his attorney. Concerning 4 mess., 3 bov. land and 1a. meadow in Spondon. John had these of the gift of Robert and Alice to hold to himself and his heirs of the chief lord etc forever. Robert warranted for himself and his heirs. John gave 20 marks of silver. (219)

917. Westminster. Octave of Midsummer 1373. P: Innocent Trotte of Litton. D: William Sellyok and Emma h.w. Concerning a moiety of 2 mess. and 39a. land in Litton. Innocent had these of the gift of William and Emma who remised and quitclaimed of, and warranted for, themselves and the heirs of Emma to Innocent and his heirs. Innocent gave 10 marks of silver. (220)

918. Westminster. Octave of Michaelmas 1374. P: Robert Mold, clerk, William de Burleye, chaplain, and Richard de Thurmundeleye, chaplain. D: Henry Frannceys and Agnes h.w. Concerning a moiety of 1 mess., 1 toft, 60a. land 5a. meadow and 2s 3d rent in Chaddesden. Henry and Agnes acknowledged these to be the right of Robert and they remised and quitclaimed of themselves and the heirs of Agnes to Robert, William and Richard and the heirs of Robert. The plaintiffs gave 20 marks of silver. (221)

919. Westminster. The morrow of Martinmas 1374. P: Richard de Haloum, vicar of the church of Baseford, and Thomas de Haloum, chaplain. D: Thomas de Holt of Maperley and Constance h.w. Concerning 2 mess., 60a. land, and 10a. meadow in Stanley, Ketilston, Morley and Maperley. Thomas and Constance acknowledged these to be the right of Richard who, with Thomas de Haloum, had them of their gift. They remised and quitclaimed the tenements of, and warranted for, themselves and the heirs of Constance to Richard and Thomas and the heirs of Richard. Richard and Thomas gave 100 marks of silver. (222)

920. Westminster. Quindene of Michaelmas 1374. Octave of Trinity 1375. P: Maude, widow of Walter de Monte Gomery, chivaler. D: Robert de Huggeford and Margery h.w. Concerning a moiety of 1 mess., 42a. land, 6a. meadow and 9a. pasture in Sudbury. Maude had 2 parts of these of the gift of Robert and Margery who remised and quitclaimed of themselves and the heirs of Margery to Maude and her heirs forever. They also granted that the third part which John de Longeley and Clarice h.w. held as Clarice's dowry of the inheritance of Margery and which ought to revert to Robert and Margery on the death of Clarice, should remain instead to Maude and her heirs to hold of the chief lord etc forever. Robert and Margery warranted for themselves and Margery's heirs. Maude gave 20 marks of silver. (223)

921. Westminster. The morrow of Martinmas 1375. P: Thomas de Castelton, vicar of the church of Wyrkesworth. D: Ralph Fremon of Roulesley and Elizabeth h.w. Concerning 2 mess., 7 bov. land and 3a. meadow in Brassyngton. Thomas had these of the gift of Ralph and Elizabeth to hold to himself and his heirs of the chief lord etc forever. Ralph and Elizabeth warranted for themselves and Elizabeth's heirs. Thomas gave 100 marks of silver. (224)

922. Westminster. Octave of the Purification 1376. P: William Hunt, parson of the church of Gotham, Adam de Horsley, clerk, William de Dethek, Robert Laverok, John de Hynkersell, chaplain, Richard de Southewell, chaplain, and John de Paistonhurst by John de Oxton, attorney for William, William, John, Richard and John. D: John Laverok of Chesterfeld and Isabel h.w. Concerning 10 mess., 200a. land, 30a. meadow, 6a. woodland and 10 marks rent in Chesterfeld, Boythorp, Brampton, Linacre, Neubold, Hulme, Dronfeld, Dunston, Langley, Whityngton, Magna Tapton, Parva Tapton, Brimyngton, Staveley and Staveleyromley. John and Isabel acknowledged these to be the right of Adam who, with the other plaintiffs, had them of their gift. They remised and quitclaimed of, and warranted for, themselves and the heirs of Isabel to the plaintiffs and the heirs of Adam. The plaintiffs gave £200. (225)

923. Westminster. Quindene of Hilary 1376. P: John atte Kirke of Kynwoldmersshe. D: Roger de Waltham of Notyngham and Emma h.w. Concerning 3 mess., 40a. land and 10a. meadow in Kynwoldmersshe. John had these of the gift of Roger and Emma who remised and quitclaimed of, and warranted for, themselves and the heirs of Emma to John and his heirs. John gave 100 marks of silver. (226)

924. Westminster. Quindene of Trinity 1375. P: Henry de Coggeshale, chivaler, Thomas de Morhall, clerk, John James, Thomas de Grendon, clerk, and Nicholas de Baukewell. D: Henry de Braillesford, chivaler. Concerning the manors of Braillesford and Wyngerworth and the advowson of the church of Braillesford. Westminster. Quindene of Easter 1376, after the death of Henry de Coggeshale. The other 4 plaintiffs, the deforciant and the tenements as before. Henry de Braillesford acknowledged the manors and advowson to be the right of Thomas de Morhall who, with the other plaintiffs, had the manor of Braillesford and the advowson of the gift of Henry to hold to themselves and the heirs of Thomas de Morhall of the chief lord etc forever. Henry de Braillesford also granted for himself and his heirs that the manor of Wyngerworth which Roger Harecourt and Margaret h.w. held for Margaret's life of the inheritance of Henry and which ought to revert to Henry and his heirs on the death of Margaret, should remain instead to the plaintiffs and the heirs of Thomas de Morhall to hold as above. Henry warranted for himself and his heirs. The plaintiffs gave 200 marks of silver. (227)

925. Westminster. Quindene of Easter 1376. Octave of Trinity 1376. P: Ralph de Stathum and Goditha h.w. D: John Flegh and Margery h.w. Concerning a moiety of the manor of Caldlowe. John and Margery acknowledged the moiety to be the right of Ralph and they remised and quitclaimed it of themselves and the heirs of Margery to Ralph, Goditha and the heirs of Ralph. Ralph and Goditha gave 100 marks of silver. (228)

926. Westminster. Octave of Trinity 1376. P: William de Nedham. D: Henry Sharp of Fairefeld and Ellen h.w. Concerning 1 mess. and 15½a. land in Overgrene and Nethergrene. William had these of the gift of Henry and Ellen who remised and quitclaimed of, and warranted for, themselves and the heirs of Ellen to William and his heirs. William gave 20 marks of silver. (229)

927. Westminster. Quindene of Trinity 1376. P: Nicholas de Tissyngton. D: Richard Saundressone of Rippeleye and Joan h.w. Concerning 13a. land in Duffeld. Nicholas had the land of the gift of Richard and Joan who remised and quitclaimed of, and warranted for, themselves and the heirs of Joan to Nicholas and his heirs. Nicholas gave 10 marks of silver. (230)

928. Westminster. Michaelmas three weeks 1376. P: Robert de Wardlowe of Assheford. D: Thomas Rider of Allorwas and Joan h.w. Concerning 1 mess. and 3a. land in Baukwell. Robert had these of the gift of Thomas and Joan who remised and quitclaimed of, and warranted for, themselves and the heirs of Joan to Robert and his heirs. Robert gave 10 marks of silver. (231)

929. Westminster. Octave of Michaelmas 1375. Octave of Michaelmas 1376. P: William Leche of Derby and Agnes h.w. D: John de Holand of Derby, chaplain, and Robert de Weston, chaplain. Concerning 1 mess. in Derby. John and Robert acknowledged the messuage to be the right of William and they granted for themselves and the heirs of John that the messuage, which Joan, widow of Robert Alybon, held for life of the inheritance of John and which ought to revert to John, Robert and John's heirs on the death of Joan, should remain instead to William, Agnes and William's heirs to hold of the chief lord etc forever. John and Robert warranted for themselves and the heirs of John. William and Agnes gave 10 marks of silver. (232)

930. Westminster. Quindene of Hilary 1377. P: John de Stanhop and Elizabeth h.w. D: John Waltiers and Joan h.w. Concerning the manor of Bursyngcote. John and Joan acknowledged the manor to be the right of Elizabeth and they remised and quitclaimed it of themselves and the heirs of Joan to John, Elizabeth and her heirs who then agreed to pay 50s of silver each year at the feast of the Nativity of St John the Baptist and also at the feast of the Lord's Birth during Joan's lifetime and if John and Elizabeth or the heirs of Elizabeth should default in these payments at any term it will be lawful to distrain *[by the same terms as in 869]*. After Joan's death John, Elizabeth and Elizabeth's heirs will be quit of the annual payments. (233)

931. Westminster. Octave of Michaelmas 1376. Quindene of Easter 1377. P: Robert de Langton. D: John de Luton and Christian h.w. Concerning 2 bov. land in Birchewode. Robert had the land of the gift of John and Christian who remised and quitclaimed of, and warranted for, themselves and the heirs of Christian to Robert and his heirs. Robert gave 20 marks of silver. (234)

RICHARD II

CP/25/39/39

932. Westminster. Easter three weeks 1377. Octave of Hilary 1378. P: Roger son of Richard de Riseley. D: Ralph de Onthorp and Margaret h.w. Concerning 1 mess., 2½ bov. land and 3a. meadow in Breydeston. Roger had these of the gift of Ralph and Margaret who remised and quitclaimed of, and warranted for, themselves and the heirs of Margaret to Roger and his heirs. Roger gave 20 marks of silver. (1)

933. Westminster. The morrow of the Purification 1378. Quindene of Easter 1378. P: Robert de Derby. D: Thurstan de la Boure and Margaret h.w. Concerning a moiety of 2 mess. and 20a. 1 rood of land and a fourth part of a mill in Mornesale and Britterichefeld. Robert had these of the gift of Thurstan and Margaret to hold to himself and his heirs of the chief lord etc forever. Thurstan and Margaret warranted for themselves and the heirs of Margaret. Robert gave 20 marks of silver. (2)

934. Westminster. Quindene of Hilary 1378. Quindene of Easter 1378. P: Richard Braylesford of Shardelowe. D: Richard Gournay of Shardelowe and Maude h.w. Concerning 1 mess. and 1a. land in Wylne and Shardelowe. Richard Braylesford had these of the gift of Richard and Maude to hold to himself and his heirs of the chief lord etc forever. Richard and Maude warranted for themselves and the heirs of Maude. Richard Braylesford gave 100 shillings of silver. (3)

935. Westminster. Octave of Hilary 1378. P: Richard Beveregge of Chestrefeld. D: William de Hampton of Thurleston and Maude h.w. Concerning 2 mess., 1 toft, 2a. land and a moiety of a mess. in Chestrefeld. William and Maude remised and quitclaimed of, and warranted for, themselves and the heirs of Maude to Richard and his heirs. Richard gave 20 marks of silver. (4)

936. Westminster. Quindene of Michaelmas 1377. P: Robert Martell and Roger de Baucwell. D: John de Asshborne, citizen and goldsmith of London, and Joan h.w. Concerning 1 mess., 1 toft, 20a. land, 1a. meadow, 1a. woodland and a moiety of a toft in Chestrefeld, Boythorp and Walton next Chestrefeld. John and Joan acknowledged these to be the right of Robert, rendered them to Robert and Roger to hold to themselves and the heirs of Robert of the chief lord etc forever, and warranted for themselves and the heirs of Joan. Robert and Roger gave 20 marks of silver. (5)

937. Westminster. Quindene of Easter 1378. Octave of Trinity 1378. P: William son of Nicholas de Hadfeld. D: Thomas son of William Hudeson and Ellen h.w. Concerning 1 mess., 12a. land, 6a. meadow and 8a. pasture in Glossop. Thomas and Ellen granted and rendered these to William to hold to himself and the heirs of his body of the chief lord etc forever. Successive remainders to Richard and Roger, sons of William, and the heirs of their bodies. Remainder to the right heirs of William. Thomas and Ellen warranted for themselves and the heirs of Ellen. William gave 20 marks of silver. (6)

938. Westminster. Octave of Midsummer 1378. P: Oliver de Barton and Alice h.w. D: Robert de Swynarton, chivaler, and Joan h.w. Concerning the manor of Williamthorp. Robert and Joan acknowledged this to be the right of Oliver, who, with Alice, had it of their gift. They remised and quitclaimed

55

of, and warranted for, themselves and the heirs of Joan to Oliver, Alice and Oliver's heirs. Oliver and Alice gave 200 marks of silver. (7)

939. Westminster. Quindene of Michaelmas 1378. P: Oliver de Barton and Alice h.w. D: Nicholas de Bakewell and Joan h.w. Concerning the manor of Williamthorp excepting 1 mess., 50a. land, 6a. meadow and 40s rent within the manor. Nicholas and Joan acknowledged this to be the right of Oliver who, with Alice, had it of their gift. They remised and quitclaimed of, and warranted for, themselves and the heirs of Nicholas to Oliver, Alice and Oliver's heirs. Oliver and Alice gave 100 marks of silver. (8)

940. Westminster. Quindene of Michaelmas 1378. P: John Cokayn, John de Aston and John de Somersale, chaplain. D: John del Pentrie and Alice h.w. Concerning 11 mess. and 3a. land in Dovvebrugge. John and Alice acknowledged these to be the right of John de Aston and they remised and quitclaimed of themselves and the heirs of Alice to the plaintiffs and the heirs of John de Aston. The plaintiffs gave 100 marks of silver. (9)

941. Westminster. The morrow of Ascension 1380. P: Thomas de Pykkesthorp parson of the church of Braylesford, John de Fyndern and Thomas de Wombewell. D: Henry de Braylesford, chivaler. Concerning the manor of Braylesford, 10 marks rent and an eighth part of a knight's fee in Bradeley. Henry acknowledged these to be the right of Thomas de Pykkesthorp who, with John and Thomas de Wombewell, had them of Henry's gift. The plaintiffs then granted and rendered them to Henry to hold of the chief lord etc for his life. Remainder to John Basset of Chedele, chivaler, and Joan h.w. and the heirs of her body. Remainder to the right heirs of Henry. (10)

942. Westminster. Octave of Michaelmas 1379. P: Oliver de Barton and Alice h.w. D: Nicholas de Baukewell and Joan h.w. Concerning 50a. land, 6a. meadow and 40s rent in Williamthorp. Nicholas and Joan acknowledged these to be the right of Oliver who, with Alice, had them of their gift. They remised and quitclaimed of, and warranted for, themselves and the heirs of Nicholas to Oliver, Alice and Oliver's heirs. Oliver and Alice gave 100 marks of silver. (11)

943. Westminster. Quindene of Michaelmas 1379. P: John le Smyth of Tyddeswell, chaplain, and Nicholas Martyn, chaplain. D: John le Wright of Eyom and Joan h.w. Concerning 1 mess. and 1 bov. land in Eyom. John and Joan acknowledged these to be the right of Nicholas who, with John le Smyth, had them of their gift to hold to themselves and the heirs of Nicholas of the chief lord etc forever. John le Wright warranted for himself and his heirs. John and Nicholas gave 100 marks of silver. (12)

944. Westminster. Easter three weeks 1381. P: Robert Barlay, senior, Robert Barlay, junior, Ralph Barker and Thomas Gonnifray, parson of the church of Dronfeld. D: John Stafford and Joan h.w. Concerning 1 mess., 1 toft, 1 carucate 1 bov. and 4a. land, 5a. meadow, 6s rent and a moiety of a mill in Parva Longusdon, Yolgreve, Birchels and Alport. John and Joan acknowledged these to be the right of Robert Barlay, junior, who, with the other plaintiffs, had them of their gift to hold to themselves and the heirs of Robert Barlay, junior, of the chief lord etc forever. The plaintiffs gave 100 marks of silver. (13)

945. Westminster. Octave of Michaelmas 1380. P: Robert de Swyllyngton, chivaler, and Robert Gretheved, clerk. D: John de Litton and Christian h.w. Concerning the manor of Ufton. John and Christian acknowledged the manor to be the right of Robert de Swyllyngton who, with Robert Gretheved, had it of their gift. They remised and quitclaimed of, and warranted for, themselves and the heirs of Christian to Robert and Robert and the heirs of Robert de Swyllyngton. The plaintiffs gave £200. (14)

946. Westminster. Quindene of Michaelmas 1380. P: Oliver de Barton. D: John Horwode and Maude h.w. Concerning a third part of the manor of Ednesore. John and Maude granted this to Oliver and remised and quitclaimed to Oliver and his heirs whatsoever they had in the third part for the life of Maude. Oliver gave 100 marks of silver. (15)

947. Westminster. Octave of Michaelmas 1381. Octave of Hilary 1382. P: The abbot of Derleye. D: William Leche of Derby and Agnes h.w. Concerning 1 mess. in Derby. William and Agnes remised and quitclaimed of, and warranted for, themselves and the heirs of Agnes to the abbot, his successors and his church of the Blessed Mary, of Derleye. The abbot gave 20 marks of silver. (16)

948. Westminster. Michaelmas one month 1382. P: John de Aston, chaplain, and John Smyth, chaplain. D: Nicholas Sadeller of Sheffeld and Felise h.w. Concerning 1 mess., 9a. land and 9s rent in Tiddeswalle. Nicholas and Felise acknowledged these to be the right of John de Aston who, with John Smyth, had them of their gift. They remised and quitclaimed of, and warranted for, themselves and the heirs of Felise to John and John and the heirs of John de Aston. The plaintiffs gave 20 marks of silver. (17)

949. Westminster. Michaelmas one month 1382. P: John Bowere of Derby. D: Robert Dubber of Coventre and Emma h.w. Concerning 3 tofts, 18a. land and 12d rent in Derby. John had these of the gift of Robert and Emma who remised and quitclaimed of, and warranted for, themselves and the heirs of Emma to John and his heirs. John gave 20 marks of silver. (18)

950. Westminster. Quindene of Martinmas 1382. P: Anker Freschevill. D: Richard de Sutton and Alice h.w. Concerning the manor of Ailwaston. Richard and Alice remised and quitclaimed of, and warranted for, themselves and the heirs of Alice to Anker and his heirs. Anker gave 200 marks of silver. (19)

951. Westminster. Quindene of Easter 1384. P: Thomas Gunifray, clerk. D: Richard Hikson of Dore and Joan h.w, Thomas Dyker of Abney and Agnes h.w. and Robert Pigot of Leverton and Alice h.w. Concerning 1 mess. and 6½a. land in Wheston. The deforciants granted and rendered these to Thomas Gunifray to hold to himself and his heirs of the chief lord etc forever and they warranted for themselves and the heirs of Joan, Agnes and Alice. Thomas gave 10 marks of silver. (20)

952. Westminster. The morrow of Ascension 1384. P: Agnes widow of Richard de Hokenale of Ilkeston and John, her son. D: William de Haukesoke and Margery h.w. Concerning 12a. land in Shipley. William and Margery acknowledged the land to be the right of John who, with Agnes, had it of their gift. They remised and quitclaimed of, and warranted for, themselves and the heirs of Margery to John, Agnes and John's heirs. Agnes and John gave 20 marks of silver. (21)

953. Westminster. Quindene of Michaelmas 1383. P: Oliver de Barton. D: John Michel of Coventre and Eleanor h.w. Concerning the manor of Assh. Oliver had the manor of the gift of John and Eleanor who remised and quitclaimed of, and warranted for, themselves and the heirs of Eleanor to Oliver and his heirs. Oliver gave £100. (22)

954. Westminster. Octave of Martinmas 1383. P: William de Wodehous. D: Alan de Levines of Leycamstede and Cecily h.w. Concerning 1 mess. and 1 bov. land called Stonhallond, in Basselowe. William had these of the gift of Alan and Cecily who remised and quitclaimed of, and warranted for, themselves and the heirs of Cecily to William and his heirs. William gave 100 marks of silver. (23)

955. Westminster. Octave of the Purification 1383. Octave of Hilary 1385. P: Ralph de Rocheford, kt, William de Spaigne of St Botho, Thomas Eland and Robert de Cletham. D: John Bussy and Maude h.w. Concerning a moiety of the manor of Parkhall. John and Maude acknowledged the moiety to be the right of Robert who, with the other plaintiffs, had it of their gift, with the exception of 2 carucates of land, 40a. meadow, 100a. pasture and a moiety of a mess. within the moiety of the manor, to hold to themselves and the heirs of Robert of the chief lord etc forever. John and Maude also granted for themselves and the heirs of Maude that the tenements excepted above, which Oliver de Barton and Alice h.w. held for 28 years of the inheritance of Maude and which, at the end of the 28 years, ought to revert to John and Maude and Maude's heirs, should remain instead to the plaintiffs and the heirs of Robert. John and Maude warranted for themselves and the heirs of Maude. The plaintiffs gave 100 marks of silver. (24)

956. Westminster. Quindene of Hilary 1385. P: Ralph Frecchevylle, kt. D: Richard de Frormanby of Harpeham and Isabel h.w. Concerning a moiety of a toft in Chestrefeld. Richard and Isabel remised and quitclaimed of, and warranted for, themselves and the heirs of Isabel to Ralph and his heirs. Ralph gave 20 marks of silver. (25)

CP 25/1/39/40

957. Westminster. Quindene of Trinity 1385. P: Master Nicholas de Chaddesden, William de Monyasshe, vicar of the church of Duffeld, Nicholas de Knyveton, Thomas de Weddenesleye and Thomas de Stannton. D: John de Stathum and Isabel h.w. Concerning the manor of Cotton. John and Isabel acknowledged this to be the right of William who, with the other plaintiffs, had it of their gift, to hold to themselves and the heirs of William of the chief lord etc forever. Isabel warranted for herself and her heirs. The plaintiffs gave 100 marks of silver. (26)

958. Westminster. Easter one month 1383. Quindene of Easter 1385. P: John Cokayn, the uncle, William de Moneassh, vicar of the church of Duffeld, John de Aston, Henry Wallour, chaplain, and Henry de Asshebourne, clerk. D: John Cokayn of Asshebourne, the nephew. Concerning the manor of Herthull and a mill in Aldeport. John Cokayn of Asshebourne acknowledged these to be the right of Henry de Asshebourne and granted for himself and his heirs that the manor and mill, which Thomas de Wennesley held for life of his inheritance and which ought to revert to him on Thomas's death, should remain instead to the plaintiffs and the heirs of Henry de Asshebourne to hold of the chief lord etc forever. John warranted for himself and his heirs and the plaintiffs gave 100 marks of silver. (27)

959. Westminster. Quindene of Easter 1385. P: Thomas Durannt of Chestrefeld. D: Hugh Pigot of Nettelham and Agnes h.w. Concerning 1 mess., 80a. land, 4a. meadow, 3a. woodland and 4s rent in Tapton. Hugh and Agnes remised and quitclaimed of, and warranted for, themselves and Agnes's heirs to Thomas and his heirs. Thomas gave 100 marks of silver. (28)

960. Westminster. Quindene of Michaelmas 1384. P: Reginald Grey. D: Anker Freschevill and Agnes h.w. Concerning the manor of Ailwaston.

59

Anker and Agnes rendered this to Reginald to hold to himself and his heirs of the chief lord etc forever; Anker warranted for himself and his heirs. Reginald gave £200. (29)

961. Westminster. Quindene of Martinmas 1384. Easter three weeks 1385. P: John Cokayn, kt, Oliver de Barton, William de Sallowe and John son of John de Knyveton, senior. D: John Cokayn senior, John de Aston and Henry de Asshebourn, clerk. Concerning the manor of Herthull and a mill in Aldeport. The defendants acknowledged these to be the right of John Cokayn, kt, and granted for themselves and the heirs of Henry that the manor and mill, which Thomas de Wenneslay held for life of the inheritance of Henry and which ought to revert to the defendants and the heirs of Henry on the death of Thomas, should remain instead to the plaintiffs and the heirs of John Cokayn to hold of the chief lord etc forever. The plaintiffs gave £100. (30)

962. Westminster. Octave of Michaelmas 1385. Quindene of Hilary 1386. P: Richard Beveregge of Chestrefeld. D: Richard de Rossyngton and Maude h.w. Concerning 2 mess., 9 shops, a toft, 16a. land and 1a. meadow in Chestrefeld, Wyngreworth, Newebold, Dunston and Tappeton. Richard and Maude granted for themselves and the heirs of Maude that these tenements, which Richard Beveregge and Joan h.w. held for Joan's life of the inheritance of Maude and which ought to revert to Richard and Maude and Maude's heirs on the death of Joan, should remain instead to Richard Beveregge and his heirs to hold of the chief lord etc forever. Richard and Maude warranted for themselves and Maude's heirs. Richard Beveregge gave 100 marks of silver. (31)

963. Westminster. Quindene of Easter 1386. P: Thomas Stathum and Elizabeth h.w. D: Thomas Witty, parson of the church of Braydeshale, John Parke and Goditha, widow of Ralph de Stathum. Concerning the manor of Caldelowe. Thomas Stathum acknowledged the manor to be the right of Goditha who, with the other defendants, granted and rendered it to Thomas and Elizabeth to hold to themselves and the heirs of their bodies of the defendants and the heirs of Goditha, paying therefor one rose each year at the feast of the Nativity of St John the Baptist for all services etc due to the defendants and the heirs of Goditha and doing to the chief lord etc. Successive remainders to the heirs of the body of Thomas Stathum and to Richard, his brother, and the heirs of his body. Reversion to the defendants and the heirs of Goditha. (32)

964. Westminster. Quindene of Trinity 1387. P: Oliver de Barton. D: William de Hulton of Derby and Margaret h.w. Concerning a messuage in Derby. Oliver had this of the gift of William and Margaret who remised and quitclaimed of, and warranted for, themselves and the heirs of Margaret to Oliver and his heirs. Oliver gave £20. (33)

965. Westminster. Quindene of Trinity 1386. Octave of Michaelmas 1386. P: Thomas de Wennesley, kt, Roger Harecourt, Thomas Hunt, William del Lowe and William de Adderley. D: John de Annesley, chivaler, and Isabel h.w. Concerning 12 mess., 9½ bov. 1½a. land, 7s rent and a third part of 2 mess., 1 bov. 80a. land, 15a. meadow and 12a. pasture in Ekynton, Duffeld, Beaurepeire, Mogynton and Henore, a third part of the manor of Rodburne and the advowsons of the churches of Rodburne and Mogynton and a fourth part of the advowson of the church of Ekynton. John and Isabel acknowledged these to be the right of William de Adderley and rendered them to the plaintiffs to hold to themselves and the heirs of William de Adderley of the chief lord etc forever. John and Isabel warranted for themselves and the heirs of Isabel to the plaintiffs and the heirs of William de Adderley. The plaintiffs gave £100. (34)

966. Westminster. Octave of Michaelmas 1387. P: Thomas Tochet, parson of the church of Makworth, and John Elme. D: Thomas de Tapley of Derby and Margaret h.w. Concerning 1 mess. in Derby. Thomas and Margaret acknowledged the messuage to be the right of Thomas Tochet who, with John, had it of their gift. They remised and quitclaimed of, and warranted for, themselves and the heirs of Margaret to Thomas and John and Thomas's heirs. Thomas Tochet and John gave 10 marks of silver. (35)

967. Westminster. Octave of Trinity 1389. P: John de Glossop of Chapell in le Frith. D: Stephen del Brome of Huklowe and Ellen h.w. Concerning 1 mess. in Boudon. John had this of the gift of Stephen and Ellen who remised and quitclaimed of, and warranted for, themselves and the heirs of Ellen to John and his heirs. John gave 10 marks of silver. (36)

968. Westminster. Octave of Michaelmas 1389. P: Benedict Oliver. D: John le Souter of Whithalugh and Alice h.w. Concerning 1 mess. and 4a. land in Boudon. Benedict had these of the gift of John and Alice who remised and quitclaimed of, and warranted for, themselves and the heirs of Alice to Benedict and his heirs. Benedict gave 10 marks of silver. (37)

969. Westminster. Quindene of Hilary 1390. P: William Fairlet of Makworth. D: Adam Prynce and Joan h.w. Concerning 1 mess., 12a 1 rood land and 1½ roods meadow in Makworth. William had these of the gift of Adam and Joan who remised and quitclaimed of, and warranted for, themselves and the heirs of Joan to William and his heirs. William gave 10 marks of silver. (38)

970. Westminster. Octave of the Purification 1391. Quindene of Easter 1391. P: John de Outeby, parson of the church of Keteryng. D: Thomas de

Outeby and Joan h.w. Concerning 6 mess., 4 tofts, 100a. land, 10a. meadow and 4 marks rent in Derby and Osmundeston. John had these of the gift of Thomas and Joan and he granted and rendered them to them to hold to themselves and the heirs of their bodies of the chief lord etc forever. Successive remainders to the heirs of the body of Joan and to the right heirs of Thomas. (39)

971. Westminster. The morrow of Ascension 1391. Octave of Trinity 1391. P: Thomas Foliambe and Robert Langham. D: Thomas Stafford, chivaler, and Alice h.w. and Nicholas Langeford, chivaler, and Margery h.w. Concerning £12 rent derived from the manors of Penkeston and Normanton. The defendants acknowledged the rent to be the right of Robert who, with Thomas Foliambe, had it by their grant to hold and receive each year, one half at the feast of Pentecost, the other half at the feast of St Martin, from the hands of the defendants and the heirs of Alice and Margery to Thomas, Robert and Robert's heirs. *[Distraint clause as in 869.]* Thomas and Robert gave £100. (40)

972. Westminster. The morrow of Ascension 1391. Octave of Trinity 1391. P: Robert Langham. D: Thomas Stafford, chivaler, and Alice h.w. and Nicholas Langeford, chivaler, and Margery h.w. Concerning the advowson of the church of Normanton. The defendants acknowledged this to be the right of Robert and remised and quitclaimed of themselves and the heirs of Alice and Margery to Robert and his heirs. Robert gave 100 marks of silver. (41)

973. Westminster. Quindene of Hilary 1390. Octave of Midsummer 1390. P: John Bate of Sallowe. D: John Tenerey of Eyton and Margaret h.w. Concerning 2 bov. land and 1a. meadow in Longeyton. John and Margaret acknowledged these to be the right of John Bate who had 1 bov. land and the 1a. meadow of their gift to hold to himself and his heirs of the chief lord etc forever. John and Margaret also granted for themselves and the heirs of John that the remaining 1 bov. land, which Maude, widow of William Anot, and her daughter Agnes held for their lives of the inheritance of John Tenerey and which ought to revert to John, Margaret and John's heirs on the deaths of Maude and Agnes, should remain instead to John Bate and his heirs. John, Margaret and John's heirs warranted. John Bate gave 20 marks of silver. (42)

974. Westminster. Octave of Michaelmas 1390. P: William Groos of Derby and Deonise h.w. D: Richard de Trowell and Hawis h.w. Concerning 4 mess. and 2½a. land in Derby and Chaddesden. Richard and Hawis acknowledged these to be the right of William who, with Deonise, had them of their gift. They remised and quitclaimed of, and warranted for, themselves and the heirs of Hawis to William, Deonise and William's heirs. William and Deonise gave £20. (43)

975. Westminster. Quindene of Easter 1392. P: John Wemme and Ann h.w. D: William Truttok, chaplain, and John Nayl, chaplain. Concerning 2 mess. and 1 shop in Derby. John and Ann acknowledged these to be the right of John Nayl who, with William, had them of their gift and they remised and quitclaimed of, and warranted for, themselves and the heirs of Ann to William, John Nayl and John's heirs. William and John gave 10 marks of silver. (44)

976. Westminster. Quindene of Michaelmas 1391. P: John Shagh of Somersale. D: William de Croft and Agnes h.w. Concerning 32a. land, 4a. meadow and 3a. woodland in Walton and Brompton. John had these of the gift of William and Agnes who remised and quitclaimed of, and warranted for, themselves and the heirs of Agnes to John and his heirs. John gave 20 marks of silver. (45)

977. York. Michaelmas one month 1392. Westminster. Octave of Hilary 1393. P: Thomas Bagenald of Makworth. D: William Birchovere of Spondon and Joan h.w. Concerning a toft, 32a. land and 2a. meadow in Makworth. Thomas had these of the gift of William and Joan who remised and quitclaimed of, and warranted for, themselves and the heirs of Joan to Thomas and his heirs. Thomas gave 20 marks of silver. (46)

978. Westminster. The morrow of Ascension 1393. P: John Brewode, parson of the church of Roddeburne and Richard Tayllour of Trusleye. D: Henry Phelipot of Marketon and Maude h.w. Concerning 1 mess., 33a. land, 4½a. meadow and a rent of ½lb pepper in Makworth and Marton. Henry and Maude acknowledged these to be the right of John who, with Richard, had them of their gift. They remised and quitclaimed of, and warranted for, themselves and the heirs of Maude to John, Richard and the heirs of John. John and Richard gave 20 marks of silver. (47)

979. York. Octave of Martinmas 1392. Westminster. Octave of Hilary 1393. P: William Shepherd of Shardelowe. D: John Spayne and Margery h.w. Concerning 1 mess. and 10a. land in Shardelowe and Aston. William had these of the gift of John and Margery who remised and quitclaimed of, and warranted for, themselves and the heirs of Margery to William and his heirs. William gave 20 marks of silver. (48)

980. Westminster. Quindene of Easter 1394. P: John Cokayn of Berwardecote and Ida h.w. D: William Burton and Margery h.w. Concerning a moiety of 1 mess., 1 carucate land and 16s rent in Berwardecote, Brunaldeston and Hatton. William and Margery acknowledged these to be the right of John who, with Ida, had them of their gift. They remised and quitclaimed of themselves and the heirs of Margery to John and Ida and John's heirs. John and Ida gave 100 marks of silver. (49)

981. Westminster. Quindene of Easter 1394. P: John Cokayn of Berwardecote and Ida h.w. D: Robert Shyppley and Eleanor h.w. Concerning a moiety of 1 mess., 1 carucate land and 16s rent in Berwardecote, Brunaldeston and Hatton. Robert and Eleanor acknowledged these to be the right of John who, with Ida, had them of their gift. They remised and quitclaimed of themselves and the heirs of Eleanor to John, Ida and John's heirs. John and Ida gave £20. (50)

CP 25/1/39/41

982. Westminster. Quindene of Easter 1393. Michaelmas one month 1393. P: Simon Couper of Whetecroft, Henry Raulyn of Whetecroft, John Jakson of Etwalle and Richard de Halle of Alkemonton, chaplain. D: John Couper of Whetecroft and Margery h.w. Concerning 1 mess., 2 tofts, 3 bov. land, 6a. meadow and 2s rent in Brynaston. John and Margery granted these to the plaintiffs together with the homage and services of Robert Doidsawt and Isabel h.w. and their heirs of all the tenements which they held of John and Margery. They rendered them to the plaintiffs to hold to themselves and the heirs of John Jakson of the chief lord etc forever, paying therefor to John and Margery for their lives, 19 shillings of silver each year, half at the feast of St Michael and the other half at the feast of the Annunciation of the Blessed Mary. *[Distraint clause in 869.]* After the deaths of John and Margery the plaintiffs and the heirs of John Jakson shall be quit of these payments. John, Margery and Margery's heirs warranted. The plaintiffs gave 100 marks of silver. (51)

983. Westminster. Quindene of Easter 1395. Octave of Trinity 1395. P: Ralph de Percy, chivaler. D: Ralph de Crumwell, chivaler, and Maude h.w. Concerning the manor of Dronfeld. Ralph and Maude granted and rendered the manor to Ralph de Percy to hold to himself and the heirs of his body of them and the heirs of Maude paying therefor each year one rose at the feast of the Nativity of St John the Baptist for all services etc due to them and Maude's heirs and doing to the chief lord etc. Reversion to Ralph, Maude and Maude's heirs. Ralph de Percy gave 100 marks of silver. (52)

984. Westminster. Quindene of Easter 1395. P: Thomas de Stanton and Joan h.w. D: John Haukeswelle of Derby and Margaret h.w. and William, son of John Haukeswelle of Derby, and Agnes h.w. Concerning 1 mess. in Derby. The defendants acknowledged this to be the right of Thomas and they remised and quitclaimed of, and warranted for, themselves and the heirs of Margaret and Agnes to Thomas, Joan and Thomas's heirs. Thomas and Joan gave 10 marks of silver. (53)

985. Westminster. Quindene of Easter 1395. P: John Cokayn of Berewardcote and Ida h.w. D: William del Hyll of Ansty, otherwise called William Parker, and Ellen h.w. Concerning 1 toft, 3 bov. land and 2a. meadow in Berewardcote and Etewell. William and Ellen acknowledged these to be the right of John who, with Ida, had them of their gift. They remised and quitclaimed of, and warranted for, themselves and the heirs of Ellen to John, Ida and John's heirs. John and Ida gave £20. (54)

986. Westminster. The morrow of All Souls 1394. P: Thomas de Wendesley, chivaler, Thurstann atte Boure of Tyddeswell, John Redser, clerk, and Nicholas del Leghes of Eyoum. D: Nicholas Pycworth of Helowe and Margaret h.w. Concerning the manor of Helowe. Nicholas and Margaret acknowledged the manor to be the right of John and rendered it to the plaintiffs to hold to themselves and the heirs of John of the chief lord etc forever. Nicholas and Margaret warranted for themselves and the heirs of Margaret. The plaintiffs gave 100 marks of silver. (55)

987. Westminster. Octave of Martinmas 1394. Octave of Hilary 1395. P: William Sklater of Derby and Lucy h.w. D: William Hilton of Derby and Margaret h.w. Concerning 1 mess. in Derby. William and Margaret acknowledged the messuage to be the right of William Sklater and they remised and quitclaimed of, and warranted for, themselves and the heirs of Margaret to William, Lucy and William's heirs. William and Lucy gave 10 marks of silver. (56)

988. Westminster. The morrow of Ascension 1396. Octave of Trinity 1396. P: Adam Haselbache. D: William, son of Hugh de Asshover, and Joan h.w. Concerning 1 mess., 18a. land, 4a. meadow and 2a. woodland in Tannesley. Adam had these of the gift of William and Joan who remised and quitclaimed of, and warranted for, themselves and the heirs of Joan to Adam and his heirs. Adam gave 20 marks of silver. (57)

989. Westminster. Quindene of Martinmas 1396. Octave of Hilary 1397. P: Henry Howeland of Estwayte. D: Richard de Grene and Maude h.w. Concerning 1 mess., 1 toft and 2 bov. 7a. land in Denby. Henry had these of the gift of Richard and Maude who remised and quitclaimed of, and warranted for, themselves and the heirs of Maude to Henry and his heirs. Henry gave 20 marks of silver. (58)

990. Westminster. Quindene of Martinmas 1396. Octave of Hilary 1397. P: William Ledbeter, chaplain, John Andrewe, chaplain, and John del Dale, chaplain. D: John de Penyston and Felise h.w. Concerning 13a. land in Bubenhull. John and Felise acknowledged this to be the right of William who, with the other plaintiffs, had it of their gift. They remised and quitclaimed of, and warranted for, themselves and the heirs of Felise to the plaintiffs and the heirs of William. The plaintiffs gave 10 marks of silver. (59)

991. Westminster. Quindene of Easter 1388. P: Maude, widow of Reginald Graye of Shirland, Reginald de Croppehill, William Horbyri, clerk, John Barley, clerk, and Hugh Draper by Thomas Oxenbrig, attorney for Maude, Reginald, William and Hugh. D: John del Mersshe, chaplain. Concerning 10 mess., 200a. land, 30a. meadow, 6a. woodland and 10 marks rent in Chestrefeld, Boythorp, Brampton, Linacre, Neubold, Hulme, Dronfeld, Dunston, Langley, Whityngton, Magna Tapton, Parva Tapton, Brimyngton, Staveley and Staveley Romley. Later, Octave of Midsummer 1396, after the deaths of Maude, Reginald and William. John del Mersshe acknowledged the rent and tenements to be the right of John Barley and he rendered to the plaintiffs the tenements and 24s 4d of the rents. He granted to them 8 marks 2s 4d rents and the homage and services of 51 people listed below to hold to themselves and the heirs of John Barley of the chief lord etc forever. John del Mersshe warranted for himself and his heirs. The plaintiffs gave 100 marks of silver. The 51 people whose homage and services were granted to the plaintiffs were: the Master of the Hospice of St Leonard at Chestrefeld and Thomas, the keeper of the Chantry of St Michael in the church of Chestrefeld and their successors, John Bate, John del Asshes, John Manger, William Lorimer, John Broune, William Longstaffe, chaplain, Adam Broune, Ralph Barker, Hugh Draper of Chestrefeld and Cecily h.w., William Marsshall, Mary de Tapton, John de Bughton and Elizabeth h.w., Cecily, widow of Roger son of Henry, Alice Knyffesmyth, Roger Manger, Henry Clerke, John del Wode, John de Norton, Thomas Durannt, John de Silkeston, William Beveregg, John Caunt and Joan h.w., Robert de Wityngton, John de Blythe, Robert de Tapton, Richard de Kylvyngton and Margery h.w., Thomas del Chapell and Alice h.w., John Alcok, William Ferrour and Margaret h.w., Robert de Collay, Agnes, widow of Roger atte Barre, John de Tappeton, Robert Dandeson, Thomas de Derton and Joan h.w., Henry de Maunsfeld, Henry Bate, Roger de Baugnell, Robert Cokerell, Richard Northe and Joan h.w., William de Calall and William Lowe and their heirs. (60)

992. Westminster. The morrow of Ascension 1397. Octave of Trinity 1397. P: Thomas Walton, clerk. D: Philip Maubank and Joan h.w. Concerning 4 mess., 2 carucates and 140a. land, 12a. meadow and 20a. woodland in Barleburgh, Whytewell and Cloun. Philip and Joan acknowledged these to be the right of Thomas and rendered them to him to hold to himself and his heirs of the chief lord etc forever. Thomas gave 200 marks of silver. (61)

993. Westminster. Easter one month 1397. Octave of Trinity 1397. P: William de Leek, John de Oxton and Edmund Cooke of Thurgarton. D: John Brommale and Maude h.w. Concerning 1 mess., 3 bov. land and 6a. woodland in Elmeton. John and Maude acknowledged these to be the right of Edmund who, with John and William, had them of their gift. They remised and quitclaimed of themselves and the heirs of Maude to the plaintiffs and the heirs of Edmund. The plaintiffs gave 20 marks of silver. (62)

994. Westminster. Octave of Trinity 1397. P: John Foucher and Isabel h.w. D: Robert de Merkaston and Maude h.w. Concerning 3½a. land and 2½a. meadow in Twyford and Steynton. Robert and Maude acknowledged these to be the right of John who, with Isabel, had them of their gift. They remised and quitclaimed of, and warranted for, themselves and the heirs of Maude to John, Isabel and John's heirs. John and Isabel gave 10 marks of silver. (63)

995. Westminster. Easter one month 1397. Octave of Trinity 1397. P: John Broun of Matlok. D: Thomas Porter and Alice h.w. Concerning 1 mess. in Wyrkysworth. John had the messuage of the gift of Thomas and Alice who remised and quitclaimed of, and warranted for, themselves and the heirs of Thomas to John and his heirs. John gave 10 marks of silver. (64)

996. Westminster. Quindene of Michaelmas 1391. Octave of Hilary 1398. P: William, son of Thomas Roundell of Tuttebury. D: Ralph de Hiton of Sudbury and Isabel h.w., Thomas del Lee of Sudbury and Agnes h.w. and Henry Smyth of Marchyngton sub Nedwod and Maude h.w. Concerning 1 mess., 6a. land and 1a. meadow in Merston. The defendants acknowledged these to be the right of William and they rendered them to him to hold to himself and his heirs of the chief lord etc forever. They also warranted for themselves and the heirs of Isabel, Agnes and Maude. William gave 20 marks of silver. (65)

997. Westminster. The morrow of Ascension 1398. P: William Bradeshawe, junior. D: Adam Warde of Tyddeswell and Agnes h.w. Concerning 50a. land in Hope. William had this of the gift of Adam and Agnes who remised and quitclaimed of, and warranted for, themselves and the heirs of Agnes to William and his heirs. William gave £20. (66)

998. Westminster. The morrow of Ascension 1398. Quindene of Trinity 1398. P: Thomas Tochet, clerk, Robert de Foliambe, clerk, and William Arowesmyth, clerk. D: John de Chelaston and Agnes h.w. Concerning 4 mess., 55a. land, 7a. meadow and a moiety of a mess. in Makeworth and Marketon. John and Agnes acknowledged these to be the right of Thomas and they rendered 4 mess., 40a. land and 4a. meadow to the plaintiffs to hold to themselves and the heirs of Thomas of the chief lord etc forever. They also granted for themselves and the heirs of Agnes that 15a. land, 5a. meadow and the moiety of the messuage in Marketon, which John de Tapton and Agnes h.w. held for her life of the inheritance of Agnes, John de Chelaston's wife, and which ought to revert to John and Agnes and Agnes's heirs on the death of Agnes, John de Tapton's wife, should remain instead to the plaintiffs and the heirs of Thomas. John, Agnes and Agnes's heirs warranted. The plaintiffs gave 100 marks of silver. (67)

999. Westminster. Quindene of Michaelmas 1397. P: William de Bagshagh. D: William Ragge of Stadun and Maude h.w. Concerning 12a. land in Bowedon. William had this of the gift of William and Maude who remised and quitclaimed of, and warranted for, themselves and the heirs of Maude to William and his heirs. William de Bagshagh gave 20 marks of silver. (68)

1000. Westminster. Octave of Michaelmas 1397. P: Henry de Coton, clerk, and Thomas de Tykhull and Agnes h.w. D: Thomas de Stannton and Joan h.w. Concerning 2 mess., 72a. land, 8a. meadow and 11s 6d rent in Aston upon Trent next Weston. Thomas and Joan acknowledged these to be the right of Thomas de Tykhull who, with Agnes and Henry, had them of their gift. They remised and quitclaimed of, and warranted for, themselves and the heirs of Thomas to the plaintiffs and the heirs of Thomas de Tykhull. The plaintiffs gave 100 marks of silver. (69)

1001. Westminster. Octave of Michaelmas 1397. P: John de Trowell. D: John Dowe and Cecily h.w. Concerning 1 mess. and 2 bov. land in Ilkeston. John de Trowell had these of the gift of John and Cecily who remised and quitclaimed of, and warranted for, themselves and the heirs of Cecily to John and his heirs. John de Trowell gave 20 marks of silver. (70)

1002. Westminster. Quindene of Michaelmas 1390. Quindene of Hilary 1399. P: Thomas Tochet, parson of the church of Mackeworth, William Brenlaston and John Nayle, chaplain. D: John Bromhale and Maude h.w. Concerning 5 mess., 7 shops, 3 tofts, 133a. land, 9a. meadow, 10a. woodland, 18d rent and a moiety of a mess. in Chastrefeld, Tapton, Brymyngton, Newebolt, Elmeton and Aylwaston. The plaintiffs acknowledged these to be the right of John Bromhale and they rendered to John and Maude 2 mess., 1 toft, 78a. land, 2a. meadow and the woodland to hold to themselves and the heirs of John of the chief lord etc forever. They also granted for themselves and the heirs of John Nayle that 3 mess., the shops, 2 tofts, 55a. land, 7a. meadow, the rent and the moiety of the mess., which John Boughton and Elizabeth h.w. held for her life of the inheritance of John Nayle and which ought to revert to the plaintiffs and the heirs of John

Nayle on the death of Elizabeth, should remain instead to John, Maude and John's heirs. John and Maude gave 100 marks of silver. (71)

1003. Westminster. Easter one month 1399. P: Henry Bothe of Parva Over. D: William Buyldyng of Parva Over and Alice h.w. Concerning 1 toft, 32a. land, 2a. meadow and a moiety of 1 rood of land in Parva Over, Twyford, Brynaston and Normanton. Henry had these of the gift of William and Alice and he rendered them to them to hold to themselves for their lives of Henry and his heirs paying therefor each year one rose at the feast of the Nativity of St John the Baptist for all services etc and doing to the chief lord etc. Reversion to Henry and his heirs. (72)

1004. Westminster. The morrow of Martinmas 1398. Octave of Hilary 1399. P: Robert, abbot of Beauchief. D: John Bassett, kt, and Joan h.w. Concerning 70a. pasture in Byrched. John and Joan acknowledged the pasture to be the right of Robert and his church of St Thomas Martyr at Beauchief and they remised and quitclaimed of, and warranted for, themselves and the heirs of Joan to Robert, his successors and his church. The abbot gave £20. (73)

1005. Westminster. Easter one month 1399. P: William Tyrry of Cubley. D: John Leggealden of Derby and Joan h.w. Concerning 5 mess., 14½a. land and 4a. 3 roods meadow in Derby. William had these of the gift of John and Joan who remised and quitclaimed of, and warranted for, themselves and the heirs of Joan to William and his heirs. William gave 100 marks of silver. (74)

1006. Westminster. The morrow of Martinmas 1398. P: The abbot of Welbek. D: John de Barleburgh and Agnes h.w. Concerning 8 mess., 25 bov. land and 23s rent in Dukmanton. John and Agnes acknowledged these to be the right of the abbot and his church of St James at Welbek who had them of their gift. They remised and quitclaimed of, and warranted for, themselves and the heirs of Agnes to the abbot, his successors and his church. The abbot gave 200 marks of silver. (75)

1007. Westminster. The morrow of Martinmas 1398. P: Ralph Barkere of Dore. D: John Bassett, kt, and Joan h.w. Concerning the advowson of the church of Dronfeld. John and Joan acknowledged the advowson to be the right of Ralph and remised and quitclaimed of, and warranted for, themselves and the heirs of Joan to Ralph and his heirs. Ralph gave £100. (76)

CP 25/1/39/42

1008. Westminster. Easter one month 1401. P: Denis de Rollesley. D: John Pewetrell of Mapirley and Joan h.w. Concerning 3 mess., 3 bov. 6a. land, 4a. meadow and 20d rent in Kersyngton. John and Joan remised and quitclaimed of themselves and the heirs of Joan to Denis and his heirs. Denis gave 20 marks of silver. (1)

1009. Westminster. Quindene of Hilary 1402. P: William de Nedham and John de Nedham. D: John Laverok and Margaret h.w. Concerning 1 mess. and 32a. land in Wormhill and the office of one forester in le Chaumpeyn. John and Margaret acknowledged these to be the right of William and they rendered them to William and John to hold to themselves and the heirs of William of the chief lord etc forever, paying therefor each year to John and Margaret for their lives, 40s, one half at the feast of the Annunciation of the Blessed Mary and the other half at the feast of St Michael. *[Distraint clause as in 869.]* After the deaths of John and Margaret, William and John Nedham and William's heirs will be quit of these payments. John and Margaret warranted for themselves and the heirs of Margaret. William and John gave 20 marks of silver. (2)

1010. Westminster. The morrow of Ascension 1402. P: Thomas Rempston, chivaler, John Leek, chivaler, Simon Bache, clerk, Thomas Herdwyk, clerk, John le Leventhorp, John Bonyngton, Thomas Somercotes and William Repyngton. D: John Cokayn, the uncle, and Ida h.w. Concerning the manor of Berwardecotes. John and Ida acknowledged the manor to be the right of John Bonyngton who, with the other plaintiffs, had it of their gift. They remised and quitclaimed of themselves and the heirs of John to the plaintiffs and the heirs of John Bodyngton. The plaintiffs gave 100 marks of silver. (3) *[John's name is spelt 'Bodyngton' 3 times and 'Bonyngton' twice.]*

1011. Westminster. The morrow of the Purification 1402. Octave of Trinity 1402. P: William de Coton of Ridewarehampstall and Agnes h.w. D: John de Coton and Elizabeth h.w. Concerning the manor of Boyleston and 10 mess., 10 bov. land, 6a. meadow and 6a. woodland in Rossynton and Norbury, and the advowson of half the church of Boyleston. John acknowledged these to be the right of Agnes who, with William, had the manor and the advowson of the gift of John and Elizabeth. William and Agnes granted and rendered the manor and the advowson to John and Elizabeth to hold to themselves and the heirs of their bodies of William, Agnes and Agnes's heirs paying therefor one rose at the feast of the Nativity of St John the Baptist for all services etc and doing to the chief lord etc. William and Agnes also granted for themselves and the heirs of Agnes that the tenements, which Thomas Fitzherberd and Nicholas Fitzherberd held for the life of Thomas of the inheritance of Agnes and which ought to revert to William and Agnes and Agnes's heirs on the death of Thomas, should remain instead to John, Elizabeth and John's heirs. Reversion to William, Agnes and Agnes's heirs. (4)

1012. Westminster. Michaelmas one month 1402. P: Thomas Waterhouse. D: Alfred de Lathebury, chivaler, and Alana h.w. Concerning 1 mess., 20a. land and 6a. meadow in Duffeld. Alfred and Alana remised and quitclaimed of, and warranted for, themselves and the heirs of Alana to Thomas and his heirs. Thomas gave 20 marks of silver. (5)

1013. Westminster. The morrow of Martinmas 1403. P: Thurstan del Boure, John del Boure of Qwitfeld, William del Wode, chaplain, and Thomas Horsley, chaplain. D: Robert de Stannton of Osslaston and Isabel h.w. and Nicholas Clerk of Derby and Agnes h.w. Concerning the manor of Parva Longesdon and 11 mess., 118a. land, 10a. meadow, 200a. pasture, 5a. woodland and 10s rent and a moiety of a mill and a rent of $\frac{1}{2}$lb cummin in Parva Longesdon and Magna Longesdon, Moensall and Tunstede. The defendants acknowledged these to be the right of Thurstan who, with the other plaintiffs, had the manor, 10 mess., 100a. land, the pasture, the woodland, the moiety and the rents of their gift. They remised and quitclaimed of themselves and the heirs of Isabel and Agnes to the plaintiffs and the heirs of Thurstan. The defendants also granted for themselves and the heirs of Isabel and Agnes that 1 mess. and 18a. land, [which Arthur] de Rolleston [held for life] of the inheritance of Isabel and Agnes and which ought to revert to the defendants and the heirs of Isabel and Agnes [on Arthur's death], should remain instead to the plaintiffs and the heirs of Thurstan to hold [of the chief lord] etc forever. [The defendants warranted and the plaintiffs gave £200.] (6) *[Damaged]*

1014. Westminster. Easter one month 1405. P: William Leche and William Smyth. D: John Charnelles and Margaret h.w. and William Lynet and Elizabeth h.w. Concerning 7 mess., 80a. land and 20a. meadow in Lytton, Abney and Whyston. The defendants acknowledged these to be the right of William Leche and they rendered them to him and William Smyth to hold to themselves and the heirs of William Leche of the chief lord etc forever. The defendants warranted for themselves and the heirs of Margaret and Elizabeth to the plaintiffs and the heirs of William Leche. The plaintiffs gave 100 marks of silver. (7)

1015. Westminster. Octave of Hilary 1405. P: John Makeworth, clerk, John Brewode, clerk, and William Arowesmyth, clerk. D: Edward del Park and Isabel h.w. Concerning 3 mess., 6 bov. land, 4a. meadow and 5s rent in Makworth and Marton. Edward and Isabel acknowledged these to be the right of John Makeworth who, with the other plaintiffs, had them of their gift. They remised and quitclaimed of, and warranted for, themselves and the heirs of Isabel to the plaintiffs and the heirs of John Makeworth. The plaintiffs gave 20 marks of silver. (8)

1016. Westminster. Octave of Hilary 1405. P: John Lathebury and Elizabeth h.w. D: Alfred Lathebury and Alana h.w. Concerning 7 mess., 160a. land, 20a. meadow and a moiety of a mill in Hethehouses and Neuton Sulne and fishing rights in the waters of the Trent in Neuton Sulne. Alfred and Alana granted and rendered these to John and Elizabeth to hold to themselves and the heirs of their bodies of Alfred, Alana and Alfred's heirs paying therefor, each year, one rose at the feast of the Nativity of St John the Baptist for all services etc due to Alfred, Alana and Alfred's heirs and doing to the chief lord etc. Reversion to Alfred, Alana and Alfred's heirs. John and Elizabeth gave 100 marks of silver. (9)

1017. Westminster. The morrow of the Purification 1405. P: John Andrewe, chaplain, Peter Pole and William Smyth. D: John Penystone and Felise h.w. Concerning 1 mess., 2 bov. land and 10a. meadow in Bubynhill. John and Felise acknowledged these to be the right of John Andrewe and they rendered them to the plaintiffs to hold to themselves and the heirs of John Andrewe of the chief lord etc forever. John and Felise warranted for themselves and the heirs of Felise to the plaintiffs and the heirs of John Andrewe. The plaintiffs gave 20 marks of silver. (10)

1018. Westminster. Octave of Hilary 1406. P: Benedict de Asshton. D: William de Ekkels and Ellen h.w. Concerning 1 mess. and 3½a. land in Kynder. William and Ellen rendered these to Benedict to hold to himself and his heirs of the chief lord etc forever, and they warranted for themselves and the heirs of Ellen to Benedict and his heirs. Benedict gave 10 marks of silver. (11)

1019. Westminster. Octave of Hilary 1406. P: Robert Wodderove. D: Richard Gonnifray, clerk. Concerning 2 mess., 34½a. land in Wormhull and 2 serjeanties within the forest of High Peak. Richard granted and rendered these to Robert to hold to himself and the heirs of his body of Richard and his heirs paying therefor, each year, one rose at the feast of the Nativity of St John the Baptist for all services etc due to Richard and his heirs and doing to the chief lord etc. Remainder to William Wodderove of Hope and the heirs of his body. Reversion to Richard and his heirs. Robert gave £20. (12)

1020. Westminster. Octave of Hilary 1406. P: Thomas de Langley, clerk, Thomas de Gresley, chivaler, Robert de Twyford, esq. John de Stannton and Roger de Wyngreworth. D: Thomas Roley and Robert Glade and Joan h.w. Concerning 4 mess. in Chestrefeld and Derby and the manor of Wyngreworth except 1 mess., 3 bov. land, 2 tofts and a garden within the manor. The defendants acknowledged these to be the right of Roger and they granted for themselves and the heirs of Thomas and Joan that the tenements and manor, with exceptions, which Roger Bradeshawe and Elizabeth h.w., formerly wife of William de Crawshawe, held for the life of Elizabeth of the inheritance of Thomas and Joan and which ought to revert to the defendants and the heirs of Thomas and Joan on Elizabeth's death, should remain instead to the plaintiffs and the heirs of Roger to hold of the chief lord etc forever. The defendants and the heirs of Thomas and Joan warranted to the plaintiffs and the heirs of Roger who gave 200 marks of silver. (13)

1021. Westminster. The morrow of Martinmas 1405. Octave of Hilary 1406. P: Richard Fyton and Richard Lyversegge. D: William de Clayton and Alice h.w. Concerning 1 mess., 20a. land, 3a. meadow and 6a. woodland in Bouedon in the Peak. William and Alice acknowledged these to be the right of Richard Fyton who, with Richard Lyversegge, had them of their gift. The plaintiffs granted and rendered the tenements to William and Alice to hold of the chief lord etc for their lives. Successive remainders to John de Clayton, son of William and Alice, and the heirs of his body, to his brother William and the heirs of his body, to the heirs of the bodies of William and Alice and to the right heirs of Alice. (14)

1022. Westminster. Octave of the Purification 1407. P: John Makworth, clerk, and Thomas Makworth and Alice h.w. D: William de la Pole and Margery h.w. Concerning the manor of Asshe next Sutton in the county of Derby, and 3 mess., 200a. land, 20a. meadow, 20a. pasture and 20s rent in Asshe next Sutton. William and Margery acknowledged these to be the right of John and they remised and quitclaimed of themselves and the heirs of William to John, Thomas, Alice and the heirs of John. The plaintiffs gave £100. (15)

1023. Westminster. Octave of Martinmas 1406. P: Geoffrey Lother and Robert Pudsay. D: Hugh Suward, junior, and Alice h.w. Concerning 3 mess., 1 toft, 3½ bov. 40a. land and 8a. meadow in Kynewaltmerssh, Ekyngton and Barleburgh. Hugh and Alice acknowledged these to be the right of Geoffrey who, with Robert, had them of their gift. They remised and quitclaimed of, and warranted for, themselves and the heirs of Alice to Geoffrey, Robert and Geoffrey's heirs. Geoffrey and Robert gave 20 marks of silver. (16)

1024. Westminster. Octave of Hilary 1408. P: Thomas Stokes of Stotfeld, senior, and John Cartwryght of Stretton, senior. D: Thomas Dexter of

Stretton next Appulby and Margaret h.w. Concerning 3 mess., 3 virgates land and 20a. meadow in Stretton and Okethorp. Thomas and Margaret acknowledged these to be the right of Thomas Stokes who, with John, had them of their gift. They remised and quitclaimed of, and warranted for, themselves and the heirs of Margaret to Thomas, John and the heirs of Thomas. Thomas and John gave 20 marks of silver. (17)

1025. Westminster. The morrow of Ascension 1408. Octave of Trinity 1408. P: Henry de Coton. D: Henry del Bothe and Elizabeth h.w. Concerning 1 mess. and 1 dovecot in Derby. Henry de Coton had these of the gift of Henry and Elizabeth who remised and quitclaimed of, and warranted for, themselves and the heirs of Elizabeth to Henry and his heirs. Henry gave 20 marks of silver. (18)

1026. Westminster. Octave of Hilary 1409. P: William Leche of Ednesouere and John Andrewe, chaplain. D: Henry del Heye and Deonise h.w. Concerning 1 mess., 34a. land and 3a. meadow in Pillesley. Henry and Deonise acknowledged these to be the right of William and rendered them to William and John to hold to themselves and the heirs of William of the chief lord etc forever. They also warranted for themselves and the heirs of Deonise. William and John gave 10 marks of silver. (19)

1027. Westminster. Octave of the Purification 1409. P: John Macworth, clerk, Thomas Gresley, kt, Thomas Tykhill, John Fyndern and William Fyndern. D: Nicholas de Rocheford. Concerning 6 mess., 100a. land, 30a. meadow and 20a. pasture in Asshe. Nicholas acknowledged these to be the right of John Macworth and he rendered them to the plaintiffs to hold to themselves and the heirs of John Macworth of the chief lord etc forever. He also warranted for himself and his heirs. The plaintiffs gave 100 marks of silver. (20)

1028. Westminster. Easter one month 1409. P: James de Stathum. D: Richard de Berde. Concerning the manor of Berde. James had the manor of the gift of Richard and he granted and rendered it to Richard to hold of the chief lord etc for his life. Successive remainders to Peter, son of John de Legh, and Emma, Richard's daughter, and the heirs of their bodies and to the right heirs of Richard. (21)

1029. Westminster. Michaelmas three weeks 1409. P: John de Makworth, clerk, Ellis de Stokke and Thomas del Stokke of Derby. D: Henry del Bothe and Isabel h.w. Concerning 2 mess. and a moiety of 3 mess. in Derby. Henry and Isabel acknowledged these to be the right of Thomas who, with the other plaintiffs, had them of their gift. They remised and quitclaimed of, and warranted for, themselves and the heirs of Isabel to the plaintiffs and the heirs of Thomas. The plaintiffs gave 10 marks of silver. (22)

1030. Westminster. The morrow of the Purification 1410. P: Robert Smeton, chaplain, Richard de Barton, chaplain, and Richard Broun of Repyngdon. D: John Hanneson of Repyngdon, barker, and Agnes h.w. Concerning a moiety of 1 mess., 1 virgate and 4a. land and 2½a. meadow in Repyngdon. John and Agnes acknowledged the moiety to be the right of Richard Broun and they rendered it to the plaintiffs to hold to themselves and the heirs of Richard Broun of the chief lord etc forever. They also warranted for themselves and the heirs of Agnes. The plaintiffs gave 10 marks of silver. (23)

1031. Westminster. The morrow of the Purification 1410. Quindene of Easter 1410. P: Henry del Bothe, Ralph de Barton and Geoffrey de Hulme. D: Randolph de Barton and Joan h.w. Concerning 4 mess., 200a. land, 20a. meadow and 20s rent in Egynton, Hilton and Asshe. Randolph and Joan acknowledged these to be the right of Henry and they rendered them to the plaintiffs to hold to themselves and the heirs of Henry of the chief lord etc forever. They also warranted for themselves and the heirs of Joan. The plaintiffs gave 100 marks of silver. (24)

1032. Westminster. Octave of Midsummer 1410. P: William Cartere of Bronaldeston. D: John Laurence of Leycestre. Concerning 1 mess., 16a. land and 1½a. meadow in Etewell. William had these of the gift of John who remised and quitclaimed of, and warranted for, himself and his heirs to William and his heirs. William gave 20 marks of silver. (25)

1033. Westminster. The morrow of All Souls 1409. P: William Warde. D: Joan, widow of Roger del Bernes. Concerning 1 mess., 20a. land, 3a. meadow and 2a. woodland in Glossop. William had these of the gift of Joan who remised and quitclaimed of, and warranted for, herself and her heirs to William and his heirs. William gave 10 marks of silver. (26)

1034. Westminster. The morrow of Martinmas 1410. P: Hugh de Wylughby, son of Hugh de Wylughby, and Joan h.w. D: Hugh de Wylughby, son of Edward de Wylughby. Concerning the manor of Rysley. Hugh son of Edward acknowledged the manor to be the right of Hugh son of Hugh who, with Joan, had it of his gift. He remised and quitclaimed of, and warranted for, himself and his heirs to Hugh, Joan and Hugh's heirs. Hugh and Joan gave 100 marks of silver. (27)

1035. Westminster. The morrow of Martinmas 1410. P: William Benge of Repyngton, clerk, and Roger Lanne of Kyrcolston. D: Richard de Crafte of Cortelyngstoke and Joan h.w. Concerning 3 mess., 2 tofts and 3a. land in Repyngton. Richard and Joan acknowledged these to be the right of William who, with Roger, had them of their gift. They remised and quitclaimed of, and warranted for, themselves and the heirs of Joan to

William, Roger and William's heirs. William and Roger gave 20 marks of silver. (28)

1036. Westminster. Octave of Midsummer 1412. P: Adam Byggyng, vicar of the church of Hertyngdon, and William Hoggeson, vicar of the church of Yolgreve. D: Roger Raueson and Joan h.w. Concerning 1 mess. and 20a. land in Fernydale and Roglymedewe within the soc of Hertyngdon and also the bailiwick of Urlesfryth. Roger and Joan acknowledged these to be the right of Adam who, with William, had them of their gift to hold to themselves and the heirs of Adam of the chief lord etc forever. Roger and Joan warranted for themselves and the heirs of Joan. Adam and William gave 20 marks of silver. (29)

1037. Westminster. Octave of Midsummer 1412. P: Sanchia Blound and Ralph Halley. D: Roger Raueson and Joan h.w. Concerning 1 mess. and 40a. land in Nedham Green and Stavedon. Roger and Joan acknowledged these to be the right of Ralph who, with Sanchia, had them of their gift to hold to themselves and the heirs of Ralph of the chief lord etc forever. Roger and Joan warranted for themselves and the heirs of Joan. Sanchia and Ralph gave 20 marks of silver. (30)

1038. Westminster. Octave of Midsummer 1412. P: William Bulclogh. D: Roger Raueson and Joan h.w. Concerning 2 tofts and 22a. land in Fayrefeld. William had these of the gift of Roger and Joan to hold to himself and his heirs of the chief lord etc forever. Roger and Joan warranted for themselves and the heirs of Joan. William gave 10 marks of silver. (31)

1039. Westminster. Quindene of Michaelmas 1412. P: William Fleccher of Tunstede. D: Henry Shene of Norbury and Ellen h.w. Concerning 1 mess. and 8a. land in Wormehill. Henry and Ellen rendered these to William to hold to himself and his heirs of the chief lord etc forever. They warranted for themselves and the heirs of Ellen. William gave 20 marks of silver. (32)

1040. Westminster. The morrow of the Purification 1413. P: Reginald Shaghe. D: William de Horbere and Beatrice h.w. Concerning 1 mess., 20a. land, 2a. meadow and 2a. woodland in Henore. Reginald had these of the gift of William and Beatrice who remised and quitclaimed of, and warranted for, themselves and the heirs of Beatrice to Reginald and his heirs. Reginald gave £20. (33)

1041. Westminster. Octave of Martinmas 1412. P: Henry de Knyveton, kt, Richard Lane of Hyde, William Fyndern of the county of Essex, John Lever, citizen and saddler of London, Roger Normanton of Horsley and John de Fynderne son of John de Fynderne of the county of Derby. D: John de Strauley, kt, and Joan h.w. Concerning the manor of Repyngdon called Strauleyespart. John de Strauley and Joan acknowledged this to be the right of John de Fynderne who, with the other plaintiffs, had it of their gift to hold to themselves and the heirs of John de Fynderne of the chief lord etc forever. John and Joan warranted for themselves and the heirs of John. The plaintiffs gave 50 marks of silver. (34)

HENRY V

CP 25/1/39/43

1042. Westminster. Octave of the Purification 1414. P: John Besand, chaplain, Thomas Stanley of Duffeld and Thomas de Derby, draper. D: William del Heye of Stonystanton and Alice h.w. Concerning 1 mess. in Derby. William and Alice acknowledged the messuage to be the right of John and they remised and quitclaimed of, and warranted for, themselves and the heirs of William to the plaintiffs and the heirs of John. The plaintiffs gave 100 marks of silver. (1)

1043. Westminster. Quindene of Trinity 1414. P: Richard Stathum and Richard Denton. D: John Sperham and Emma h.w. Concerning 2 mess. in Derby. John and Emma acknowledged the messuages to be the right of Richard Stathum who, with Richard Denton, had them of their gift. They remised and quitclaimed of, and warranted for, themselves and the heirs of John to the plaintiffs and the heirs of Richard Stathum. The plaintiffs gave 20 marks of silver. (2)

1044. Westminster. Michaelmas three weeks 1414. P: John Nicol and Joan h.w. D: Richard Shepey and Emma h.w. Concerning 1 mess. in Derby. Richard and Emma acknowledged the messuage to be the right of John who, with Joan, had it of their gift. They remised and quitclaimed of, and warranted for, themselves and the heirs of Emma to John, Joan and John's heirs. John and Joan gave 20 marks of silver. (3)

1045. Westminster. Octave of Michaelmas 1414. P: Roger Leche, kt, and Catherine h.w. D: John de Strelley of Haselbache, kt. Concerning the manor of Netherhaddon. John acknowledged the manor to be the right of Roger and he granted for himself and his heirs that the manor which John Barley held for life of the inheritance of John and which ought to revert to John and his heirs on the death of John Barley should remain instead to

Roger, Catherine and Roger's heirs to hold of the chief lord etc forever. John and his heirs warranted. Roger and Catherine gave 100 marks of silver. (4)

1046. Westminster. The morrow of Martinmas 1415. P: John del Stone of Kersyngton. D: John Burgulon of Lyttel Weston and Maude h.w. Concerning 8a. land and 4a. meadow in Kersyngton. John and Maude remised and quitclaimed of, and warranted for, themselves and the heirs of Maude to John del Stone and his heirs. John del Stone gave 20 marks of silver. (5)

1047. Westminster. The morrow of Ascension 1415. Octave of Trinity 1415. P: Philip Leche, kt, Adam de Neubyggyng, clerk, and William Pyrton, clerk. D: Edward Foliambe, esq. Concerning the manors of Elton and Tyddeswell and 400a. land and 40a. meadow in Wormehill, Lytton, Burton and Abney. Edward acknowledged these to be the right of William and he rendered them to the plaintiffs to hold to themselves and the heirs of William of the chief lord etc forever. Edward warranted for himself and his heirs. The plaintiffs gave 500 marks of silver. (6)

1048. Westminster. Octave of Midsummer 1416. P: Peter de la Pole, William Holmesfeld, vicar of the church of Tyddeswell, and John Andrewe, chaplain. D: Robert Rokell and Margaret h.w. Concerning 5 mess. and 6a. land in Tyddeswell. Robert and Margaret acknowledged these to be the right of William who, with the other plaintiffs, had them of their gift to hold to themselves and the heirs of William of the chief lord etc forever. Robert and Margaret warranted for themselves and the heirs of Margaret. The plaintiffs gave 100 marks of silver. (7)

1049. Westminster. Octave of Midsummer 1416. P: William Holmesfeld, vicar of the church of Tyddeswell, Robert Duffeld, chaplain, John Andrewe, chaplain, and Thomas, son of William Bagshawe. D: Robert Abbot of Bobenhill and Cecily h.w. Concerning 1 mess. and 9 bov. land in Bobenhill and Baslowe. Robert and Cecily acknowledged these to be the right of William who, with the other plaintiffs, had them of their gift. They remised and quitclaimed of, and warranted for, themselves and the heirs of Cecily to the plaintiffs and the heirs of William. The plaintiffs gave 100 marks of silver. (8)

1050. Westminster. Octave of Martinmas 1417. P: Thomas Frannceys, esq. D: Robert Frannceys, chivaler, and Isabel h.w. Concerning the manor of Bulton. Thomas had the manor of the gift of Robert and Isabel who remised and quitclaimed of, and warranted for, themselves and the heirs of Robert to Thomas and his heirs. Thomas gave 100 marks of silver. (9)

1051. Westminster. The morrow of Martinmas 1418. P: Robert Chaloner of Sheffeld and Richard, his son. D: John Roulay of Retford and Isabel h.w.

Concerning 1 mess. in Chestrefeld. John and Isabel acknowledged the messuage to be the right of Robert who, with Richard, had it of their gift. They remised and quitclaimed of, and warranted for, themselves and the heirs of Isabel to Robert, Richard and Robert's heirs. Robert and Richard gave 10 marks of silver. (10)

1052. Westminster. The morrow of Ascension 1419. P: William Babyngton and Margery h.w. D: John Trussebut, esq. Concerning the manor of Blakwell. John acknowledged the manor to be the right of William who, with Margery, had it of his gift. He remised and quitclaimed of, and warranted for, himself and his heirs to William, Margery and William's heirs. William and Margery gave 100 marks of silver. (11)

1053. Westminster. The morrow of Ascension 1419. Octave of Trinity 1419. P: Thomas, son of Ellis del Stokke of Derby, and Agnes h.w. D: Ellis del Stokke of Derby and Cecily h.w. Concerning 8 mess. in Derby. Thomas and Agnes acknowledged the messuages to be the right of Cecily. Ellis and Cecily granted and rendered them to Thomas and Agnes to hold to themselves and the heirs of their bodies of Ellis and Cecily and the heirs of Cecily forever, paying therefor each year one rose at the feast of the Nativity of St John the Baptist for all services etc due to Ellis, Cecily and Cecily's heirs and doing to the chief lord etc. Reversion to Ellis, Cecily and Cecily's heirs. (12)

1054. Westminster. The morrow of Martinmas 1420. P: John Walker, parson of the church of Estbriggeford, and Thomas Babyngton. D: William Hardewyk of Hardewyk. Concerning a moiety of 2 mess., 2 carucates land, 20a. meadow and 6a. woodland in Callale. William acknowledged these to be the right of John who, with Thomas, had them of his gift. He remised and quitclaimed of, and warranted for, himself and his heirs to John, Thomas and John's heirs. John and Thomas gave 20 marks of silver. (13)

1055. Westminster. Octave of Martinmas 1420. P: William Pyrton, Henry de Bothe and Ellis de Stokkys. D: John Neem, chaplain. Concerning 6 mess., 12 bov. 7a. land, 20a. meadow, 10a. pasture and 6a. woodland in Neweton Sulne and Repyngdon. John acknowledged these to be the right of William who, with the other plaintiffs, had them of his gift. He remised and quitclaimed of, and warranted for, himself and his heirs to the plaintiffs and the heirs of William. The plaintiffs gave 100 marks of silver. (14)

1056. Westminster. Michaelmas one month 1420. P: The abbot of the church of the Blessed Mary at Basyngwerk. D: Robert de Hadfeld and Joan h.w. and John Staveley and Agnes h.w. Concerning 5 mess., 100a. land, 40a. meadow, 100a. pasture, 20a. woodland, 10a. heath and 10a. marsh in Glassop and Hadfeld. The defendants acknowledged these to be the right of the abbot and they remised and quitclaimed of, and warranted for, themselves and the heirs of Joan and Agnes to the abbot and his successors. The abbot gave 100 marks of silver. (15)

1057. Westminster. Octave of Midsummer 1420. Octave of Michaelmas 1420. P: William Babyngton, Nicholas Wymbyssh, clerk, John Horspole, clerk, Nicholas Conyngston, Roger Hosewyf and Walter Taillard. D: Thomas Loundres and Joan h.w. Concerning the manor of Meysham called Berford Maner. Thomas and Joan acknowledged the manor to be the right of Walter and they granted for themselves and the heirs of Joan that the manor, which Elizabeth, widow of Baldwin Berford, chivaler, held for life of the inheritance of Joan and which ought to revert to Thomas and Joan and Joan's heirs on the death of Elizabeth, should remain instead to the plaintiffs and the heirs of Walter to hold of the chief lord etc forever. Thomas and Joan warranted for themselves and the heirs of Joan. The plaintiffs gave 100 marks of silver. (16)

1058. Westminster. Easter one month 1421. P: John Wyld of Abbeney. D: Thomas del Bank of Alkemonton and Joan h.w. Concerning 1 mess. and 16a. land in Offerton. Thomas and Joan remised and quitclaimed of, and warranted for, themselves and the heirs of Joan to John and his heirs. John gave 20 marks of silver. (17)

1059. Westminster. Quindene of Trinity 1421. P: Edward Fitzwilliam, esq. and Thomas Chamberleyn. D: John Gra, kt, and Margaret h.w. Concerning the manors of Wynfeld and Tybbesshelf. John and Margaret acknowledged the manors to be the right of Thomas who, with Edward, had them of their gift. Edward and Thomas then granted and rendered them to John and Margaret to hold to themselves and the heirs of their bodies of the chief lord etc forever. Successive remainders to the heirs of Margaret's body and to the right of John Herez, kt. (18)

HENRY VI

CP 25/1/39/44

1060. Westminster. The morrow of Ascension 1422. Octave of Hilary 1423. P: Richard Lyversegge. D: John del Bothe, junior, and Joan h.w. Concerning 10 mess., 6 virgates 13 bov. 30a. land, 36a. meadow and 18d rent in Twyford, Stayneston, Egynton and Etwell. Richard had 8 mess., 10 bov. 6 virgates 30a. land, the meadow and the rent of the gift of John and

Joan. These he granted and rendered to John and Joan to hold to themselves and the heirs of Joan of the chief lord etc forever. He also granted for himself and his heirs that the remaining 2 mess. and 3 bov. land in Stayneston, which Robert Smyth, Emma h.w. and John their son held for life of the inheritance of Richard and which ought to revert to Richard and his heirs on the deaths of Robert, Emma and John, should remain instead to John del Bothe and Joan and Joan's heirs. (1)

1061. Westminster. Quindene of Midsummer 1422. Octave of Trinity 1423. P: Henry Bothe and William Pyrton. D: Hugh de Strauley, esq. Concerning the manor of Netherhaddon. Hugh acknowledged the manor to be the right of William who, with Henry, had it of his gift. He remised and quitclaimed of, and warranted for, himself and his heirs to Henry, William and William's heirs. Henry and William gave 100 marks of silver. (2)

1062. Westminster. Easter one month 1423. P: William Couper of Derby, Walter Draper of Burton and Thomas Milner of Derby, hewer. D Henry del Bothe and Isabel h.w. Concerning 2 mess. and 6½a. land in Derby. Henry and Isabel acknowledged these to be the right of William who, with the other plaintiffs, had them of their gift. They remised and quitclaimed of, and warranted for, themselves and the heirs of Isabel to the plaintiffs and the heirs of William. The plaintiffs gave 10 marks of silver. (3)

1063. Westminster. Easter one month 1424. Octave of Trinity 1424. P: John Wilde of Abney. D: William Bradshawe and Maude h.w. Concerning 1 mess. and 50a. land in Overofforton and Netherofforton. John had these of the gift of William and Maude who remised and quitclaimed of, and warranted for, themselves and the heirs of William to John and his heirs. John gave 20 marks of silver. (4)

1064. Westminster. The morrow of Martinmas 1424. Octave of Hilary 1425. P: William Keterych and Deonise h.w. D: John Bradshawe and Agnes h.w. Concerning 4 mess., 7a. land and a moiety of 4 mess. in Derby. John and Agnes acknowledged these to be the right of Deonise who, with William, had them of their gift. William and Deonise granted and rendered 2 mess. and the moiety to John and Agnes for their lives and 2 mess. and the land to Agnes for her life, to hold of William, Deonise and the heirs of Deonise paying therefor each year one rose at the feast of the Nativity of St John the Baptist for all services etc due to them and doing to the chief lord etc. Reversion to William, Deonise and the heirs of Deonise. (5)

1065. Westminster. The morrow of Midsummer 1425. P: John Cursun of Croxhale. D: John Creweker and Agnes h.w. Concerning the manor of Twyford. John Cursun had the manor of the gift of John and Agnes and he granted and rendered it to them to hold to themselves and the heirs of the body of John, of himself and his heirs paying therefor each year one rose at the feast of the Nativity of St John the Baptist for all services etc due to John Cursun and his heirs and doing to the chief lord etc. Reversion to John Cursun and his heirs. (6)

1066. Westminster. Easter one month 1426. P: William Bolere of Bowedon and John Tailllour, chaplain. D: William Bradwall of Fayrfelde and Margaret h.w. Concerning 1 mess. and 5a. land in Wormhill. William and Margaret acknowledged these to be the right of William Bolere who, with John, had them of their gift. They remised and quitclaimed of, and warranted for, themselves and the heirs of Margaret to William, John and William's heirs. William and John gave 10 marks of silver. (7)

1067. Westminster. Octave of Martinmas 1425. P: Thomas Buxstones and William Brome, chaplain. D: William Baily of Leek and Emma h.w. Concerning 1 mess. and 8a. land in Chelmardon. William and Emma acknowledged these to be the right of Thomas who, with William Brome, had them of their gift. They remised and quitclaimed of themselves and the heirs of Emma to Thomas, William and Thomas's heirs. William and Thomas gave 10 marks of silver. (8)

1068. Westminster. Quindene of Hilary 1427. P: John, son of Henry Bothe, John de Bradshagh, Robert del Stok, John de Irton and Geoffrey de Holme. D: Thomas del Stok and Agnes h.w. Concerning the manor of Erleston. Thomas and Agnes acknowledged the manor to be the right of John son of Henry who, with the other plaintiffs, had it of their gift. They remised and quitclaimed of, and warranted for, themselves and the heirs of Agnes to the plaintiffs and the heirs of John son of Henry. The plaintiffs gave 100 marks of silver. (9)

1069. Westminster. Octave of Midsummer 1426. Octave of Michaelmas 1426. P: Ellis del Stok, John Lawe, vicar of the church of St Michael, Derby, and John Fox, chaplain. D: John Sparham and Agnes h.w. Concerning 1 mess. and 20a. land in Derby. John and Agnes acknowledged these to be the right of Ellis who, with the other plaintiffs, had it of their gift. They remised and quitclaimed of, and warranted for, themselves and the heirs of John to the plaintiffs and the heirs of Ellis. The plaintiffs gave 20 marks of silver. (10)

1070. Westminster. Michaelmas three weeks 1426. P: John Stathum of Morley. D: William Wygley of Werkesworth and Agnes h.w. Concerning 1 mess., 2 tofts and 3 bov. land in Caldelowe. John had these of the gift of William and Agnes who remised and quitclaimed of, and warranted for, themselves and the heirs of Agnes to John and his heirs. John gave 100 marks of silver. (11)

1071. Westminster. Michaelmas one month 1427. Quindene of Easter 1428. P: Alan Daweson. D: Richard Dagull of Neubold and Margery h.w.

Concerning 1 mess., 1 virgate land and 1 rood meadow in Repyngdon. Alan had these of the gift of Richard and Margery who remised and quitclaimed of, and warranted for, themselves and the heirs of Margery to Alan and his heirs. Alan gave 20 marks of silver. (12)

1072. Westminster. Michaelmas one month 1427. P: William Fox, chaplain. D: Richard Vernonn, kt, and Benedicta h.w. Concerning the manors of Basselowe and Hasilbache. William had the manors of the gift of Richard and Benedicta who remised and quitclaimed of, and warranted for, themselves and the heirs of Benedicta to William and his heirs. William then granted and rendered the manors to Richard to hold (a) the manor of Basselowe except 5 mess., a water mill, 5 bov. land and 36s 4d rent within the manor, to himself and his heirs for the life of Joan, widow of Richard Vernonn, kt, father of Richard; and (b) the manor of Hasilbache together with the tenements excepted in (a), to himself and his heirs for the life of Isabel, widow of Fulk de Penbrugge, kt, of the chief lord etc. Successive remainders to Richard Vernonn, esq. and Elizabeth h.w. and the heirs of the body of Richard and to Richard son of Richard. (13)

1073. Westminster. The morrow of All Souls 1427. Octave of Hilary 1428. P: Bernard Rydwars, clerk. D: Robert Hodegray and Margery h.w. Concerning a moiety of 1 mess. in Derby. Bernard had the moiety of the gift of Robert and Margery who remised and quitclaimed of, and warranted for, themselves and the heirs of Margery to Bernard and his heirs. Bernard gave 20 marks of silver. (14)

1074. Westminster. The morrow of Martinmas 1428. P: Robert Throstell, Robert Forbour and Thomas Pulter, chaplain. D: Robert Wermynton of Herbarowe and Alice h.w. Concerning 1 mess. in Derby. Robert and Alice acknowledged the messuage to be the right of Robert Throstell who, with the other plaintiffs, had it of their gift. They remised and quitclaimed of, and warranted for, themselves and the heirs of Alice to the plaintiffs and the heirs of Robert Throstell. The plaintiffs gave 10 marks of silver. (15)

1075. Westminster. Octave of Martinmas 1429. Quindene of Easter 1430. P: John de Assheton, chaplain, and William del Brom, chaplain. D: William Biakwall and Emma h.w. Concerning 1 mess. and 12a. land in Herdwykwall. William and Emma acknowledged these to be the right of John who, with William Brom, had them of their gift. They remised and quitclaimed of, and warranted for, themselves and the heirs of Emma to John, William and John's heirs. John and William gave 20 marks of silver. (16)

1076. Westminster. Octave of Martinmas 1429. P: John Cursonn, esq. D: Richard Vernonn, kt. Concerning 6 virgates land and 10a. meadow in Croxhale called Croxhaleholme. John had these of the gift of Richard who remised and quitclaimed of himself and his heirs to John and his heirs. John gave £20. (17)

1077. Westminster. Octave of the Purification 1432. Octave of Trinity 1432. P: John Coton, junior, and Joan h.w. D: John Coton, senior, and Elizabeth h.w. Concerning the manor of Boyleston called Cotonmaner, 10 mess., 10 bov. land, 8a. meadow and 8a. woodland in Rosyngton and Norbury and the advowson of half the church of Boyleston. John, senior, and Elizabeth granted and rendered these to John and Joan to hold to themselves and the heirs of their bodies of John, senior, Elizabeth and John's heirs, paying therefor each year one rose at the feast of the Nativity of St John the Baptist for all services etc due to John, senior, Elizabeth and John's heirs and doing to the chief lord etc. Reversion to John, senior, Elizabeth and John's heirs. (18)

1078. Westminster. The morrow of Martinmas 1431. P: Ellis del Stok, John Jowe, clerk, and John Robyngton, chaplain. D: Agnes, widow of John de Bradshagh and William Keterich and Deonise h.w. Concerning 7 mess., 2 tofts, 52a. land and 1a. meadow in Derby. The defendants acknowledged these to be the right of Ellis who, with the other plaintiffs, had them of their gift to hold to themselves and the heirs of Ellis of the chief lord etc forever. They also warranted for themselves and the heirs of Deonise. The plaintiffs gave 100 marks of silver. (19)

1079. Westminster. The morrow of All Souls 1431. P: Thomas Babyngton, esq. and Isabel h.w. D: Thomas Chaworth, kt, William Babyngton, kt, William Ulgarthorp, esq. and John Manchester. Concerning the manors of Dethek and Lutchurch and 2 mess., 4 bov. land and 4a. meadow in Whityngton and the advowson of the chapel of St John Baptist in Dethek. Thomas Babyngton and Isabel acknowledged these to be the right of John who, with the other defendants, had them of their gift. The defendants granted and rendered them to Thomas and Isabel to hold to themselves and the heirs of their bodies of the chief lord etc forever. Remainder to the right heirs of Isabel. (20)

1080. Westminster. Quindene of Hilary 1433. P: John Savage, kt, Robert de Legh of Adelyngton, Richard Pilkyngton, Richard de Shore and John Duncalf, vicar of the church of Prestbury. D: James de Legh and Emma h.w. Concerning the manor of Berd and 5 mess., 40a. land, $2\frac{1}{2}$a. meadow and 3s 6d rent in Ollershed, Whitill, Shydyord, Hayfeld, Holywodehede and Bothum. James and Emma acknowledged these to be the right of John Duncalf who, with the other plaintiffs, had them of their gift. They remised and quitclaimed of, and warranted for themselves and the heirs of Emma to the plaintiffs and the heirs of John Duncalf. The plaintiffs gave 200 marks of silver. (21)

1081. Westminster. The morrow of All Souls 1432. P: John Broun. D: John Prest, John Marche and Agnes h.w. John Rose and Joan h.w., Richard Dalby and Agnes h.w., Richard Knyghtley and Alice h.w. and Robert Sclatier. Concerning 4 mess. and 8 virgates land in Lullyngton. John Broun had these of the gift of the defendants who remised and quitclaimed of themselves and the heirs of Agnes, Joan, Agnes and Alice to John and his heirs. John Broun gave 100 marks of silver. (22)

1082. Westminster. Easter one month 1433. P: Richard Broun and Ambrose Fissher, chaplain. D: William Baker of Swartlyngcote and Catherine h.w. Concerning 1 mess., 1 virgate land and 1a. pasture in Repyngton. William and Catherine acknowledged these to be the right of Richard who, with Ambrose, had them of their gift. They remised and quitclaimed of, and warranted for, themselves and the heirs of Catherine to Richard, Ambrose and Richard's heirs. Richard and Ambrose gave 20 marks of silver. (23)

1083. Westminster. The morrow of Martinmas 1432. P: Ralph Kyrke. D: Hugh Bredbure and Ellen h.w. Concerning 1 mess. and 9a. land in Whithalgh. Ralph had these of the gift of Hugh and Ellen who remised and quitclaimed of, and warranted for, themselves and the heirs of Ellen to Ralph and his heirs. Ralph gave 10 marks of silver. (24)

1084. Westminster. The morrow of Martinmas 1432. P: Robert Heyr, Richard Walkeden, vicar of the church of Hope, and John Alotte. D: John Hall and Alice h.w. Concerning 2 mess. and 18½a. land in Huklowe. John and Alice acknowledged these to be the right of Robert who, with the other plaintiffs, had them of their gift. They remised and quitclaimed of, and warranted for, themselves and the heirs of John to the plaintiffs and the heirs of Robert. The plaintiffs gave 20 marks of silver. (25)

CP 25/1/39/45

1085. Westminster. The morrow of Martinmas 1432. P: Richard Byngham and John Manchastre. D: John Cokayn, kt, and Isabel h.w. Concerning the manors of Harthill and Middelton next Yolgreve and a mill in Alport. John Cokayn acknowledged these to be the right of John Manchastre who, with Richard, had them of his gift to hold to themselves and the heirs of John Manchastre of the chief lord etc forever. John Cokayn warranted for himself and his heirs. Richard and John then granted and rendered the manors and mill to John Cokayn and Isabel to hold to themselves and the heirs of their bodies of the chief lord etc forever. Successive remainders to Richard Vernon, kt, and the male heirs of his body and to the right heirs of John Cokayn. (26)

1086. Westminster. Quindene of Martinmas 1433. Octave of Hilary 1434. P: Henry Pyerponnt, kt, John Pole, esq. and John Curson, esq. D: Nicholas Monntgomery, kt, and Joan h.w. Concerning the manor of Cubley and the advowson of the church of Cubley. Nicholas and Joan acknowledged these to be the right of Henry who, with the other plaintiffs, had them of their gift. The plaintiffs granted and rendered them to Nicholas and Joan to hold to themselves and the heirs of the body of Nicholas of the chief lord etc forever. Remainder to the right heirs of Nicholas. (27)

1087. Westminster. Michaelmas three weeks 1434. P: Richard Wryght and Richard Hatherfeld, chaplain. D: William Throstyll of Derby and Robert Forboure of Derby. Concerning 2 mess. in Derby. William and Robert acknowledged these to be the right of Richard Wryght who, with Richard Hatherfeld, had them of their gift. They remised and quitclaimed of, and warranted for, themselves and the heirs of Robert to the plaintiffs and the heirs of Richard Wryght. The plaintiffs gave 20 marks of silver. (28)

1088. Westminster. The morrow of Midsummer 1436. P: Richard Vernon, kt, and Richard Broun of Repyngdon. D: John Warde of Steyneston and Margery h.w. Concerning 8 mess., 16 bov. land, 16a. meadow and 60a. pasture in Welynton. John and Margery acknowledged these to be the right of Richard Vernon who, with Richard Broun, had them of their gift. They remised and quitclaimed of, and warranted for, themselves and the heirs of Margery to the plaintiffs and the heirs of Richard Vernon. The plaintiffs gave 100 marks of silver. (29)

1089. Westminster. The morrow of All Souls 1435. P: Stephen de Thorp, junior, and Joan h.w. D: Stephen de Thorp, senior. Concerning a fourth part of the manor of Hathersegge. Stephen, senior, granted and rendered the fourth part to Stephen and Joan to hold to themselves and the heirs of their bodies of the chief lord etc forever. Remainder to Robert Eyer and his heirs. Stephen, senior, warranted for himself and his heirs. Stephen and Joan gave 100 marks of silver. (30)

1090. Westminster. Michaelmas three weeks 1438. P: Ralph Cromwell, kt, Nicholas Dixon, clerk, John Tailboys, senior, William Eton, Robert Gansell, parson of the church of Cromwell, and William Stanlowe. D: William Ulkerthorp of Ulkerthorp. Concerning 1 mess., 60a. land, 12a. meadow and 10a. woodland in Ufton in the parish of South Wynfeld. William Ulkerthorp acknowledged these to be the right of Ralph who, with the other plaintiffs, had them of his gift. He remised and quitclaimed of, and warranted for, himself and his heirs to the plaintiffs and the heirs of Ralph. The plaintiffs gave 100 marks of silver. (31)

1091. Westminster. The morrow of the Purification 1441. P: Ralph Leche. D: Thomas Stokys, senior, and Elizabeth h.w. Concerning the manor of

Chattesworth. Ralph had the manor of the gift of Thomas and Elizabeth who remised and quitclaimed of, and warranted for, themselves and the heirs of Elizabeth to Ralph and his heirs. Ralph gave 100 marks of silver. (32)

1092. Westminster. Quindene of Easter 1441. P: John Curson, esq. D: John Hilton and Margaret h.w. Concerning 4 mess., 4 cottages, 100a. land, 30a. meadow and 30a. woodland in Weston Underwodd. John Curson had these of the gift of John and Margaret who remised and quitclaimed of, and warranted for, themselves and the heirs of Margaret to John Curson and his heirs. John Curson gave 100 marks of silver. (33)

1093. Westminster. Octave of Hilary 1442. P: Robert Toby and Roger Baron. D: William Taillour and Alice h.w. Concerning a moiety of the manor of Trusseley and 1 mess. and 3a. land in Egynton on le Heth. William and Alice acknowledged these to be the right of Robert who, with Roger, had them of their gift. They remised and quitclaimed of, and warranted for, themselves and the heirs of Alice to Robert, Roger and Robert's heirs. Robert and Roger gave 100 marks of silver. (34)

1094. Westminster. Quindene of Easter 1442. P: Richard Chaterley. D: John Shore. Concerning 6 mess. and 30a. land in Derby. John acknowledged these to be the right of Richard and he granted for himself and his heirs that these messuages and lands which Isabel, widow of Ralph Shore, held for life of the inheritance of John and which ought to revert to John and his heirs on her death should remain instead to Richard and his heirs to hold of the chief lord etc forever. John warranted for himself and his heirs. Richard gave 100 marks of silver. (35)

1095. Westminster. Easter three weeks 1443. P: John Stathum, esq. D: Thomas Okover of Okover, esq. Concerning the manor of Caldelowe. Thomas acknowledged the manor to be the right of John and he remised and quitclaimed of, and warranted for, himself and his heirs to John and his heirs. John gave £100. (36)

1096. Westminster. Easter one month 1443. P: Robert Clyfton, esq. William Clyfton, clerk, and Henry Etwalle. D: Ralph de la Pole and Joan h.w. Concerning 4 mess., 200a. land, 30a. meadow, 10a. pasture and 7s 4d rent in Etwalle, Birnaston and Berwardcote. Ralph and Joan acknowledged these to be the right of Henry who, with Robert and William, had them of their gift. They remised and quitclaimed of, and warranted for, themselves and the heirs of Joan to the plaintiffs and the heirs of Henry. The plaintiffs gave 100 marks of silver. (37)

1097. Westminster. Easter three weeks 1443. P: Thomas Curson, esq. D: Thomas Knyveton and Margaret h.w. Concerning the manor of Myrkaston and 3 mess., 106a. land and a moiety of a water mill in Myrkaston and Mogynton. Thomas Curson had these of the gift of Thomas Knyveton who remised and quitclaimed of, and warranted for, himself and his heirs to Thomas Curson and his heirs. Thomas Curson then granted and rendered the manor and tenements to Thomas and Margaret to hold of the chief lord etc for their lives. Successive remainders to Nicholas, to Thomas, to Robert and to John, sons of Thomas and Margaret, and the heirs of their bodies, and to the right heirs of Thomas Knyveton. (38)

1098. Westminster. Michaelmas three weeks 1442. P: Robert Eyre and Richard Walkeden, vicar of the church of Hope. D: John Birmyngeham and Alice h.w. and John Wodehouse and Margery h.w. Concerning 1 mess. and 9a. land in Parva Huklowe. The defendants acknowledged these to be the right of Robert who, with Richard, had them of their gift. They remised and quitclaimed of, and warranted for, themselves and the heirs of Alice and Margery to Robert, Richard and Robert's heirs. Robert and Richard gave £20. (39)

1099. Westminster. Octave of Michaelmas 1442. P: Richard Whitehals and John Whitehals, chaplain. D: Emma, Widow of John Topcliff. Concerning 2 mess., 1a. land and 40d rent in Derby. Emma acknowledged these to be the right of Richard who, with John, had them of her gift. She remised and quitclaimed of, and warranted for, herself and her heirs to Richard, John and Richard's heirs. Richard and John gave £20. (40)

1100. Westminster. The morrow of Martinmas 1443. P: Richard Vernon, kt. D: William Woley and Emma h.w. Concerning 4 mess., 4 tofts, 200a. land, 20a. meadow, 20a. pasture and 4a. woodland in Roworth in alto Pecco within the parish of Glossop. Richard had these of the gift of William and Emma who remised and quitclaimed of, and warranted for, themselves and the heirs of Emma to Richard and his heirs. Richard gave 100 marks of silver. (41)

1101. Westminster. Easter three weeks 1444. P: Ralph Ston. D: John Haghton of Kersyngton and William Alsop of Ireton. Concerning 1 mess., 4 bov. land and 20a. meadow in Kersyngton. Ralph had these of the gift of John and William who remised and quitclaimed of, and warranted for, themselves and the heirs of William to Ralph and his heirs. Ralph gave £20. (42)

1102. Westminster. The morrow of the Purification 1445. P: Roger Toppelesse and John Toppelesse. D: Thomas Marmyon and Agnes h.w. Concerning 1 mess., 2 tofts, 52a. land and 12a. meadow in Alsope and Perwyche. Thomas and Agnes acknowledged these to be the right of John who, with Roger, had them of their gift. They remised and quitclaimed of, and warranted for, themselves and the heirs of Agnes to Roger, John and John's heirs. Roger and John gave £50. (43)

1103. Westminster. The morrow of the Purification 1445. P: William, bishop of Lincoln, John, viscount Beaumont, John Sutton, lord Dudley, John Portyngton, one of the king's justices of common pleas, John Tailboys, esq. Richard Alred, esq. Thomas Palmer, John Saucheverell, esq. William Stanlowe and John Leynton. D: William Ferers, kt, and Elizabeth h.w. Concerning the manor of Breydeshale called Le Netherhale and 16 mess., 40a. land, 58a. meadow, 220a. pasture, 2a. woodland and 16s rent in Breydeshale. William and Elizabeth acknowledged these to be the right of the bishop who, with the other plaintiffs, had them of their gift. They remised and quitclaimed of, and warranted for, themselves and the heirs of Elizabeth to the plaintiffs and the heirs of the bishop. The plaintiffs gave 200 marks of silver. (44)

1104. Westminster. Michaelmas one month 1445. P: Robert Stafford, esq. D: John Stafford of Eyom and Margaret h.w. Concerning 2 mess. and 1 carucate land in Eyom called Eyom Clyff or Midilton Clyff. Robert acknowledged these to be the right of Margaret who, with John, had them of his gift. John and Margaret granted and rendered them to Robert to hold for 50 years from the feast of St Michael last past, of themselves and the heirs of Margaret paying therefor each year 26s 8d in silver, one half at the feast of St Martin and the other half at the feast of Pentecost for all services etc due to John, Margaret and Margaret's heirs and doing to the chief lord etc John and Margaret warranted. Reversion to John, Margaret and Margaret's heirs. (45)

1105. Westminster. Octave of Trinity 1448. P: Robert Eyre and Richard Walkeden, vicar of the church of Hope. D: Thomas Padley and Rose h.w. Concerning a quarter part of 3 mess., 50a. land and 10a. meadow in Hope and Bradwall. Thomas and Rose acknowledged the quarter part to be the right of Robert who, with Richard, had it of their gift. They remised and quitclaimed of, and warranted for, themselves and the heirs of Rose to Robert, Richard and Robert's heirs. Robert and Richard gave 100 marks of silver. (46)

1106. Westminster. Michaelmas one month 1447. P: Robert Yonge. D: John Hotost and Margaret h.w. Concerning 4 mess., 4 tofts, 300a. land, 10a. meadow, 10a. pasture, 12a. woodland, 10s rent and a rent of 1lb cummin in Saxton, Scartlyngwell and Barkeston. Robert had these of the gift of John and Margaret who remised and quitclaimed of themselves and the heirs of Margaret to Robert and his heirs and warranted against Edmund, abbot of St Peters, Westminster and his successors. Robert gave 100 marks of silver. (47)

1107. Westminster. Quindene of Michaelmas 1447. P: Thomas Babyngton, esq. D: Henry Etwalle and Mary h.w. Concerning 1 mess., 36a. land, 4a. meadow and 4a. pasture in Etwalle. Henry and Mary acknowledged these to be the right of Thomas and granted for themselves and the heirs of Mary that these tenements, which Joan Elkesley held for her life of the inheritance of Henry and which ought to revert to Henry, Mary and the heirs of Henry *[sic]* on the death of Joan, should remain instead to Thomas and his heirs to hold of the chief lord etc forever. Henry and Mary warranted for themselves and the heirs of Mary. Thomas gave £20. (48)

1108. Westminster. Octave of Michaelmas 1448. P: Robert Middelton. D: William Nedham. Concerning 1 mess. and 32a. land in Wormehill and the office of one forester in Le Chaumpeyne in alto Pecco. Robert had these of the gift of William who remised and quitclaimed of, and warranted for, himself and his heirs to Robert and his heirs. Robert gave £20. (49)

1109. Westminster. The morrow of Midsummer 1453. P: John Lowe, clerk, John Riggeway, clerk, William Benet, clerk, Henry Bancroft and William Bancroft. D: Thomas Robert, brasyer, and Emma h.w. Concerning 2 mess. and 3a. land in Derby. Thomas and Emma acknowledged these to be the right of William Bancroft who, with the other defendants, had them of their gift. They remised and quitclaimed of, and warranted for, themselves and the heirs of Emma to the plaintiffs and the heirs of William Bancroft. The plaintiffs gave 40 marks of silver. (50)

1110. Westminster. Octave of the Purification 1454. Quindene of Easter 1454. P: Henry Stathom, esq. D: William Burton and Catherine h.w. Concerning 1 mess. and 2a. land in Derby. Henry had these of the gift of William and Catherine who remised and quitclaimed of, and warranted for, themselves and the heirs of Catherine to Henry and his heirs. Henry gave £20. (51)

1111. Westminster. Octave of Midsummer 1457. P: Robert Blakwall. D: Ralph de Kyrke and Christian h.w. Concerning 2 mess. and 26½a. land in Stadon and Cowedale. Robert had these of the gift of Ralph and Christian who remised and quitclaimed of, and warranted for, themselves and the heirs of Christian to Robert and his heirs. Robert gave 40 marks of silver. (52)

1112. Westminster. Octave of Midsummer 1457. P: Henry Pole and John Brokhey, parson of the parish church of Rodburn. D: William Morton of Mapurley, gent., and Alice h.w. and Margaret Twyford. Concerning 1 mess., 6 tofts and 180a. land in Kirkelongley. The defendants acknowledged these to be the right of Henry who, with John, had the messuage, 3 tofts and 90a. land of their gift to hold to themselves and the heirs of Henry of the chief lord etc forever. The defendants granted for themselves and the heirs of Alice that 3 tofts and 90a. land which Geoffrey Radcliff and Cecily h.w. held for the life of Cecily of the inheritance of Alice and which ought to revert to the defendants and the heirs of Alice on Cecily's death should remain instead to Henry, John and Henry's heirs. The defendants warranted. Henry and John gave 40 marks of silver. (53)

EDWARD IV — RICHARD III

CP 25/1/39/46

1113. Westminster. The morrow of the Purification 1463. P: Margaret, widow of Richard Coton. D: John Coton of Rydware, senior, and Joan h.w. Concerning the manor of Boyleston called Cotonmaner and 10 mess., 10 bov. land, 8a. meadow and 8a. woodland in Boyleston, Rossyngton and Norbury and the advowson of half the church of Wyleston. John and Joan granted and rendered these to Margaret to hold of themselves and the heirs of John, for her life, paying therefor one rose at the feast of the Nativity of St John the Baptist for all service etc due to John, Joan and John's heirs and doing to the chief lord etc. Reversion to John, Joan and John's heirs. (1)

1114. Westminster. Michaelmas one month 1467. P: John Meyneley, clerk, John Bothe, esq. Ralph Saucheverell, esq. Ralph Ulkerthorp, esq. John Steppyngstones, clerk, William Benet, clerk, and Thomas Monyassh, clerk. D: Ralph Pole, esq. and Elizabeth h.w. Concerning 2 mess. and 4 gardens in Derby. Ralph and Elizabeth acknowledged these to be the right of John Meyneley who, with the other plaintiffs, had them of their gift. They remised and quitclaimed of, and warranted for, themselves and the heirs of Elizabeth to the plaintiffs and the heirs of John Meyneley. The plaintiffs gave 100 marks of silver. (2)

1115. Westminster. Octave of Midsummer 1468. Octave of Michaelmas 1468. P: Thomas Revell. D: William Bate, esq. and Alice h.w. Concerning 7 mess., 91a. land, 30a. meadow, 40a. pasture and 20a. woodland in Thwathewayte, Chesterfeld, Brampton, Brymyngton, Tapton, Whityngton, Newebold and Boythorp. Thomas had these of the gift of William and Alice who remised and quitclaimed of, and warranted for, themselves and the heirs of Alice to Thomas and his heirs. Thomas gave 200 marks of silver. (3)

1116. Westminster. Easter one month 1469. P: Nicholas Fitzherbert, Ralph Fitzherbert and Nicholas Stathom. D: John Curson of Ketelston and Joan h.w. Concerning the manor of Bentley called Hungrybentley, 8 mess., 200a. land, 20a. meadow, 100a. pasture and 20a. woodland in Bentley. John and Joan acknowledged these to be the right of Nicholas Stathom who, with the other plaintiffs, had them of their gift. They remised and quitclaimed of, and warranted for, themselves and the heirs of Joan to the plaintiffs and the heirs of Nicholas Stathom. The plaintiffs gave 200 marks of silver. (4)

1117. Westminster. Easter one month 1470. P: William Merlege. D: Richard Stanesby and Joan h.w. Concerning 3 mess. and 10a. land in Derby. William had these of the gift of Richard and Joan who remised and quitclaimed of, and warranted for, themselves and the heirs of Richard to William and his heirs. William gave 40 marks of silver. (5)

1118. Westminster. Michaelmas three weeks 1472. P: Henry Stathum of Morley. D: Henry Willyamson of Cossall and Margaret h.w. Concerning 1 toft and 20a. land in Chaddesdene called Cardellesfeld or Braudewode. Henry Stathum had these of the gift of Henry and Margaret who remised and quitclaimed of themselves and the heirs of Margaret to Henry Stathum and his heirs, and warranted against Henry, abbot of Derley and his successors. Henry Stathum gave 20 marks of silver. (6)

1119. Westminster. The morrow of the Purification 1474. P: Walter Blount, kt, Robert Clyfton, kt, and Nicholas Fitzherberd, esq. D: Robert Wyllughby, esq. and Margaret h.w. Concerning the manor of Aylwaston. Robert and Margaret acknowledged the manor to be the right of Walter who, with the other plaintiffs, had it of their gift. They remised and quitclaimed of, and warranted for, themselves and the heirs of Margaret to the plaintiffs and the heirs of Walter. the plaintiffs gave £300. (7)

1120. Westminster. The morrow of All Souls 1473. P: John Babyngton, esq. D: Henry Plumptre and Maude h.w. Concerning 2 mess., 80a. land, 12a. meadow, 20a. woodland and 100a. pasture in Cryche, Playstowe, Shukthorne and Legh. John had these of the gift of Henry and Maude who remised and quitclaimed of themselves and the heirs of Maude to John and his heirs, and warranted against Thomas, abbot of Westminster and his successors. John gave 40 marks of silver. (8)

1121. Westminster. The morrow of All Souls 1473. P: Robert Barley, senior, esq. D: Henry Grey, kt, lord Grey, and Margaret h.w. Concerning the manor of Stooke in le Peke, 100a. land, 40a. meadow, 30a. pasture and 20a. woodland in Stooke in le Peke. Robert had these of the gift of Henry and Margaret who remised and quitclaimed of, and warranted for, themselves and the heirs of Margaret to Robert and his heirs. Robert gave 200 marks of silver. (9)

1122. Westminster. The morrow of the Purification 1475. P: John Babyngton of Dethek, esq. D: William Strete and Maude h.w. Concerning 5 mess., 40a. land, 10a. meadow, 30a. pasture and 4a. woodland in Pleystowe, Shukthorn and le Lee. John had these of the gift of William and Maude who remised and quitclaimed of, and warranted for, themselves and the heirs of Maude to John and his heirs. John gave £40. (10)

1123. Westminster. The morrow of All Souls 1476. P: Robert Potter. D: Richard Halewode and Margery h.w. Concerning 4 mess., 5 gardens and 33a. land in Derby and Normanton next Derby. Robert had these of the gift of Richard and Margery who remised and quitclaimed of, and warranted for, themselves and the heirs of Margery to Robert and his heirs. Robert gave 40 marks of silver. (11)

1124. Westminster. Quindene of Midsummer 1477. Octave of Michaelmas 1477. P: Thomas Poutrell, Ralph Fitzherberd and William Poutrell. D: Maude, widow of Gervase Clifton, kt, kinswoman and one of the heirs of Ralph Cromwell lately of Cromwell, kt, and Robert Ratclyff and Joan h.w. kinswoman and the other heir of Ralph. Concerning the manor of Westhalom and 1 mess., 2 bov. land, 4a. meadow and 50a. pasture in Westhalom and Mapurley and the advowson of the church of Westhalom. The defendants acknowledged these to be the right of Thomas and they remised and quitclaimed of, and warranted for, themselves and the heirs of Maude and Joan to the plaintiffs and the heirs of Thomas. The plaintiffs gave 40 marks of silver. (12)

1125. Westminster. The morrow of Martinmas 1478. P: Richard Blakwall. D: Thomas Stadon and Joan h.w. Concerning 1 mess. and 14a. land in Sternedall, Cowedale and Stadon. Richard had these of the gift of Thomas and Joan who remised and quitclaimed of, and warranted for, themselves and the heirs of Joan to Richard and his heirs. Richard gave 40 marks of silver. (13)

1126. Westminster. Quindene of Easter 1480. P: Bartholomew Kendale, John Shepey, William Kendale, John Kendale, Richard Reynold and John Fouler. D: William Bate and Alice h.w. Concerning 8 mess., 1 toft, 40a. land, 10a. meadow, 10a. pasture and 8s rent in Melbourn and Kynges Neweton. William and Alice acknowledged these to be the right of Bartholomew who, with the other plaintiffs, had them of their gift. They remised and quitclaimed of, and warranted for, themselves and the heirs of Alice to the plaintiffs and the heirs of Bartholomew. The plaintiffs gave £40. (14)

1127. Westminster. The morrow of Midsummer 1480. P: Richard Hethecote. D: Thomas Hampton of Leycestre and James Hethecote, senior. Concerning 1 mess., 8a. land and 9a. pasture in Chesterfeld, Tapton and Neubold. Thomas and James acknowledged these to be the right of Richard and they remised and quitclaimed of, and warranted for, themselves and the heirs of Thomas to Richard and his heirs. Richard gave 40 marks of silver. (15)

1128. Westminster. Octave of the Purification 1480. Quindene of Easter 1480. P: Robert Rigby. D: Hugh Rigby and Isabel h.w. Concerning 1 mess., 1 toft, 3 virgates land, 8a. meadow and 3a. pasture in Melburne and Neweton. Robert had these of the gift of Hugh and Isabel who remised and quitclaimed of, and warranted for, themselves and the heirs of Isabel to Robert and his heirs. Robert then granted and rendered the tenements to Hugh and Isabel to hold to themselves for their lives of himself and his heirs paying therefor each year one rose at the feast of the Nativity of St John the Baptist for all services etc due to Robert and his heirs and doing to the chief lord etc. Reversion to Robert and his heirs. (16)

1129. Westminster. Octave of Martinmas 1481. P: Nicholas Knyveton. D: Robert Gilbert and Joan h.w. Concerning 100a. land in Knyveton. Nicholas had the land of the gift of Robert and Joan who remised and quitclaimed of, and warranted for, themselves and the heirs of Joan to Nicholas and his heirs. Nicholas gave £40. (17)

1130. Westminster. The morrow of Ascension 1484. P: Thomas Pouterell and John Coton. D: Nicholas Whithals and Emma h.w. and William Whithals of Chesterfeld. Concerning 2 mess., 1a. land and 40d rent in Derby. The defendants acknowledged these to be the right of Thomas who, with John, had them of their gift. They remised and quitclaimed of, and warranted for, themselves and the heirs of Emma to Thomas, John and Thomas's heirs. Thomas and John gave 40 marks of silver. (18)

1131. Westminster. Quindene of Midsummer 1484. P: Marion Dawekyn, widow. D: John Clough and Elizabeth h.w. Concerning 32a. land in Pygtor in the parish of Wormehull. Marion had the land of the gift of John and Elizabeth who remised and quitclaimed of, and warranted for, themselves and the heirs of Elizabeth to Marion and her heirs. Marion gave 20 marks of silver. (19)

1132. Westminster. Octave of the Purification 1483. Quindene of Easter 1484. P: Henry Foliambe, esq. D: Robert Lacy and Margaret h.w. Concerning a sixth part of 4 mess., 100a. land, 20a. meadow and 24a. pasture in Hope and Castelton. Henry had the sixth part of the gift of Robert and Margaret who remised and quitclaimed of, and warranted for, themselves and the heirs of Margaret to Henry and his heirs. Henry gave 40 marks of silver. (20)

1133. Westminster. Octave of Midsummer 1485. P: Richard Page. D: John Babyngton, kt, and Elizabeth h.w. Concerning 2 mess. and 2½ bov. 4a. land in Carlyngthawyte. Richard had these of the gift of John and Elizabeth who remised and quitclaimed of, and warranted for, themselves and the heirs of Elizabeth to Richard and his heirs. Richard gave 40 marks of silver. (21)

HENRY VII

CP 25/39/47

1134. Westminster. Octave of the Purification 1486. P: John Rollesley of Rollesley, junior. D: Robert Barley of Chesterfield, son of John Barley, and Alice h.w. Concerning 18 mess., 12 tofts, 100a. land, 30a. meadow, 40a. pasture, 4a. woodland and 100a common in Chesterfield, Newebold, Brampton, Dronfield, Tapton and Boythorp. John had these of the gift of Robert and Alice who remised and quitclaimed of, and warranted for, themselves and the heirs of Alice to John and his heirs. John gave £100. (1)

1135. Westminster. Quindene of Michaelmas 1487. P: John Wyot. D: Lawrence Lowe and Humphrey Lowe and Margaret h.w. Concerning the manor of Denby and 40 mess., 20 tofts, 200a. land, 100a meadow, 50a. woodland, 50a. gorse and heath, 200a. marsh, 15s rent and a rent of 1lb of cumin in Denby and Kylburne. John had these of the gift of the defendants and he granted and rendered them to Lawrence for life with remainder to Humphrey and Margaret for the life of Humphrey, to hold, without impeachment of waste, of the chief lord etc. Successive remainders to the male heirs of the body of Lawrence, to Lawrence's brother, George Lowe, and the male heirs of his body, to George's brother, Thomas Lowe, and the male heirs of his body, to the heirs of the bodies of Humphrey and Margaret, to Richard Newton of Newton next Wydford and the male heirs of his body and to the right heirs of Lawrence. (2)

1136. Westminster. Quindene of Martinmas 1487. Octave of Hilary 1488. P: John Litton, chaplain, and Robert Litton, his brother. D: Ralph Hagh and Anastase h.w. Concerning 3 mess. and 3½ bov. 2a. land in Wynster.

Ralph and Anastase acknowledged these to be the right of John who, with Robert, had them of their gift. They remised and quitclaimed of, and warranted for, themselves and the heirs of Anastase to John and Robert and the heirs of John. John and Robert gave £40. (3)

1137. Westminster. Easter three weeks 1488. P: Christopher Bury, chaplain, and Thomas Adenburgh. D: Ewyn Butterworth and Joan h.w. Concerning 1 mess., 30a. land, 10a. meadow, 14a. pasture, 12a. woodland and 13a. gorse and heath in Denby. Ewyn and Joan acknowledged these to be the right of Thomas who, with Christopher, had them of their gift. They remised and quitclaimed of, and warranted for, themselves and the heirs of Joan to Thomas, Christopher and the heirs of Thomas. Christopher and Thomas gave £40. (4)

1138. Westminster. Easter three weeks 1488. P: Christopher Bury, chaplain, and Thomas Adenburgh. D: German Neweham and Ellen h.w. Concerning 2 mess., 60a. land, 12a. meadow, 20a. pasture, 20a. woodland and 13a. gorse and heath in Denby. German and Ellen acknowledged these to be the right of Thomas who, with Christopher, had them of their gift. They remised and quitclaimed of, and warranted for, themselves and the heirs of Ellen to Thomas, Christopher and the heirs of Thomas. Christopher and Thomas gave £40. (5)

1139. Westminster. Octave of Martinmas 1489. P: Henry Vernon. D: Thomas Alen and Elizabeth h.w. Concerning 1 mess., 60a. land, 10a. meadow and 60a. pasture in Wheston, Wormehill and Tyddeswall. Henry had these of the gift of Thomas and Elizabeth who remised and quitclaimed of themselves and the heirs of Elizabeth to Henry and his heirs. Henry and Elizabeth also warranted for themselves and the heirs of Elizabeth to Henry and his heirs against John, abbot of St Peters, Westminster and his successors. Henry gave £20. (6)

1140. Westminster. Quindene of Hilary 1491. P: Richard Blakwall. D: Richard Couper and Joan h.w. Concerning 2 mess., and 14½a. land in Cowedale. Richard Blakwall had these of the gift of Richard and Joan who remised and quitclaimed of, and warranted for, themselves and the heirs of Joan to Richard Blakwall and his heirs. Richard then granted the tenements to Richard and Joan and rendered them to them to hold for their lives paying one rose each year at the feast of the Nativity of St John the Baptist for all services etc pertaining to Richard Blakwall and his heirs and doing to the chief lord etc. Reversion to Richard Blakwall and his heirs. (7)

1141. Westminster. Quindene of Martinmas 1491. P: Henry Vernonn. D: Hugh Shert and Catherine h.w. Concerning 2 mess., 80a. land, 20a. meadow and 20a. pasture in Bowedon. Henry had these of the gift of Hugh and

Catherine who remised and quitclaimed of, and warranted for, themselves and the heirs of Hugh to Henry and his heirs. Henry gave 40 marks of silver. (8)

1142. Westminster. Easter one month 1493. P: Robert Skorer, chaplain, and William Kyme, clerk. D: Richard Stephenson and Alice h.w. and John Savage and Margaret h.w. Concerning 1 mess., 100a. land, 16a. meadow and 40a. pasture in Ilkeston and Morley. The deforciants acknowledged these to be the right of Robert who, with William, had them of their gift. Richard and Alice remised and quitclaimed of themselves and the heirs of Alice to Robert and William and the heirs of Robert and they warranted for themselves and the heirs of Alice against John, abbot of St Peters, Westminster and his successors. Robert and William then granted and rendered the tenements to John and Margaret to hold to themselves and the heirs of their bodies of the chief lord etc forever. Successive remainders to the heirs of the body of Margaret and to Ralph Savage of Newested and his heirs. (9)

1143. Westminster. The morrow of All Souls 1493. P: Ralph Shirley, kt. D: Thomas Balgy. Concerning 1 mess., 100a. land, 40a. meadow, 20a. pasture and a bailiwick of forester in Hope in Alto Pecco. Ralph had these of the gift of Thomas who remised and quitclaimed of, and warranted for, himself and his heirs to Ralph and his heirs. Ralph gave 100 marks of silver. (10)

1144. Westminster. Easter one month 1494. P: Henry Vavasour, kt, William Vavasour of Baddesworth, esq. William Marshall and William Bell. D: Henry Gray, lord Gray, kt, and Catherine h.w. Concerning the manors of Langwathbasset and Houghton. Henry Gray and Catherine acknowledged these to be the right of William Marshall who, with the other plaintiffs, had them of their gift. They remised and quitclaimed of, and warranted for, themselves and the heirs of Henry to the plaintiffs and the heirs of William Marshall. The plaintiffs gave 100 marks of silver. (11)

1145. Westminster. Easter one month 1494. P: John Walker. D: Robert Smalley and Lucy h.w. Concerning 5a. pasture in Braydsall. John had the pasture of the gift of Robert and Lucy who remised and quitclaimed of, and warranted for, themselves and the heirs of Lucy to John and his heirs. John gave £10. (12)

1146. Westminster. The morrow of Martinmas 1494. P: Thomas Babyngton of Dethykke, Henry Babyngton, clerk, Arnold Babyngton and Ralph Pole. D: Robert Jouell and Agnes h.w. Concerning 2 mess., 4 tofts, 6 bov. and 100a. land, 24a. meadow, 100a. pasture and 40a. woodland in Alferton and Somercotis. Robert and Agnes acknowledged these to be the right of Thomas who, with the other plaintiffs, had them of their gift. They remised and quitclaimed of, and warranted for, themselves and the heirs of Agnes to the plaintiffs and the heirs of Thomas. The plaintiffs gave 100 marks of silver. (13)

1147. Westminster. The morrow of the Purification 1495. P: Nicholas Knyveton, junior, esq. D: John Assheby and John Wymondeswold. Concerning 2 mess., 100a. land, 100a. meadow, 200a. pasture, 12a. woodland and 10s rent in Wyneley, Duffeld, Mogynton and Wyndeley Riche. Nicholas had these of the gift of John and John who remised and quitclaimed of, and warranted for, themselves and the heirs of John Assheby to Nicholas and his heirs. Nicholas gave £20. (14)

1148. Westminster. Octave of Midsummer 1496. P: William Litton and Thomas Hunt. D: Robert Blakwall and Mary h.w. Concerning 4 mess., 32a. land and 4a. meadow in Monyasshe, Flagge, Chelmerdon, Cowedale, Stadon, Buxston and Fayrefeld. Robert and Mary acknowledged these to be the right of William who, with Thomas, had them of their gift. They remised and quitclaimed of, and warranted for, themselves and the heirs of Robert to William and Thomas and William's heirs. William and Thomas then granted and rendered the tenements to Robert and Mary to hold to themselves and the heirs of Robert of the chief lord etc forever. (15)

1149. Westminster. The morrow of All Souls 1497. P: Humphrey Bradburn, esq. D: Edward Blount, kt. Concerning 1 mess., 100a. land, 12a. meadow, 200a. pasture and 4a. woodland in Holand, Bradley and Fulwode. Humphrey had these of the gift of Edward who remised and quitclaimed of, and warranted for, himself and his heirs to Humphrey and his heirs. Humphrey gave 40 marks of silver. (16)

1150. Westminster. The morrow of All Souls 1497. P: Nicholas Knyveton, esq. D: Edward Blount, kt. Concerning 2 mess., 200a. land, 60a. meadow, 300a. pasture, 20a. woodland and 13s 4d rent in Wyndeley, Wyndeley Hill, Duffeld and Haselwode. Nicholas had these of the gift of Edward who remised and quitclaimed of, and warranted for, himself and his heirs to Nicholas and his heirs. Nicholas gave 100 marks of silver. (17)

1151. Westminster. Octave of Midsummer 1498. P: Henry Vernon, kt. D: Roger Wentworth, kt, and Anne h.w. Concerning the manor of Bakewell and 10 mess., 50a. land, 100a. meadow, 300a. pasture, 40a. woodland, 1000a. marsh, gorse and heath and 100s rent in Bakewell and Darley in le Peke. Henry had these of the gift of Roger and Anne who remised and quitclaimed of, and warranted for, themselves and the heirs of Anne to Henry and his heirs. Henry gave 40 marks of silver. (18)

1152. Westminster. The morrow of Martinmas 1498. P: George, earl of Shrewsbury, Edward Hastynges, kt, lord Hastynges and Christopher Ursewyk, clerk. D: Robert Morten and Alice h.w. and John Morten and Margery h.w. Concerning the manor of Mapurley and 6 mess., 3 toft, 200a. land, 40a. meadow, 240a. pasture, 30a. woodland and 4 marks rent in Mapurley and Brayston. The deforciants acknowledged these to be the right of the earl who, with Edward and Christopher, had them of their gift. They remised and quitclaimed of, and warranted for, themselves and the heirs of Alice and Margery to the plaintiffs and the heirs of the earl. The plaintiffs gave £200. (19)

1153. Westminster. Easter three weeks 1499. P: George, earl of Shrewsbury, Richard Knyveton, Thomas Babyngton and Thomas Thorley, chaplain. D: Richard Eyr and Margery h.w. Concerning 8 mess., 4 tofts, 2 crofts, 18a. land and 1½a. meadow in Chesterfeld, Haslond, Newbold, Boythorp, Dronfeld, Brampton and Tapton. Richard and Margery acknowledged these to be the right of the earl who, with the other plaintiffs, had them of their gift. They remised and quitclaimed of, and warranted for, themselves and the heirs of Margery to the plaintiffs and the heirs of the earl. The plaintiffs gave 100 marks of silver. (20)

1154. Westminster. Octave of Midsummer 1499. P: Nicholas Bawekewell of Ulkerthorp, William Bawekewell, John Bawekewell and Hugh Bawekewell. D: Robert Smalley and Lucy h.w. Concerning 1 mess., 2 tofts, 60a. land, 10a. meadow, 12a. pasture and 2s rent in Chaddesden. Robert and Lucy acknowledged these to be the right of Nicholas who, with the other plaintiffs, had them of their gift. They remised and quitclaimed of, and warranted for, themselves and the heirs of Lucy to the plaintiffs and the heirs of Nicholas. The plaintiffs gave 40 marks of silver. (21)

1155. Westminster. Octave of the Purification 1500. Quindene of Easter 1500. P: George, earl of Shrewsbury, Thomas Talbot, Richard Knyveton and Thomas Jakes. D: Robert Gylbert, Thomas Fox and Ellen h.w. Concerning 12 mess., 10 tofts, 20 virgates of land, 20a. meadow, 300a. pasture, 20a. woodland, 200a. marsh and 20s rent in Dronfeld, Cooldaston, Letfeld, Chasterfeld, Norton, Grenehill, Newebold, Tapton and Hekyngton. The deforciants acknowledged these to be the right of the earl who, with the other plaintiffs, had them of their gift. They remised and quitclaimed of, and warranted for, themselves and the heirs of Ellen to the plaintiffs and the heirs of the earl. The plaintiffs gave £100. (22)

1156. Westminster. Easter one month 1500. P: Henry Vernon, kt, John Cokayn, esq. Richard Knyveton, esq. Humphrey Okeover, esq. John Fitzherbert, esq. John Knyveton, esq. Robert Bradshawe, Henry Prynce, clerk, and Richard Cutler, chaplain. D: William Taberer and Douce h.w. Concerning 5 mess., 3 tofts, 60a. land, 12a. meadow, 20a. pasture and 6a. woodland in Asshebourne, Offecote and Underwode. William and Douce acknowledged these to be the right of Humphrey who, with the other plaintiffs, had them of their gift. They remised and quitclaimed of, and warranted for, themselves and the heirs of Douce to the plaintiffs and the heirs of Humphrey. The plaintiffs gave 40 marks of silver. (23)

1157. Westminster. Quindene of Midsummer 1500. The morrow of All Souls 1500. P: Richard Knyveton and John Knyveton. D: John Irlond. Concerning 4 mess., 10 virgates land, 40a. meadow, 200a. pasture, 20a. woodland, 50a. heath and 50a. marsh in Yildersley. John Irlond acknowledged these to be the right of Richard who, with John Knyveton, had them of his gift. He remised and quitclaimed of, and warranted for, himself and his heirs to Richard and John and Richard's heirs. Richard and John gave 100 marks of silver. (24)

1158. Westminster. Octave of the Purification 1501. P: Henry Wylloughby, kt. D: Humphrey Lowe and Margaret h.w. Concerning 1 mess., 300a. land, 32a. meadow and 12a. pasture in Cold Eyton, Offecote and Underwode. Henry had these of the gift of Humphrey and Margaret who remised and quitclaimed of, and warranted for, themselves and the heirs of Margaret to Henry and his heirs. Henry gave £40. (25)

1159. Westminster. Quindene of Easter 1501. Octave of Trinity 1501. P: Henry Foliambe. D: Thomas Durrant and Agnes h.w. Concerning 5 mess., 2 shops, 60a. land, 15a. pasture and 2a. woodland in Chestrefeld, Newebold and Brampton. Henry had these of the gift of Thomas and Agnes who remised and quitclaimed of, and warranted for, themselves and the heirs of Thomas to Henry and his heirs. Henry gave £100. (26)

1160. Westminster. Easter one month 1501. Octave of Trinity 1501. Petens: John Monntgomery, kt. Defendant: John Ireland and Elizabeth h.w. Concerning the manor of Yildersley and 7 mess., 3 toft, 40 virgates land, 60a. meadow, 300a. pasture, 40a. woodland, 200a. heath, 200a. marsh and 40s rent in Yildersley. John Monntgomery had these of the gift of John and Elizabeth who remised and quitclaimed of, and warranted for, themselves and the heirs of John to John Monntgomery and his heirs. John Monntgomery gave 200 marks of silver. (27)

1161. Westminster. Michaelmas one month 1501. P: Richard Knyveton, Robert Cuny and John Porte. D: Robert Coke and Benedict h.w. Concerning 1 mess., 30a. land, 10a. meadow, 10a. pasture and 6a. woodland in Bubnell and Baslowe. Robert and Benedict acknowledged these to be the right of Richard who, with Robert Cuny and John, had them of their gift.

They remised and quitclaimed of, and warranted for, themselves and the heirs of Benedict to the plaintiffs and the heirs of Richard. The plaintiffs gave 40 marks of silver. (28)

1162. Westminster. Octave of Martinmas 1501. P: Thomas Babyngton, Henry Babyngton, clerk, and Thomas Fitzherbert, clerk. D: Edward Doile and Anne h.w. Concerning 3 mess., 2 tofts, 200a. land, 60a. meadow, 100a. pasture and 10s rent in Lutchirch, Osmaston, Derby and Normanton. Edward and Anne acknowledged these to be the right of Thomas Babyngton who, with the other plaintiffs, had them of their gift. They remised and quitclaimed of, and warranted for, themselves and the heirs of Anne to the plaintiffs and the heirs of Thomas Babyngton. The plaintiffs gave 100 marks of silver. (29)

1163. Westminster. Quindene of Martinmas 1501. Octave of Hilary 1502. P: Richard, bishop of Durham, Robert Willoughby de Broke, kt, Giles Daubeney de Daubeney, kt, Reginald Gray, kt, Thomas Lovell, kt, Thomas Rowthale, clerk, John Mordaunt, James Hobert, Richard Empson and Thomas Lucas. D: John Seynt John, kt, Henry Willoughby, kt, Thomas Leke, esq. and Roger Johnson. Concerning the castle and manor of Codnore and the manors of Hennore, Lasco and Langley and 100 mess., 1000a. land, 200a. meadow, 4000a. pasture, 200a. woodland and £40 rent in Codnore, Hennore, Lasco and Langley. The defendants acknowledged these to be the right of Thomas Rowthale who, with the other plaintiffs, had them of their gift. They remised and quitclaimed of themselves and the heirs of John Seynt John to the plaintiffs and the heirs of Thomas Rowthale. They also warranted for themselves and the heirs of John Seynt John against John, abbot of the monastery of St Peter, Westminster and his successors. The plaintiffs gave £1000. (30)

1164. Westminster. Octave of the Purification 1502. Quindene of Easter 1502. P: Humphrey Bradburne, esq. D: Edward Salysbury. Concerning 1 mess., 80a. land and 12a. meadow in Perwyche. Humphrey had these of the gift of Edward who remised and quitclaimed of, and warranted for, himself and his heirs to Humphrey and his heirs. Humphrey gave £20. (31)

1165. Westminster. The morrow of Midsummer 1502. P: Henry Foliambe, senior, esq. D: Laurence Lyversage and Margaret h.w. Concerning 1 mess. in Derby. Henry had the messuage of the gift of Laurence and Margaret who remised and quitclaimed of, and warranted for, themselves and the heirs of Margaret to Henry and his heirs. Henry gave £20. (32)

1166. Westminster. Octave of Midsummer 1502. P: Hugh Revell. D: Richard Page, William Page and Alice h.w. Concerning 4 mess., 200a. land,

100a. meadow and 200a. pasture in Carlyngwayt. Hugh had these of the gift of the defendants who remised and quitclaimed of, and warranted for, themselves and the heirs of Alice to Hugh and his heirs. Hugh gave 100 marks of silver. (33)

1167. Westminster. The morrow of All Souls 1503. P: Roger Eyre, Philip Eyre and James Bayresford, clerk. D: John Rocclyff, kt, and Margaret h.w. and Elizabeth Sothyll, widow. Concerning 2 mess., 2 tofts, 3 crofts, 100a. land, 3a. meadow, 200a. pasture and 4a. woodland in Newebold. The defendants acknowledged these to be the right of Roger who, with Philip and James, had them of their gift. They remised and quitclaimed of, and warranted for, themselves and the heirs of Margaret to the plaintiffs and the heirs of Roger. The plaintiffs gave £40. (34)

1168. Westminster. The morrow of Martinmas 1503. P: Ralph Agard, Thomas Rolston and William Monnyng, clerk. D: Ralph Pole and Emma h.w. and Thomas Smyth and Joan h.w. Concerning 2 mess., 1 toft, 50a. land, 10a. meadow and 1a. pasture in Egynton on Le Heth, Merston next Tutbury and Wyllyngton. The defendants acknowledged these to be the right of William who, with Ralph and Thomas, had them of their gift. They remised and quitclaimed of, and warranted for, themselves and the heirs of Emma and Joan to the plaintiffs and the heirs of William. The plaintiffs gave 40 marks of silver. (35)

1169. Westminster. The morrow of Martinmas 1503. P: Edward Mather. D: Edward Bown and Alice h.w. Concerning 1 mess., 30a. land and 1a. meadow in Mattelok and Hasker. Edward Mather had these of the gift of Edward and Alice who remised and quitclaimed of, and warranted for, themselves and the heirs of Alice to Edward Mather and his heirs. Edward Mather gave *[Damaged]* marks of silver. (36)

1170. Westminster. Octave of Martinmas 1503. P: Ralph Delker, esq. John Knyveton, John Porte and Henry Proctour, clerk. D: Thomas Twyford, esq. Concerning 62a. pasture in Kyrkelongley. Thomas acknowledged the pasture to be the right of John Knyveton who, with the other plaintiffs, had it of his gift. He remised and quitclaimed of, and warranted for, himself and his heirs to the plaintiffs and the heirs of John Knyveton. The plaintiffs gave £40. (37)

1171. Westminster. Octave of Martinmas 1504. P: William Hastynges, esq. Richard Knevyton, esq. John Porte and Thomas Thorley, clerk. D: William Blount, lord Mountjoy, and Elizabeth h.w. Concerning the manors of Totley, Hasylwode and Lutchurche and 12 mess., 10 tofts, 300a.land, 100a. meadow, 200a. pasture, 40a. woodland, 50a. marsh, 50a. heath and 40s rent in Totley, Hasylwode, Lutchurche, Brusshefeld and Languisdon and also common pasture for 24 cows and 1 bull within the park of Shothyll in Shothyll. William Blount and Elizabeth acknowledged these to be the right of William Hastynges and they remised and quitclaimed of themselves and the heirs of Elizabeth to the plaintiffs and the heirs of William Hastynges. They also warranted for themselves and the heirs of Elizabeth against John, abbot of St Peters, Westminster, and his successors. The plaintiffs gave 300 marks of silver. (38)

1172. Westminster. The morrow of the Purification 1505. P: Thomas Cockayn, esq. William Bothe, esq. John Porte and Edmund Baker. D: Ralph Byrde. Concerning 1 mess., 1 dovecot, 1 garden and 2a. pasture in Derby. Ralph acknowledged these to be the right of John who, with the other plaintiffs, had them of his gift. He remised and quitclaimed of, and warranted for, himself and his heirs to the plaintiffs and the heirs of John. The plaintiffs gave 20 marks of silver. (39)

1173. Westminster. Easter one month 1505. P: Thomas Hobbys, clerk, Henry Hornby, clerk, Charles Bothe, clerk, and John Neuton, clerk. D: William Assheby, esq. and Agnes h.w. Concerning the manor of Chelardeston and 16 mess., 70a. land, 300a. meadow, 50a. pasture, 6a. woodland and 50s rent in Chelardeston and Osmundeston. William and Agnes acknowledged these to be the right of John and they remised and quitclaimed of, and warranted for, themselves and the heirs of Agnes to the plaintiffs and the heirs of John. The plaintiffs gave 200 marks of silver. (40)

1174. Westminster. The morrow of Martinmas 1505. P: Ralph Shepard, clerk, and Thomas Bentley. D: Thomas Twyford. Concerning 2 mess., 12a. land, 3a. meadow, 25a. pasture and 3s rent in Kyrkelongley. Thomas Twyford acknowledged these to be the right of Ralph who, with Thomas Bentley, had them of his gift. He remised and quitclaimed of, and warranted for, himself and his heirs to Ralph, Thomas and Ralph's heirs. Ralph and Thomas gave 100 marks of silver. (41)

1175. Westminster. Octave of Martinmas 1505. P: Harold Stannton, Ralph Lemyngton and Thomas Beamonnt. D: Thomas Molet. Concerning a moiety of the manors of Overhall and Netherhall and a moiety of 12 mess., 300a. land, 80a. meadow, 160a. pasture, 300a. woodland, 1 mill and 10s rent in Hartyshorne and Smythesby. Thomas Molet acknowledged these to be the right of Harold who, with Ralph and Thomas, had them of his gift. He remised and quitclaimed of, and warranted for, himself and his heirs to the plaintiffs and the heirs of Harold. The plaintiffs gave 200 marks of silver. (42)

1176. Westminster. The morrow of the Purification 1506. P: Richard Knyveton. D: John Knyveton. Concerning 59a. pasture in Bradley and

Ofcote. Richard had the pasture of the gift of John who remised and quitclaimed of, and warranted for, himself and his heirs to Richard and his heirs. Richard gave £40. (43)

1177. Westminster. The morrow of Midsummer 1506. P: Richard Knyveton, esq. Ralph Delnye, esq. John Rolseley and Humphrey Knyveton. D: John Gilbert. Concerning 1 mess., 40a. land, 1a. meadow and 16a. pasture in Medilton. John Gilbert acknowledged these to be the right of Humphrey who, with the other plaintiffs, had them of his gift. He remised and quitclaimed of, and warranted for, himself and his heirs to the plaintiffs and the heirs of Humphrey. The plaintiffs gave £20. (44)

1178. Westminster. The morrow of All Souls 1507. P: Maurice Barkeley, kt, and Richard Sutton, gent. D: Hugh Heppals and Isabel h.w. Concerning 40a. land and 10a. pasture in Lokhawe. Hugh and Isabel acknowledged these to be the right of Richard who, with Maurice, had them of their gift. They remised and quitclaimed of, and warranted for, themselves and the heirs of Isabel to Maurice, Richard and Richard's heirs. Maurice and Richard gave £20. (45)

1179. Westminster. The morrow of Martinmas 1507. P: Richard Hethecote. D: Thomas Twell and Margery h.w. Concerning 1 mess., 12a. land, 2a. meadow and 6a. pasture in Buxston. Richard had these of the gift of Thomas and Margery who remised and quitclaimed of, and warranted for, themselves and the heirs of Margery to Richard and his heirs. Richard gave 40 marks of silver. (46)

1180. Westminster. Quindene of Hilary 1508. P: Henry Vernon, kt. D: John Carr. Concerning 5 mess., 300a. land, 50a. meadow, 100a. pasture and 14a. woodland in Nethershatton, Overton, Derwent and Monffreth in the parish of Hope and Hathursege. Henry had these of the gift of John who remised and quitclaimed of himself and his heirs to Henry and his heirs. John also warranted for himself and his heirs against John, abbot of the monastery of the Blessed Peter, Westminster, and his successors. Henry gave £100. (47)

1181. Westminster. Easter one month 1508. Octave of Midsummer 1508. P: Thomas Babyngton, Thomas Fitzherbert, clerk, John Fitzherbert, Anthony Fitzherbert, Ralph Babyngton, clerk, and Roland Babyngton. D: Richard Byngham and Anne h.w. Concerning 5 mess., 6 tofts, 200a. land, 20a. meadow, 200a. pasture and 20a. woodland in Codnore and Loscowe. Richard and Anne acknowledged these to be the right of Thomas Babyngton who, with the other plaintiffs, had them of their gift. They remised and quitclaimed of, and warranted for, themselves and the heirs of Anne to the plaintiffs and the heirs of Thomas Babyngton. The plaintiffs gave £60. (48)

HENRY VIII

CP 25/2/6/29

1182. Westminster. Quindene of Martinmas 1509. P: Henry Vernon, kt. D: Henry Wylloughby, kt. Concerning 1 mess., 300a. land, 42a. meadow and 300a. pasture in Colde Eyton, Ofcote, Underwode, Asshborne and Workyswerth. Henry Vernon had these of the gift of Henry Wylloughby who remised and quitclaimed of, and warranted for, himself and his heirs to Henry Vernon and his heirs. Henry Vernon gave £80. (1)

1183. Westminster. Octave of Martinmas 1509. P: Henry Vernon, kt. D: Cuthbert Langton and Joan h.w. Concerning the manor of Birchils and 3 mess., 100a. land, 20a. meadow, 100a. pasture and 26s 8d rent in Birchils, Hassop and Bakewell. Henry had these of the gift of Cuthbert and Joan who remised and quitclaimed of, and warranted for, themselves and the heirs of Joan to Henry and his heirs. Henry gave £60. (2)

1184. Westminster. Octave of Martinmas 1510. P: Brian Stapilton, kt, William Wymondsold, Bartholomew Smalley, John Caunt, chaplain, William Cresewell, chaplain, and John Mewer, chaplain. D: William Palisser and Agnes h.w. Concerning 1 mess., 1 toft, 1 garden, 40a. land, 10a. meadow and 8a. pasture in Elvaston and Thurleston. William Palisser and Agnes acknowledged these to be the right of Brian who, with the other plaintiffs, had them of their gift. They remised and quitclaimed of, and warranted for, themselves and the heirs of Agnes to the plantiffs and the heirs of Brian. The plaintiffs gave £40. (3)

1185. Westminster. Octave of Martinmas 1511. P: Henry Vernon, kt. D: Thomas Sacheverell. Concerning 4 mess., 70a. land, 20a. meadow, 200a. pasture, 10a. woodland and 4s 11d rent in Ibull next Werkysworth. Henry had these of the gift of Thomas who remised and quitclaimed of, and warranted for, himself and his heirs to Henry and his heirs. Henry gave 100 marks of silver. (4)

1186. Westminster. Quindene of Michaelmas 1512. P: John Porte, Robert Blagge, Thomas Cokayn, esq. German Pole, esq. Richard Dawne, esq. Thomas Porte, clerk, and Thomas Myddelton, gent. D: Richard Warren and Joan h.w. Concerning 4a. meadow in Merston. Richard Warren and Joan acknowledged the meadow to be the right of John who, with the other plaintiffs, had it of their gift. They remised and quitclaimed of, and warranted for, themselves and the heirs of Joan to the plaintiffs and the heirs of John. The plaintiffs gave £14. (5)

1187. Westminster. The morrow of the Purification 1513. P: Henry Vernon, kt. D: Edward Bradschawe and Alice h.w. Concerning 1 mess., 1 garden and ½a. land in Derby. Henry had these of the gift of Edward and Alice who remised and quitclaimed of, and warranted for, themselves and the heirs of Alice to Henry and his heirs. Henry gave £40. (7)

1188. Westminster. The morrow of Ascension 1513. P: John Hunt, Roland Babyngton, Henry Bullokke, clerk, John Bullokke, Richard Blakwall and Ralph Blakwall. D: Thomas Tykkell and Elizabeth h.w. Concerning the manor of Shardelowe and 10 mess., 6 tofts, 600a. land, 100a. meadow, 300a. pasture, 4a. woodland, 200a. heath and 40s rent in Shardlowe, Aston and Wylne. Thomas and Elizabeth acknowledged these to be the right of John Hunt who, with the other plaintiffs, had them of their gift. They remised and quitclaimed of, and warranted for, themselves and the heirs of Thomas to the plaintiffs and the heirs of John Hunt. The plaintiffs gave 40 marks of silver. (8)

1189. Westminster. Easter one month 1513. P: Alexander Beynham, kt, Christopher Beynham, esq. Giles Grevile, esq. Richard Cornewale, esq. John Abrahale, esq. John Bradshawe, gent., William Walwyn, gent., Robert Norwyche, gent., Henry Stathum, gent., Thomas Cokys, gent., John Skydemore, gent., John Arnold, gent., William Lanwarne, gent., Thomas Duckemanton, gent., Humphrey Meverell, gent., Nicholas Grace, husbandman, and Thomas Bradshawe, husbandman. D: John Knyfton. Concerning the manor of Wyndeley Hill and 6 mess., 1 toft, 340a. land, 146a. meadow, 86a. pasture, 52a. woodland and 23s 4d rent in Wyndley, Wyndleyhill, Duffeld, Mogyngton, Ireton, Hasylwode, Wyndeleyryche, Undirwode, Ofcote and Kneton. John Knyfton acknowledged these to be the right of William Walwyn and he remised and quitclaimed of, and warranted for, himself and his heirs to the plaintiffs and the heirs of William Walwyn. The plaintiffs gave £600. (9)

1190. Westminster. The morrow of Midsummer 1513. P: Thomas Wylne, son and heir of John Wylne and Margaret h.w. D: John Wylne, senior, and Margaret h.w. Concerning 2 mess., 1 toft, 100a. land, 6a. meadow and 80a. pasture in Melburne and Normanton next Derby. Thomas had these of the gift of John and Margaret who remised and quitclaimed of, and warranted for, themselves and the heirs of Margaret to Thomas and his heirs. Thomas then granted and rendered the tenements to John and Margaret to hold for their lives, without impeachment of waste, of the chief lord etc paying therefor each year to Thomas and his heirs, one red rose at the feast of the Nativity of St John the Baptist for all services etc pertaining to John *[sic; recte Thomas]* and his heirs. Reversion to Thomas and his heirs. (10)

1191. Westminster. The morrow of the Purification 1514. P: Ralph Shirley, kt. D: John Wylne and Margaret h.w. Concerning the advowson and the right of presentation to the precentorship of one chaplain and his successors in the honour of St Catherine, virgin, founded in the church of St Michael, archangel, of Melbourne together with the prebend of the same. Ralph had these of the gift of John and Margaret who remised and quitclaimed of themselves and the heirs of Margaret to Ralph and his heirs. They also warranted against John, abbot of the monastery of St Peter, Westminster and his successors. Ralph gave 200 marks of silver. (11)

1192. Westminster. Octave of Martinmas 1514. P: Richard Hogh, William Fayrebarne and Henry Hurt, chaplain. D: Robert Wynter. Concerning 1 mess., 1 garden, 30a. land and 6a. meadow in Weston on Trent. Robert acknowledged these to be the right of Richard who, with the other plaintiffs, had them of his gift. He remised and quitclaimed of, and warranted for, himself and his heirs to the plaintiffs and the heirs of Richard. The plaintiffs gave £50. (12)

1193. Westminster. Easter three weeks 1515. P: Richard Rolston, clerk. D: Richard Francess, esq. Concerning 3 mess., 1 cottage, 4 virgates 1 bov. land, 1 toft and 6a. meadow in Stanton. Richard Rolston had these of the gift of Richard Francess who remised and quitclaimed of, and warranted for, himself and his heirs to Richard Rolston and his heirs. Richard Rolston gave 100 marks of silver. (13)

1194. Westminster. Easter three weeks 1515. P: George Blakwall, son and heir apparent of Robert Blakwall, John Hunt, John Gell and Thomas Bagshawe. D: John Castell. Concerning 3 mess., 60a. land, 20a. meadow and 20a. pasture in Blakwall, Tadyngton and Presclyff. John Castell acknowledged these to be the right of George who, with the other plaintiffs, had them of his gift. He remised and quitclaimed of, and warranted for, himself and his heirs to the plaintiffs and the heirs of George. The plaintiffs gave 100 marks of silver. (14)

1195. Westminster. Michaelmas three weeks 1515. P: Robert Cleyton. D: Richard Barber and Catherine h.w. Concerning a third part of 1 mess., 40a. land, 6a. meadow, 10a. pasture and 4a. woodland in Kynder within the parish of Glossop. Robert had the third part of the gift of Richard and Catherine who remised and quitclaimed of, and warranted for, themselves and the heirs of Catherine to Robert and his heirs. Robert gave 40 marks of silver. (15)

1196. Westminster. Octave of Martinmas 1515. P: Godfrey Foliambe, esq. D: Thomas Barton and Ellen h.w. Concerning 1 mess., 12a. land and 20a. pasture in Tiddeswall. Godfrey had these of the gift of Thomas and Ellen who remised and quitclaimed of, and warranted for, themselves and the heirs of Ellen to Godfrey and his heirs. Godfrey gave £40. (16)

1197. Westminster. Quindene of Hilary 1516. P: Godfrey Folyamb. D: Humphrey Peryent and Joan h.w. Concerning 3 mess., 200a. land, 40a.

meadow, 30a. pasture, 100a. heath and 6a. woodland in Wygley and Phalange. Godfrey had these of the gift of Humphrey and Joan who remised and quitclaimed of, and warranted for, themselves and the heirs of Joan to Godfrey and his heirs. Godfrey gave £30. (17)

1198. Westminster. The morrow of Midsummer 1516. P: Godfrey Foliambe, esq. D: John Bright and Ann h.w. Concerning 3 mess., 200a. land, 40a. meadow, 30a. pasture, 6a. woodland and 100a. heath in Wigley and Phalange. Godfrey had these of the gift of John and Ann who remised and quitclaimed of, and warranted for, themselves and the heirs of Ann to Godfrey and his heirs. Godfrey gave £40. (18)

1199. Westminster. Michaelmas three weeks 1516. P: Richard Sutton, esq. D: Richard Pylkyngton of Robyngton, son and heir of Robert Pylkyngton. Concerning 8 mess., 100a. land, 20a. meadow, 100a. pasture, 40a. woodland and 20s rent in Mellor within the parish of Glossop. Richard Sutton had these of the gift of Richard Pylkyngton who remised and quitclaimed of, and warranted for, himself and his heirs to Richard Sutton and his heirs. Richard Sutton gave 100 marks of silver. (19)

1200. Westminster. The morrow of Ascension 1517. P: Robert More. D: John Smyth. Concerning 16a. pasture and 4a. woodland in Ekyngton. John acknowledged these to be the right of Robert and he granted for himself and his heirs that this land, which John Cade and Elizabeth h.w. held for the life of Elizabeth of the inheritance of John Smyth and which, on the death of Elizabeth, ought to revert to John Smyth and his heirs, should remain instead to Robert and his heirs to hold of the chief lord etc forever. John Smyth warranted for himself and his heirs. Robert gave £40. (20)

1201. Westminster. The morrow of Ascension 1517. P: James Berefford. D: Thomas Kynwolmarshe and Cecily h.w. Concerning 6 mess., 11 bov. land and 41s 5d rent in Wynster, the profit of a certain mine and the office of barmaster of all the mines there. Thomas and Cecily remised and quitclaimed these of themselves and the heirs of Cecily to James and his heirs. They warranted against John, abbot of the monastery of St Peter, Westminster, and his successors. James gave 100 marks of silver. (21)

1202. Westminster. Quindene of Trinity 1517. P: Henry Sacheverell, kt, John Porte, esq. Robert Jeykynson, clerk, Edward Baker, Roger More and Edward Pennannt. D: Thomas Hylton. Concerning 3 mess., 100a. land, 20a meadow, 40a. pasture, 2a. woodland and 5s rent in Workesworth, Midylton and Parwiche. Thomas acknowledged these to be the right of Robert who, with the other plaintiffs, had them of his gift. He remised and quitclaimed of, and warranted for, himself and his heirs to the plaintiffs and the heirs of Robert. The plaintiffs gave 100 marks of silver. (22)

1203. Westminter. Michaelmas three weeks 1518. P: German Pole, esq. James Basford, clerk, John Pennant, clerk, James Oxeley and Henry Aynesworth. D: Hugh Orme and Margery h.w. and Humphrey Herley and Margaret h.w. Concerning 1 mess., 2 tofts, 40a. land, 12a. meadow, 10a. pasture and 16s rent in Workesworth. The defendants acknowledged these to be the right of Henry who, with the other plaintiffs, had them of their gift. They remised and quitclaimed of, and warranted for, themselves and the heirs of Margery and Margaret to the plaintiffs and the heirs of Henry. The plaintiffs gave £40. (23)

1204. Westminster. Michaelmas three weeks 1518. P: Richard Choppyn and Gillian h.w. D: Richard Moumford and Margaret h.w. Concerning 1 mess., 1 shop and 1 garden in Derby. Richard and Gillian had these of the gift of Richard and Margaret who remised and quitclaimed of, and warranted for, themselves and the heirs of Margaret to Richard, Gillian and Richard's heirs. Richard and Gillian gave 40 marks of silver. (24)

1205. Westminster. The morrow of the Purification 1519. P: Thomas Cokayn, kt, John Porte, esq. Ralph Cantrell, clerk, Thomas Middleton and Henry Aynesworth. D: Thomas Langforth. Concerning 2 mess., 30a. land, 5a. meadow and 20a. pasture in Longforth and Bulton. Thomas Langforth acknowledged these to be the right of John who, with the other plaintiffs, had them of his gift. He remised and quitclaimed of, and warranted for, himself and his heirs to the plaintiffs and the heirs of John. The plaintiffs gave £30. (25)

1206. Westminster. Easter one month 1519. P: Robert Leversage. D: George Macworth and Ann h.w. Concerning 7 mess., 1 garden, 44a. land and ½a. meadow in Derbye. Robert had these of the gift of George and Ann who remised and quitclaimed of, and warranted for, themselves and the heirs of Ann to Robert and his heirs. Robert gave 100 marks of silver. (26)

1207. Westminster. Quindene of Trinity 1519. P: John Fitzherbert, clerk, Humphrey Fitzherbert, esq. Thomas Cumberford, esq. Thomas Purefey, esq. and Ralph Purefey, gent. D: John Fitzherbert, esq. Concerning the manor of Norbury, 20 mess., 10 tofts, 3 mills, 600a. land, 300a. meadow, 500a. pasture, 100a. woodland and 2s rent in Norbury, Rossyngton, Snelston and Cubley together with the advowson of the church of Norbury. John Fitzherbert, esq. acknowledged these to be the right of John Fitzherbert, clerk, who, with the other plaintiffs, had them of his gift. He remised and quitclaimed of, and warranted for, himself and his heirs to the plaintiffs and the heirs of John, the clerk. The plaintiffs then granted and rendered the manor, tenements and advowson to John Fitzherbert, esq. to hold of the chief lord etc without impeachment of waste, for his life. (27)

1208. Westminster. The morrow of All Souls 1519. P: Henry Ellot, Richard Ellot and John Swifte. D: John Hewet and Joan h.w. Concerning 1 toft, 4a. swamp *(terre aqua coopertis)*, 6a. meadow and 1½a. pasture in Kynwaldmersshe and a fourth part of a house called 'an Iren Smythe' in Kynwaldmersshe. John and Joan acknowledged these to be the right of Henry who, with the other plaintiffs, had them of their gift. They remised and quitclaimed of, and warranted for, themselves and the heirs of Joan to the plaintiffs and the heirs of Henry. The plaintiffs gave 50 marks of silver. (28)

1209. Westminster. Octave of Martinmas 1519. P: John Porte of Etwall, esq.and Joan Fitzherbert, widow. D: John Fitzherbert of Norbury, esq. and Roland Babyngton. Concerning the manor of Aisshe and 3 mess., 200a. land, 50a. meadow, 100a. pasture, 2a. woodland, 300a. gorse and heath and 3s 4d rent in Aisshe. John and Roland granted and rendered these to Joan Fitzherbert for her life with remainder to John Porte and his heirs by his wife Joan, to hold of John, Roland and Roland's heirs paying therefor at the feasts of the Purification of the Blessed Mary and St James, apostle, each year, for all services etc pertaining to John, Roland and Roland's heirs: (i) 40s during the life of Joan Fitzherbert; (ii) £5 after Joan's death and during the life of a certain Dorothy Fitzherbert, widow, formerly wife of Nicholas Fitzherbert, deceased; (iii) £9 after Dorothy's death; and (iv) £10 to Roland's heirs after the deaths of Joan, Dorothy and John Fitzherbert and Roland. The defendants warranted for themselves and the heirs of John Fitzherbert *[sic; recte Roland?]*. (29)

1210. Westminster. Easter one month 1520. P: John Porte, esq. Thomas Cokayn, kt, Robert Blagge, one of the barons of the King's Exchequer, Anthony Fitzherbert, serjeant-at-law of the king, John Dawney, esq. John Copwood, gent., John Middelton, gent., Edmund Baker and John Lyeth. D: Ralph Martyn and Maude h.w. and Ranulf Martyn their son. Concerning 1 mess., 20a. land, 4a. meadow, 40a. pasture and 6a. woodland in Rodebowrne. Ralph, Maude and Ranulf acknowledged these to be the right of John Porte who, with the other plaintiffs, had them of their gift. They remised and quitclaimed of, and warranted for, themselves and the heirs of Maude to the plaintiffs and the heirs of John Porte. The plaintiffs gave £40. (30)

1211. Westminster. Easter one month 1521. P: Walter Gryffith, kt, Anthony Babyngton, William Chatweyn, Humphrey Ferrers, esq. Robert Seyton, Adam Eyr, gent., Roger Netham, rector of Egenton, and Richard Sewdell, chaplain. D: William Perponnte, kt. Concerning the manor of Aysshover, 12 mess., 10 tofts, 200a. land, 20a. meadow, 40a. pasture, 40a. woodland, 500a. moorland and 100s 10d rent in Aysshover, Edynstowe,

Alton, Northege, Overton, Mylnetown, Stubbyng and Ravennest. William Perponnte acknowledged these to be the right of Anthony who, with the other plaintiffs, had them of his gift. He remised and quitclaimed of, and warranted for, himself and his heirs to the plaintiffs and the heirs of Anthony. The plaintiffs gave £300. (31)

1212. Westminster. Quindene of Trinity 1521. P: Godfrey Foliambe, kt, and Oliver Shawe, chaplain. D: George Lynakre, esq. Concerning 3 mess., 100a. land, 10a. meadow, 20a. pasture and 13s 9d rent in Hasland and Hyll. George acknowledged these to be the right of Godfrey who, with Oliver, had them of his gift. He remised and quitclaimed of, and warranted for, himself and his heirs to Godfrey, Oliver and Godfrey's heirs. Godfrey and Oliver gave £80. (32)

1213. Westminster. The morrow of the Purification 1522. P: Ellis Assheby and John Byllup. D: Ralph Constable and Ann h.w. Concerning 16 mess., 200a. land, 60a. meadow, 40a. pasture, 500a. woodland and 66s 8d rent in Barleburgh, Whytwell, Romley and Cloyne. Ralph and Ann acknowledged these to be the right of Ellis who, with John, had them of their gift. They remised and quitclaimed of, and warranted for, themselves and the heirs of Ann to Ellis, John and the heirs of Ellis. Ellis and John then granted and rendered the tenements to Ralph and Ann to hold to themselves and the male heirs of their bodies of the chief lord etc forever. Successive remainders to the heirs of the bodies of Ralph and Ann, to the heirs of the body of Ann and to the right heirs of Ralph. (33)

1214. Westminster. Quindene of Midsummer 1522. Octave of Michaelmas 1522. P: William Blount of Mountjoy, kt, Thomas Tyrell, kt, John Baldwyn, John Baker and Walter Blount, gent. D: Robert Markham and Ellen h.w. Concerning 8 mess., 100a. land, 40a. meadow, 40a. pasture and 12d rent in Saperton, Makeley, Lees, Foston, Scropton and Hone. Robert and Ellen acknowledged these to be the right of William and they remised and quitclaimed of, and warranted for, themselves and the heirs of Ellen to the plaintiffs and the heirs of William. The plaintiffs gave £300. (34)

1215. Westminster. The morrow of Ascension 1523. Octave of Trinity 1523. P: John Blount, gent., Ralph Cantrell, clerk, John Franncys, Ralph Puryfay, Walter Blount and John Mawdeley, gent. D: Edward Walpole. Concerning a third part of the manors of Colande, Oslaston, Roddesley and Wynstur, and of 20 mess., 10 tofts, 500a. land, 50a. meadow, 300a. pasture, 40a. woodland, 200a. gorse and heath and 100s rent in Colande, Oslaston, Roddesley, Wynstur, Westbroughton, Sudbury, Ullesmore, Braylesford, Thurvaston, Longford, Assheborne, Underwode and Clyfton. Edward acknowledged the third part to be the right of John Blount who, with the other plaintiffs, had it of his gift. He remised and quitclaimed of, and warranted for, himself and his heirs to the plaintiffs and the heirs of John Blount. The plaintiffs gave £160. (35)

1216. Westminster. Octave of Martinmas 1523. P: John Mundy, kt, Robert Brudenell, the king's chief justice of common pleas, Andrew Wyndesore, John Dance, kt, William Shelley, serjeant-at-law, and Richard Lyster, esq. D: John Tychet, kt, lord Audeley, and Mary h.w. Concerning the manors of Marketon, Makworth and Allestrye and 8 mess., 2 water mills, 800a. land, 200a. meadow, 800a. pasture, 500a. woodland, 700a. gorse and heath and £50 rent in Marketon, Makworth, Allestrye and Derby and also the advowson of the church of Makworth. John Tychet and Mary acknowledged these to be the right of Robert who, with the other plaintiffs, had them of their gift. They remised and quitclaimed of themselves and the heirs of John to the plaintiffs and the heirs of Robert. They also warranted for themselves and the heirs of Mary against John, abbot of the monastery of St Peter, Westminster, and his successors. The plaintiffs gave £1200. (36)

1217. Westminster. Octave of Martinmas 1523. P: John Huse, kt, Giles Huse, kt, Robert Sutton, esq. Robert Huse, esq. John Mounson, esq. Thomas Kelham, gent., and Anthony Ireby, gent. D: Robert Sheffeld, esq. Concerning 2 mess., 250a. land, 50a. meadow, 20a. pasture and 8a. woodland in Neuton and Sulney. Robert Sheffeld acknowledged these to be the right of John Huse and he granted that these tenements which Richard Savage and Elizabeth h.w. held for the life of Elizabeth of the inheritance of Robert Sheffeld and which, on the death of Elizabeth, ought to revert to himself and his heirs should remain instead to the plaintiffs and the heirs of John Huse to hold of the chief lord etc forever. Robert Sheffeld warranted for himself and his heirs. The plaintiffs gave 200 marks of silver. (37)

1218. Westminster. Easter one month 1524. P: Guy Rawlynson, Nicholas Berde and Ralph Bradbury of Olderset. D: Isabel Holynworth, widow, John Sutton and Elizabeth h.w. Concerning 1 mess., 20a. land, 2a. meadow and 16a. pasture in Bowdenhedde in the parish of le Chapell in le Fryth. The defendants acknowledged these to be the right of Guy who, with the other plaintiffs, had them of their gift. They remised and quitclaimed of themselves and the heirs of Elizabeth to the plaintiffs and the heirs of Guy. Elizabeth warranted for herself and her heirs. The plaintiffs gave £40. (38)

1219. Westminster. Quindene of Easter 1523. Octave of Trinity 1524. P: Otwell Baly and Thurstan Townesende, clerk. D: Thomas Barbour and Catherine h.w. Concerning three fourths of 2 mess., 50a. land, 10a. meadow, 4a. pasture and 3a. woodland in Shatton and Bromeside. Thomas and Catherine acknowledged these to be the right of Thurstan who, with Otwell, had them of their gift. They remised and quitclaimed of, and warranted for, themselves and the heirs of Catherine to Thurstan, Otwell and the heirs of Thurstan. Otwell and Thurstan gave £40. (39)

1220. Westminster. Easter one month 1525. P: Godfrey Foliambe, kt, Ralph Shawe, clerk, Denis Baxter, clerk, and Roger Bieston, clerk. D: Richard Cropper alias Fideler and Elizabeth h.w. Concerning 1 mess., 50a. land, 10a. meadow, 10a. pasture and 6a. woodland in Yngmanthorpe within the parish of Brampton. Richard and Elizabeth acknowledged these to be the right of Godfrey who, with the other plaintiffs, had them of their gift. They remised and quitclaimed of, and warranted for, themselves and the heirs of Elizabeth to the plaintiffs and the heirs of Godfrey. The plaintiffss gave £40. (40)

1221. Westminster. Easter one month 1525. P: John Shawe and Margaret h.w. D: John Cade. Concerning 1 mess., 30a. land, 7a. meadow and 3a. woodland in Brampton. John Cade acknowledged these to be the right of Margaret who, with John Shawe, had them of his gift. He remised and quitclaimed of, and warranted for, himself and his heirs to John, Margaret and Margaret's heirs. John and Margaret gave £40. (41)

1222. Westminster. Easter one month 1525. P: Godfrey Foliambe, kt, Ralph Shawe, clerk, Denis Baxter, and Roger Bieston, clerk. D: John Hunt. Concerning 2 mess., 120a. land, 50a. meadow, 30a. pasture and 24a. woodland in Tupton, Eggnestowe and Brymmmyngton. John acknowledged these to be the right of Godfrey who, with the other plaintiffs, had them of his gift. He remised and quitclaimed of, and warranted for, himself and his heirs to the plaintiffs and the heirs of Godfrey. The plaintiffs gave £40. (42)

1223. Westminster. Easter three weeks 1525. P: George Asshe, Roger Asshe, clerk, John Asshe and Nicholas Thornell. D: John Shentalle and Joan h.w. and Ralph Calcrofte and Elizabeth h.w. Concerning 1 mess., 3 cottages and 1 croft in Chesterfeld. The defendants acknowledged these to be the right of George who, with the other plaintiffs, had them of their gift. They remised and quitclaimed of themselves and the heirs of John Shentalle to the plaintiffs and the heirs of George. John and Joan warranted for themselves and the heirs of John. The plaintiffs then granted and rendered to Ralph and Elizabeth 20s rent derived from the tenements to have and receive each year, one half at each of the feasts of St Michael, archangel, and the Annunciation of the Blessed Virgin Mary, for the life of Elizabeth. *[Distraint clause as in 869.]* (43)

1224. Westminster. Octave of Hilary 1526. P: Christopher More, Humphrey Bolland, William Cowper, William Selyoke and William Mason, clerk. D: George Hastynges, kt, lord Hastynges. Concerning the manor of

Dronfeld and 1 water mill and £11 rent in Dronfeld, Woodhowse, Stubley, Colley, Barley, Newbold, Chasterfeld, Tapton, Calowe, Hasland and Boythorp. George acknowledged these to be the right of William Mason who, with the other plaintiffs, had them of his gift. He remised and quitclaimed of, and warranted for, himself and his heirs to the plaintiffs and the heirs of William Mason. The plaintiffs gave £200. (44)

1225. Westminster. Easter one month 1526. P: Ralph Sherley, gent. D: Thomas Wylne. Concerning 80a. pasture in Melburne. Thomas acknowledged the pasture to be the right of Ralph and he granted for himself and his heirs that this pasture, which Margaret Wylne, widow, formerly wife of John Wylne, father of Thomas, held for her life of the inheritance of Thomas and which ought to revert to Thomas on Margaret's death, should remain instead to Ralph and his heirs to hold of the chief lord etc forever. Thomas warranted for himself and his heirs. Ralph gave 40 marks of silver. (44a)

1226. Westminster. Octave of Midsummer of 1526. P: Thomas Browne. D: Arthur Dykson. Concerning 2 mess., 2a. land and 2a. pasture in Capella de le Fryth. Thomas had these of the gift of Arthur who remised and quitclaimed of, and warranted for, himself and his heirs to Thomas and his heirs. Thomas gave 40 marks of silver. (45)

1227. Westminster. Octave of Martinmas 1526. P: Henry Sacheverell, kt, George Fynderne, William Sacheverell and Robert Sacheverell. D: Robert Leversuche and Alice h.w. and John Perkyn alias Perkynson and Elizabeth h.w. Concerning 2 mess., 40a. land, 20a. pasture and 10a. meadow in Thurlaston and Elvaston. The defendants acknowledged these to be the right of Henry who, with the other plaintiffs, had them of their gift. They remised and quitclaimed of themselves and the heirs of Alice and Elizabeth to the plaintiffs and the heirs of Henry. The plaintiffs gave £30. (46)

1228. Westminster. The morrow of the Purification 1527. P: Anthony Fitzherbert, kt, one of the justices of pleas, John Fitzherbert, esq. Thomas Fitzherbert, doctor of decretals, Richard Coton and William Marten, clerk. D: William Myners. Concerning 40a. land, 20a. meadow and 40a. pasture in Hollyngton and Langford. William Myners acknowledged these to be the right of Anthony who, with the other plaintiffs, had them of his gift. He remised and quitclaimed of, and warranted for, himself and his heirs to the plaintiffs and the heirs of Anthony. The plaintiffs gave £30. (47)

1229. Westminster. The morrow of the Purification 1527. P: Geoffrey, Bishop of Coventre and Lichfield and John Rotheram, gent. D: Catherine Blythe, widow. Concerning 2 mess., 100a. land, 40a. meadow, 100a. pasture, 10a. woodland and 20a. gorse and heath in Dronfeld. Catherine acknowledged these to be the right of the bishop who, with John, had them of her gift. She remised and quitclaimed of, and warranted for, herself and her heirs to John, the bishop and his heirs. The bishop and John then granted and rendered the tenements to Catherine to hold for her life of the chief lord etc. Successive remainders to William Blythe, her son, and the heirs of his body and to the right heirs of Catherine. (48)

1230. Westminster. Quindene of Hilary 1527. P: Nicholas Holborn. D: Humphrey Shepard and Margaret h.w. Concerning 1 mess., 1 garden and 1a. land in Derby and Lutchurch. Nicholas had these of the gift of Humphrey and Margaret who remised and quitclaimed of, and warranted for, themselves and the heirs of Margaret to Nicholas and his heirs. Nicholas gave £30. (49)

1231. Westminster. Michaelmas one month 1527. P: Thomas Kynnersley, esq. John Kynnersley, John Fitzherbert, clerk, Thomas Clerke, chaplain, and Thomas Burneham. D: Robert Markeham, gent., and Ellen h.w. Concerning 2 mess., 37a. land, 4a. meadow and 16¼a. pasture in Saperton, Saperton Lees, Howne and Hatton. Robert and Ellen acknowledged these to be the right of Thomas Clerke who, with the other plaintiffs, had them of their gift. They remised and quitclaimed of, and warranted for, themselves and the heirs of Ellen to the plaintiffs and the heirs of Thomas Clerke. The plaintiffs gave £30. (50)

1232. Westminster. Quindene of Easter 1528. P: Richard Sewdell, clerk, John Walton, clerk, and Robert White, clerk. D: Anthony Walton. Concerning 1 mess., 100a. land, 20a. meadow, 100a. pasture and 20a. woodland in Barleborowe and Publey. Anthony acknowledged these to be the right of Richard who, with John and Robert, had them of his gift. He remised and quitclaimed of, and warranted for, himself and his heirs to the plaintiffs and the heirs of Richard. The plaintiffs gave £80. (51)

1233. Westminster. Easter one month 1528. P: Anthony Fitzherbert, one of the justices of common pleas, John Porte, kt, one of the justices of the King's Bench, German Pole, esq. Robert Barley, esq. Robert Lowe, Denis Lowe and William Mourten. D: Richard Paynell and Isabel h.w. Concerning 2 mess., 300a. land, 80a. meadow, 200a. pasture, 100a. woodland and 20a. heath in Denby, Fenton, Sturston and Bradley. Richard and Isabel acknowledged these to be the right of Anthony who, with the other plaintiffs, had them of their gift. They remised and quitclaimed of themselves and warranted for themselves and the heirs of Isabel to the plaintiffs and the heirs of Anthony. The plaintiffs gave 200 marks of silver. (52)

1234. Westminster. Octave of Martinmas 1528. P: John Porte, kt, one of the justices of the King's Bench, Thomas Cokayn, kt, German Pole, George

Fynderne, esq. John Porte, junior, Henry Aynesworthe and John Collumbell. D: Thomas Querneby and Elizabeth h.w. and Humphrey Querneby. Concerning 4 tofts, 4 gardens and 4a. land in Derby and Chaddesden. The defendants acknowledged these to be the right of John Porte, kt, who, with the other plaintiffs, had them of their gift. They remised and quitclaimed of, and warranted for, themselves and the heirs of Elizabeth to the plaintiffs and the heirs of John Porte, kt. The plaintiffs gave £40. (53)

1235. Westminster. Michaelmas three weeks 1528. P: Godfrey Foliambe, kt, Ralph Shawe, clerk, Denis Baxter, clerk, Oliver Shawe, clerk, and Roger Bieston, clerk. D: John Bakewell, clerk. Concerning 3 mess., 200a. land, 100a. meadow, 200a. pasture, 40a. woodland and 10s 9d rent in Brymmyngton, Whyttyngton and Tapton next Chestrefeld. John acknowledged these to be the right of Godfrey who, with the other plaintiffs, had them of his gift. He remised and quitclaimed of, and warranted for, himself and his heirs to the plaintiffs and the heirs of Godfrey. The plaintiffs gave 100 marks of silver. (54)

CP 25/2/6/30

1236. Westminster. Quindene of Easter 1528. Octave of Trinity 1529. P: George Savage, clerk, John Savage, esq. James Fuliambe, esq. and William Whithall, gent. D: John Leeke and Margaret h.w. Concerning a moiety of 3 mess., 64a. land, 12a. meadow, 20a. pasture and 40a. moorland in Thornhyll in the parish of Hope. John and Margaret acknowledged these to be the right of George and they remised and quitclaimed of, and warranted for, themselves and the heirs of Margaret to the plaintiffs and the heirs of George. The plaintiffs gave £40. (1)

1237. Westminster. The morrow of Martinmas 1529. P: William Blyth, gent., John Blyth, clerk, and Robert Alen, clerk. D: Nicholas Hewet and Joan h.w. Concerning 6 mess., 20a. land, 20a. meadow, 40a. pasture and 20a. woodland in Beighton and Mosburghe. Nicholas and Joan acknowledged these to be the right of William who, with John and Robert, had them of their gift. They remised and quitclaimed of, and warranted for, themselves and the heirs of Joan to the plaintiffs and the heirs of William. The plaintiffs gave 100 marks of silver. (2)

1238. Westminster. Quindene of Michaelmas 1529. P: Thomas Babyngton, Richard Sacheverell, Henry Sacheverell, George Fynderne, Ralph Longford, Thomas Fitzherbert, esq. William Basset, junior, esq. and Henry Cotton, gent. D: Henry Sacheverell, kt, and Isabel h.w. Concerning the manor of Hopwell and 24 mess., 800a. land, 400a. meadow, 500a.

pasture, 60a. woodland, 100a. gorse and heath and 34s 2d rent in Spondon, Chaddysdon, Elvaston, Thurlaston, Kylborne, Derby, Hopwell, Darley, Wynstore, Bolton, Asshelehey, Wyndley and Morley. Henry and Isabel acknowledged these to be the right of Thomas Fitzherbert who, with the other plaintiffs, had them of their gift. They remised and quitclaimed of, and warranted for, themselves and the heirs of Isabel to the plaintiffs and the heirs of Thomas Fitzherbert. The plaintiffs gave 800 marks of silver. (3)

1239. Westminster. Octave of Martinmas 1529. P: John Lane and Roger Newton. D: Henry Frannces, gent., and Agnes h.w. Concerning 4 mess., 4 tofts, 133a. land, 100a. meadow, 60a. pasture and 60a. gorse and heath in Stonystanton. Henry and Agnes acknowledged these to be the right of John and they remised and quitclaimed of, and warranted for, themselves and the heirs of Henry to John, Roger and the heirs of John. John and Roger gave 100 marks of silver. (4)

1240. Westminster. The morrow of Ascension 1530. Octave of Trinity 1530. P: Matthew Knyveton, esq. Thomas Rolston, esq. John Knyveton of Sturston, gent., and Robert More, clerk. D: John Knyveton of Underwode, gent. Concerning 5 mess., 5 gardens, 20a. land, 4a. meadow and 10a. pasture in Asshebourne, Offcote and Underwode. John Knyveton of Underwode acknowledged these to be the right of Matthew who, with the other plaintiffs, had them of his gift. He remised and quitclaimed of, and warranted for, himself and his heirs to the plaintiffs and the heirs of Matthew. The plaintiffs gave £50. (5)

1241. Westminster. Octave of Trinity 1530. P: Richard Anston, Richard Wilson, John Payne and Henry Knyght. D: John Dudley, kt, and Joan h.w. Concerning the manors of Okeburke otherwise called Okebroke, Chaddesden and Stanton otherwise called Staunton and 12 mess., 8 cottages, 300a. land, 60a. meadow, 200a. pasture, 140a. woodland and 6s rent in Okeburke otherwise called Okebroke, Chaddesden and Stanton. John and Joan acknowledged these to be the right of Richard Aston [*sic*] and they remised and quitclaimed of themselves and the heirs of Joan to the plaintiffs and the heirs of Richard Anston. They also warranted against John, abbot of the monastery of St Peter, Westminster, and his successors. The plaintiffs gave £320. (6)

1242. Westminster. The morrow of Martinmas 1530. P: Anthony Babyngton, esq. Walter Gryffyth, kt, William Chettewen, Humphrey Ferrers, esq. Richard Sudell, clerk, Robert Seyton and Adam Eyre. D: William Cundy and Alice h.w. Concerning 2 mess., 2a. land, ½a. meadow and 18a. pasture in Lytchurche and Derby. William and Alice acknowledged these to be the right of Anthony who, with the other plaintiffs, had them of their gift. They remised and quitclaimed of, and

117

warranted for, themselves and the heirs of Alice to the plaintiffs and the heirs of Anthony. The plaintiffs gave 80 marks of silver. (7)

1243. Westminster. The morrow of the Purification 1531. P: George Wodroffe. D: Elizabeth Vernon, widow, and Thomas Vernon. Concerning the manors of Hokelow Magna and Hope and 40 mess., 12 cottages, 1 water mill, 600a. land, 200a. meadow, 120a. pasture, 200a. heath and marsh and 20s rent in Hokelow Magna, Hope, Bradwall, Castleton and Folow. George had these of the gift of Elizabeth and Thomas who remised and quitclaimed of themselves and the heirs of Elizabeth to George and his heirs. They also warranted for themselves and the heirs of Thomas. George gave 400 marks of silver. (8)

1244. Westminster. Quindene of Trinity 1531. P: William Murell, Ralph Caldwall, Robert Curson and John Fyssher. D: John Hether, senior. Concerning 1 mess. and 1 garden in the parish of St Peter, Derby. John Hether acknowledged the messuage and garden to be the right of William who, with the other plaintiffs, had them of his gift. He remised and quitclaimed of, and warranted for, himself and his heirs to the plaintiffs and the heirs of William. The plaintiffs gave 80 marks of silver. (9)

1245. Westminster. Octave of Midsummer 1531. P: George, earl of Shrewsbury, Philip Draycotte, esq. Richard Maynwarying, esq. and John Basset, esq. D: Margaret, countess of Salisbury. Concerning the manor of Chesterfeld and 4 mess., 1 water mill, 1000a. land, 10a. meadow, 1000a. pasture, 200a. woodland, 1000a. gorse and heath and £20 rent in Chesterfeld together with the hundred of Skarysdale and the advowson of the hospice or free chapel of St Leonard at Chesterfeld. The countess acknowledged these to be the right of the earl and she remised and quitclaimed of, and warranted for, herself and her heirs to the plaintiffs and the heirs of the earl. The plaintiffs gave £440. (10)

1246. Westminster. Michaelmas three weeks 1531. P: Anthony Fitzherbert, kt, one of the justices of pleas. D: Philip Draycott, esq. and Elizabeth h.w. Concerning the manor of Norbury and 20 mess., 10 tofts, 4 mills, 600a. land, 300a. meadow, 500a. pasture, 100a. woodland, 200a. moorland and 2s rent in Norbury, Rossyngton, Snelston and Cubley and also the advowson of the church of Norbury. Philip and Elizabeth remised and quitclaimed of themselves and their heirs to Anthony and the male heirs of his body to hold of the chief lord etc forever. Successive remainders to Henry Fitzherbert and the male heirs of his body and to Humphrey Fitzherbert and the male heirs of his body. Reversion to Philip and Elizabeth and the heirs of Elizabeth. Philip and Elizabeth warranted for themselves and the heirs of Elizabeth against John, the abbot of the monastery of St Peter, Westminster and his successors. Anthony gave £1000. (11)

1247. Westminster. Michaelmas three weeks 1531. P: Nicholas Purefey and Nicholas Styrley. D: Ralph Blagden and Margaret h.w. Concerning 7 mess., 140a. land, 20a. meadow and 100a. pasture in Codnore and Loscowe and two thirds of half of 5 mess., 300a. land, 100a. meadow, 200a. pasture, 100a. woodland and 1 water mill in Ryddynges. Ralph and Margaret acknowledged these to be the right of Nicholas Purefey who, with Nicholas Styrley, had them of their gift. They remised and quitclaimed of, and warranted for, themselves and the heirs of Margaret to Nicholas Styrley and Nicholas Purefey and his heirs. The plaintiffs gave £120. (12)

1248. Westminster. Quindene of Easter 1531. P: John Seliard and William Lambkyn. D: Nicholas Frechewell, gent. Concerning 9 mess., 200a. land, 100a. meadow, 200a. pasture, 100a. woodland and 100a gorse and heath in Staley. Nicholas acknowledged these to be the right of John who, with William had them of his gift. He remised and quitclaimed of, and warranted for, himself and his heirs to John, William and John's heirs. John and William gave 200 marks of silver. (13)

1249. Westminster. Easter one month 1532. P: Otwell Bowdon. D: Humphrey Bothe and Margaret h.w. Concerning a fourth part of 2 mess., 120a. land, 8a. meadow, 20a. pasture, 8a. woodland and 40a. marsh and heath in Kynder. Otwell had these of the gift of Humphrey and Margaret who remised and quitclaimed of themselves and their heirs to Otwell and his heirs. They also warranted for themselves and the heirs of Margaret. Otwell gave £30. (14)

1250. Westminster. Quindene of Trinity 1532. P: Henry Sacheverell, kt, Richard Sacheverell, kt, Lodowick Bagot, kt, Ralph Longforth, kt, Thomas Curson, Robert Cawarden and Robert Lyteson. D: Thomas Boteler, esq. Anthony Greysley, gent., Thomas Colwiche, gent., Christopher Colwiche, gent., Robert Camden, gent., John Sawnder, Richard Wakefeld, Thomas Saunder, Ralph Webb and Hugh Yerdeley. Concerning the manor of Castell Greysley, 10 mess., 1000a. land, 100a. meadow, 100a. pasture, 100a. woodland and 60s rent in Castel Greysley, Lynton, Donasthorp, Okethorp and Shele. The defendants acknowledged these to be the right of Robert Leteson and they remised and quitclaimed of, and warranted for, themselves and the heirs of Anthony Greysley to the plaintiffs and the heirs of Robert Leteson. The plaintiffs gave £300. (15)

1251. Westminster. Quindene of Trinity 1532. P: George, earl of Shrewsbury, George, earl of Huntyngdon, Richard Sacheverell, kt, John Salter, Walter Wrottesley and Humphrey Symond. D: Thomas Boteler, esq. Anthony Greysley, gent., Thomas Colwiche, gent., Christopher Colwiche, gent., Robert Camden, gent., John Sawnder, Richard Wakefeld, Thomas Saunder, Ralph Webb and Hugh Yerdeley. Concerning the manors of

Draklowe and Caldwall and 4 mess., 100a. land, 500a. meadow, 1000a. pasture, 60a. woodland, 1000a. gorse and heath and 20s rent in Draklowe, Caldwall, Stapynhyll and Walton. The defendants acknowledged these to be the right of Humphrey Symond and the remised and quitclaimed of, and warranted for, themselves and the heirs of Anthony Greysley to the plaintiffs and the heirs of Humphrey. The plaintiffs gave £1200. (16)

1252. Westminster. Easter one month 1533. P: William Hastingys, esq. Henry Sacheverell, kt, John Vernon, esq. Arthur Eyre, esq. William Home and William Hatfeld, clerk. D: Henry Bekewell. Concerning 8a. land in Ulgarthorp. Henry Bekewell acknowledged the land to be the right of William Hastingys who, with the other plaintiffs, had it of his gift. He remised and quitclaimed of, and warranted for, himself and his heirs to the plaintiffs and the heirs of William Hastingys. The plaintiffs gave £20. (17)

1253. Westminster. Quindene of Easter 1533. P: Richard Bradshawe. D: Nicholas Archer and Ann h.w. Concerning 5 mess., 60a. land, 12a. meadow and 6a. pasture in Darbe, Osmaston and Normanton. Richard had these of the gift of Nicholas and Ann who remised and quitclaimed of, and warranted for, themselves and the heirs of Ann to Richard and his heirs. Richard gave 200 marks of silver. (18)

1254. Westminster. Octave of Martinmas 1533. P: Thomas Watterton, Thomas Reasby, Lionel Reasby and Alexander Swyft. D: Robert Swyft, junior, and Ellen h.w. daughter and heiress of Nicholas Wykersley, esq. Concerning 2 mess., 100a. land, 20a. pasture, 20a. meadow and 100a. woodland in Haversege. Robert and Ellen acknowledged these to be the right of Thomas Watterton who, with the other plaintiffs, had them of their gift. They remised and quitclaimed of themselves and the heirs of Ellen to the plaintiffs and the heirs of Thomas Watterton. They also warranted for themselves and the heirs of Robert. The plaintiffs gave £100. (19)

1255. Westminster. The morrow of Martinmas 1533. P: John Smyth, esq. William Whorwood, gent., Alan Hord, gent., John Aleyn, junior, citizen and mercer of London, Christopher Aleyn, citizen and mercer of London, and Edward Brysley. D: John Busshey, esq. Concerning the manor of Parkehall in Northwynfeld and 40 mess., 6 cottages, 1000a. land, 300a. meadow, 300a. pasture, 100a. woodland and 40s rent in Northwynfeld, Pylseley, Brampton, Assher and Morton. John Busshey acknowledged these to be the right of John Smyth who, with the other plaintiffs, had them of his gift. He remised and quitclaimed of, and warranted for, himself and his heirs to the plaintiffs and the heirs of John Smyth. The plaintiffs gave £340. (20)

1256. Westminster. Easter three weeks 1534. P: Thomas Heyther, Richard Birde, Thomas Newton, gent., John Heyther, junior, and William Bulkeley.

D: William Blount, kt, lord Mountyoye. Concerning 1 mess. and 1 garden in Derby. William Blount acknowledged the messuage and garden to be the right of Thomas Heyther who, with the other plaintiffs, had them of his gift. He remised and quitclaimed of, and warranted for, himself and his heirs to the plaintiffs and the heirs of Thomas Heyther. The plaintiffs gave £40. (21)

1257. Westminster. Quindene of Midsummer 1529. Octave of Trinity 1534. P: Nicholas Garleke, son of John and Margaret Garleke. D: John Garleke and Margaret h.w. Concerning 8 mess., 120a. land, and 120a. meadow in Whitffeld, Whitffeld Hurst and Herdykwall. Nicholas had these of the gift of John and Margaret who remised and quitclaimed of themselves and the heirs of Margaret to Nicholas and his heirs. They warranted for themselves and the heirs of Margaret against themselves and her heirs. Nicholas then granted and rendered to John an annuity of 13s 4d derived from 5 mess., 100a. land and 100a. meadow in Whitffeld and Whitffeld Hurst, part of the tenements aforesaid, to hold and receive in two equal portions at the feasts of the Annunciation of the Blessed Virgin Mary and St Michael, archangel, for the life of John. *[Distraint clause as in **869**.]* Nicholas also granted and rendered to Margaret 3 mess., 20a. land and 20a. meadow in Herdykwall (except 3a. land then in the tenure of Robert Torre) and also a third part of the aforesaid 5 mess., 100a. land and 100a. meadow in Whitffeld and Whitffeld Hurst to hold to herself of the chief lord etc for her life without impeachment of waste. After the deaths of John and Margaret the tenements are to remain to Nicholas and his heirs. Should Nicholas die without heirs of his body then the tenements in Whitffeld and Whitffeld Hurst to remain to the right heirs of John whilst those in Herdykwall are to remain to the right heirs of Margaret. (22)

1258. Westminster. Michaelmas three weeks 1534. P: John Selyok, John Parker, John Swalowe and Robert Croke, clerk. D: Stephen Constable, esq. and Elizabeth h.w. Concerning the manor of Barleburgh and 16 mess., 4 cottages, 300a. land, 60a. meadow, 160a. pasture, 500a. woodland and 66s rent in Barleburgh, Whytwell, Romley and Clowne. Stephen and Elizabeth acknowledged these to be the right of John Selyok who, with the other plaintiffs, had them of their gift. They remised and quitclaimed of, and warranted for, themselves and the heirs of Elizabeth to the plaintiffs and the heirs of John Selyok. The plaintiffs gave £320. (23)

1259. Westminster. The morrow of All Souls 1534. P: Richard Rogers, citizen and clothworker of London, Edward Altham of London, clothworker, Jacob Metcalf of London, clothworker, John Rogers, Robert Sonnyng of London, draper, and Thomas Rogers. D: Richard Hewet and Alice h.w., John Hewet and Nicholas Hewet. Concerning 1 mess., 1 toft, 42a. land, 3a. meadow, and 19a. pasture in Kynwalmarsh. The defendants acknowledged these to be the right of Richard Rogers who, with the other plaintiffs, had them of their gift. They remised and quitclaimed of, and warranted for, themselves and the heirs of Alice to the plaintiffs and the heirs of Richard Rogers. The plaintiffs gave 100 marks of silver. (24)

1260. Westminster. Michaelmas one month 1534. P: William Lytton and Thomas Lytton. D: Henry Stanlowe and Alice h.w. Concerning 1 mess., 1 garden and 11a. land in Monyasshe. Henry and Alice acknowledged these to be the right of William who, with Thomas, had them of their gift. They remised and quitclaimed of, and warranted for, themselves and the heirs of Alice to William, Thomas and William's heirs. William and Thomas gave £20. (25)

1261. Westminster. Easter one month 1535. P: John Porte, kt, Thomas Cokayn, kt, John Dawne, kt, German Pole, esq. Thomas Bromeley, esq. William Newporte, gent., and George Charneley, gent. D: John Dyngley, esq. Concerning 3 mess., 6 cottages, 6 tofts, 200a. land, 40a. meadow, 100a. pasture, 3a. woodland and 500a. gorse and heath together with an eighth part of the manor of Repton alias Repyngdon and a water mill and £9 rent in Repton and Mylton. John Dyngley acknowledged these to be the right of John Porte who, with the other plaintiffs, had them of his gift. He remised and quitclaimed of, and warranted for, himself and his heirs to the plaintiffs and the heirs of John Porte. The plaintiffs gave 200 marks of silver. (26)

1262. Westminster. The morrow of Martinmas 1535. P: William Croftys. D: Margaret Wydoson, widow, and Thomas Hether and Mudwina, h.w. Concerning 1 mess., 2 bov. land, and 6a. meadow in Longayton. William had these of the gift of the defendants who remised and quitclaimed of themselves and their heirs and warranted for themselves and the heirs of Mudwina to William and his heirs. William gave £40. (27)

1263. Westminster. The morrow of Martinmas 1535. P: Emund Goldsmyth, clerk, John Bawman and Robert Nesse. D: Ralph Wilson and Agnes h.w. Concerning 1 mess. and 9a. 3 roods land in Castelton. Ralph and Agnes acknowledged these to be the right of Robert who, with Edmund and John, had them of their gift. They remised and quitclaimed of, and warranted for, themselves and the heirs of Agnes to the plaintiffs and the heirs of Robert. The plaintiffs gave £10. (28)

1264. Westminster. Octave of Martinmas 1535. P: John Wolseley, esq. William Dethik, George Appulby, George Abney, Richard Asshe and John Purfrey. D: Richard Temple, senior, and Elizabeth h.w. and Richard Temple, junior. Concerning 2 mess., 80a. land, 15a. meadow, 40a. pasture and 2a. woodland and common pasture for 60 head of cattle and 200 sheep, in Willesley. The defendants acknowledged these to be the right of George

Abney who, with the other plaintiffs, had them of their gift. They remised and quitclaimed of, and warranted for, themselves and their heirs to the plaintiffs and the heirs of George Abney. The plaintiffs gave £40. (29)

1265. Westminster. Quindene of Martinmas 1535. Octave of Hilary 1536. P: Godfrey Foliambe, kt, Ralph Shawe, clerk, Oliver Shawe, clerk, Roger Beeston, clerk, and William Walton, chaplain. D: John Alsopp and George Alsopp and Joan h.w. Concerning a third part of 2 mess., 100a. land, 40a. meadow, 100a. pasture, 200a. woodland and 200a. gorse and heath in Calall. The defendants acknowledged the third part to be the right of Godfrey who, with the other plaintiffs, had it of their gift. They remised and quitclaimed of, and warranted for, themselves and the heirs of Joan to the plaintiffs and the heirs of Godfrey. The plaintiffs gave 50 marks of silver. (30)

1266. Westminster. Octave of Martinmas 1535. Octave of Hilary 1536. P: Thomas Cokayn, kt, John Dawne, kt, Thomas Gyfford, esq. Hugh Bretherton and Robert Lynese. D: Richard Shawe and Elizabeth h.w. Concerning 2 mess., 2 cottages, 40a. land, 4a. meadow and 6a. pasture in Chadesden, Derby, and Parva Chester. Richard and Elizabeth acknowledged these to be the right of John who, with the other plaintiffs, had them of their gift. They remised and quitclaimed of, and warranted for, themselves and the heirs of Elizabeth to the plaintiffs and the heirs of John. The plaintiffs gave £40. (31)

1267. Westminster. Quindene of Hilary 1536. P: Richard Wygley and John Wygley. D: William Tagge. Concerning 1 mess. and 13a. land in Matlok. William acknowledged the messuage and land to be the right of Richard and he granted that this messuage and land which Alice Tagge, mother of William, held for her life of the inheritance of William and which, on her death, ought to revert to William and his heirs should remain instead to Richard, John and Richard's heirs to hold of the chief lord etc forever. William and his heirs warranted. Richard and John gave £20. (32)

1268. Westminster. Octave of Trinity 1536. P: William Hollys, kt. D: Ralph Longforthe, kt. Concerning the manors of Barlebrugh alias Barlyborough, Kynwelmarsshe alias Kynnolmarsshe and Hathersedge together with 80 mess., 1000a. land, 800a. meadow, 1000a. pasture, 300a. gorse and heath and £10 rent in Barlebrugh, Kynwelmarsshe and Hathersedge. William had these of the gift of Ralph who remised and quitclaimed of, and warranted for, himself and his heirs to William and his heirs. William gave £1200. (33)

1269. Westminster. Octave of Midsummer 1536. P: Thomas Sutton, gent. D: Robert Dyxson and Ann h.w. daughter and heiress of Fulk Sutton.

Concerning 2 mess., 3 tofts, 60a. land, 6a. meadow and 100a. pasture in Overhaddon. Thomas had these of the gift of Robert and Ann who remised and quitclaimed of, and warranted for, themselves and the heirs of Ann to Thomas and his heirs. Thomas then granted and rendered to Robert and Ann an annuity of 6s 8d derived from the tenements to hold and receive during Ann's life, one half at each of the feasts of St Michael, archangel, and the Annunciation of the Blessed Virgin Mary. *[Distraint clause as in 869.]* (34)

1270. Westminster. The morrow of All Souls 1536. P: George Pyerponnt, esq. D: William Clerke. Concerning 2 mess., 60a. land, 20a. meadow, 30a. pasture, 4a. woodland and pasture for 300 head of cattle in 400a. land in Tharlesthorpe within the demesne lands of Whitewell and Barleburgh. George had these of the gift of William who remised and quitclaimed of, and warranted for, himself and his heirs to George and his heirs. George gave £80. (35)

1271. Westminster. The morrow of the Purification 1537. P: Thomas Hethcote. D: Ralph Shawe. Concerning 2 mess., 2 gardens, 20a. land, 6a. meadow, 10a. pasture and 3a. woodland in Chesterfield, Barley and Brampton. Thomas had these of the gift of Ralph who remised and quitclaimed of, and warranted for, himself and his heirs to Thomas and his heirs. Thomas gave £30. (36)

1272. Westminster. Quindene of Easter. 1536. P: George Abney, esq. and Cuthbert Taillour. D: John Brown, esq. and Alice h.w. Concerning 1 mess., 40a. land, 10a. meadow, 10a. pasture, 12a. woodland, 2s rent and common pasture for 80 sheep and 20 head of cattle in Okethorp and Wyllesley. John and Alice acknowledged these to be the right of Cuthbert who, with George, had them of their gift. They remised and quitclaimed of themselves and their heirs and warranted for themselves and the heirs of Alice to George, Cuthbert and Cuthbert's heirs. George and Cuthbert gave £30. (37)

1273. Westminster. The morrow of Midsummer 1537. P: John Pynder and Elizabeth Alen. D: John Alen. Concerning 3 mess., 100a. land, 20a. meadow, 60a. pasture, 20a. woodland and common pasture for 60 head of cattle in Hymmesworth and Norton. John Alen acknowledged these to be the right of John Pynder who, with Elizabeth, had them of his gift. He remised and quitclaimed of, and warranted for, himself and his heirs to John, Elizabeth and John's heirs. John and Elizabeth gave 100 marks of silver. (38)

1274. Westminster. Quindene of Trinity 1537. P: Godfrey Foliambe, kt. D: Ralph Rolston and Margery h.w. Concerning a moiety of a fourth part of the manor of Northegehall, 12 mess., 6 cottages, 1 dovecot, 1000a. land,

200a. meadow, 1000a. pasture, 400a. woodland, 1000a. gorse and heath and 10s rent in Northegehall, Assheover and Wyngerworth. Godfrey had these of the gift of Ralph and Margery who remised and quitclaimed of, and warranted for, themselves and the heirs of Margery to Godfrey and his heirs. Godfrey gave £30. (39)

1275. Westminster. Quindene of Trinity 1537. P: John Porte, kt, one of the justices of pleas in the King's Bench, and Henry Aynesworthe. D: Elizabeth Quarneby, widow, and Humphrey Quarneby, her son and heir. Concerning 1 mess., 1 garden, 6a. land, 8a. meadow and 10a. *[unstated, probably pasture]* in Derby and Aston. Elizabeth and Humphrey acknowledged these to be the right of John who, with Henry, had them of their gift. They remised and quitclaimed of themselves and their heirs and warranted for themselves and the heirs of Elizabeth to John, Henry and John's heirs. John and Henry gave 40 marks of silver. (40)

1276. Westminster. Quindene of Trinity 1537. P: Godfrey Foliambe, kt. D: Joan Strelley. Concerning a fourth part of the manor of Northegehall and 12 mess., 6 cottages, 1 dovecot, 1000a. land, 200a. meadow, 1000a. pasture, 400a. woodland, 1000a. gorse and heath and 10s rent in Northegehall, Asshover and Wyngerworth. Godfrey had these of the gift of Joan who remised and quitclaimed of, and warranted for, herself and her heirs to Godfrey and his heirs. Godfrey gave 100 marks of silver. (41)

1277. Westminster. The morrow of All Souls 1537. P: William Hollys, kt. D: Ralph Longford, kt, and Dorothy h.w. Concerning the manors of Barlebroughe, Kynwalmarshe alias Kynwaldmarshe and Hetherseche and 50 mess., 60 tofts, 2000a. land, 1000a. meadow, 1000a. pasture, 300a. woodland, 4000a. gorse and heath and £20 rent in Barlebroughe, Kynwalmarshe and Hetherseche together with the advowson of the church of Barlebroughe. William had these of the gift of Ralph and Dorothy who remised and quitclaimed of themselves and their heirs to William and his heirs. They warranted for themselves and the heirs of Dorothy against William, abbot of the monastery of St Peter, Westminster, and his successors. William Hollys gave £700. (42)

1278. Westminster. The morrow of All Souls 1537. P: William Hollys, gent. D: Ralph Longford, kt, and Dorothy h.w. Concerning the manors of Blakewell, Whitewell and Crossewell and 40 mess., 30 tofts, 500a. land, 300a. meadow, 200a. pasture, 20a. woodland, 500a. gorse and heath and 40s rent in Blakewell, Whitewell and Crossewell together with the advowson of the church of Whitewell. William had these of the gift of Ralph and Dorothy who remised and quitclaimed of themelves and their heirs to William and his heirs. They warranted for themselves and the heirs of

Dorothy against William, abbot of the monastery of St Peter, Westminster, and his successors. William Hollys gave £160. (43)

1279. Westminster. Quindene of Michaelmas 1537. P: Nicholas Garlyke. D: Frances Hopkynson. Concerning 3 mess., 40a. land and 12a. pasture in Hardykewall and Tyddyswall. Nicholas had these of the gift of Francis who remised and quitclaimed of himself and his heirs to Nicholas and his heirs. He also warranted for himself and his heirs against the abbot of the monastery of Burton and his successors. Nicholas gave £40. (44)

1280. Westminster. Octave of Michaelmas 1537. P: Godfrey Foliambe, kt. D: Nicholas Purefey, gent. Concerning a moiety of a fourth part of the manor of Northege Halle and 12 mess., 6 cottages, 1 dovecot, 1000a. land, 200a. meadow, 1000a. pasture, 400a. woodland, 1000a. gorse and heath and 10s rent in Northege Halle, Assheover and Wyngerworth. Godfrey had these of the gift of Nicholas who remised and quitclaimed of himself and his heirs to Godfrey and his heirs. He also warranted for himself and his heirs against William, abbot of the monastery of St Peter, Westminster, and his successors. Godfrey gave £60. (45)

1281. Westminster. The morrow of the Purification 1538. Quindene of Easter 1538. P: Richard Wyggley. D: William Tagg. Concerning a moiety of 1 mess. and 24a. land in Matlocke. Richard had the messuage and land of the gift of William who remised and quitclaimed of, and warranted for, himself and his heirs to Richard and his heirs. Richard gave 50 marks of silver. (46)

1282. Westminster. Easter one month 1538. P: John Caryngton, esq. D: William Fitzherbert, gent., and Ann h.w. Concerning 2 mess., 100a. land, 10a. meadow, 20a. pasture, 10a. woodland, 100a. gorse and heath and 300a. peat in Buggesworth. John had these of the gift of William and Ann who remised and quitclaimed of themselves and the heirs of Ann to John and his heirs and warranted for themselves and the heirs of Ann against Ann and her heirs. John gave 100 marks of silver. (47)

1283. Westminster. Easter three weeks 1538. P: Francis Brian, kt, John Porte, kt, George Greisley, kt, and Henry Sudeley, esq. D: John Yong, prior of the monastery of St Trinity, Repyngdon. Concerning 1 mess., 200a. land, 40a. meadow, 50a. pasture and 5a. woodland in Donesthorpe. The prior acknowledged these to be the right of Henry who, with the other plaintiffs, had them of his gift. He remised and quitclaimed of, and warranted for, himself and his successors to the plaintiffs and the heirs of Henry. The plaintiffs gave 100 marks of silver. (48)

1284. Westminster. Easter one month 1538. P: Michael Purefey and Humphrey Coton, gent. D: Francis Cokeyn, esq. and Dorothy h.w.

Concerning the manors of Harthill and Balyden and 50 mess., 1000a. land, 600a. meadow, 1000a. pasture, 500a. woodland, 1000a. gorse and heath and 40s rent in Harthill, Balyden and Parwyche. Francis and Dorothy acknowledged these to be the right of Michael who, with Humphrey, had them of their gift. They remised and quitclaimed of, and warranted for, themselves and the heirs of Francis to Michael, Humphrey and the heirs of Michael. Michael and Humphrey then granted and rendered the manors and tenements to Francis and Dorothy to hold of the chief lord etc without impeachment of waste, for their lives and the longer of the two. Successive remainders to Thomas, Francis and William Cokayn, heir apparent, second son and third son, respectively, of Francis and Dorothy, and the male heirs of their bodies; to Thomas Cokayn, brother of Francis the father, and to Edward Cokayn, and the male heirs of their bodies; and to the right heirs of Francis the father. (49)

1285. Westminster. Easter one month 1538. Octave of Trinity 1538. P: Robert Arnefeld. D: Thomas Arnefeld. Concerning 1 mess., 20a. land, 10a. meadow and 5a. woodland in Bowden in the parish of Glossop. Robert had these of the gift of Thomas who remised and quitclaimed of, and warranted for, himself and his heirs to Robert and his heirs. Robert gave £40. (50)

CP 25/2/6/31

1286. Westminster. Quindene of Easter 1539. P: Richard Fenton. D: James Bullok and Mary h.w. Concerning 1 mess., 20a. land, 6a. meadow, 20a. pasture, 20a. woodland and 20a. gorse and heath in Lyghtwood and Norton. Richard had these of the gift of James and Mary who remised and quitclaimed of, and warranted for, themselves and the heirs of Mary to Richard and his heirs. Richard gave £40. (1)

1287. Westminster. The morrow of Martinmas 1539. P: John Castlyn, gent., and William Castlyn, merchant. D: John Pynder and Elizabeth h.w. Concerning 3 mess., 100a. land, 20a. meadow, 40a. pasture and 20a. woodland in Hymysworth. John Pynder and Elizabeth acknowledged these to be the right of John Castlyn who, with William, had them of their gift. They remised and quitclaimed of, and warranted for, themselves and the heirs of John Pynder to John, William and the heirs of John. John and William gave £40. (2)

1288. Westminster. Quindene of Easter 1539. P: Adam Pursglove. D: Henry Bradschawe, gent., and Joan h.w. Concerning 1 mess., 1 cottage, 20a. land, 4a. meadow and 6a. pasture in Tyddeswall and Wheston. Adam had these of the gift of Henry and Joan who remised and quitclaimed of themselves and their heirs to Adam and his heirs. Henry also warranted for himself and his heirs. Adam gave £60. (3)

127

1289. Westminster. Quindene of Easter 1539. P: Edward Bonne. D: Thomas Braylysford and Robert Watkynson. Concerning 10a. land and 20a. pasture in Tupton. Edward had the land and pasture of the gift of Thomas and Robert who remised and quitclaimed of themselves and their heirs and warranted for themselves and the heirs of Thomas, to Edward and his heirs. Edward gave 20 marks of silver. (4)

1290. Westminster. Quindene of Easter 1539. P: Godfrey Foliambe, kt. Elizabeth Cade, widow. Concerning a fourth part of the manor of Northegehall and 1 dovecot, 10 mess., 12 cottages, 300a. land, 100a. meadow, 300a. pasture, 300a. woodland, 500a. gorse and heath and 10s rent in Northegehall, Asheover and Wyngerworth. Godfrey had these of the gift of Elizabeth who remised and quitclaimed of, and warranted for, herself and her heirs to Godfrey and his heirs. Godfrey gave £40. (5)

1291. Westminster. The morrow of All Souls 1540. P: Roland Babyngton, esq. and Joan h.w. D: William Randall and Elizabeth h.w., sister and heiress of Richard Peyt, son and heir of a certain Thomas and Agnes Peyt. Concerning 2 gardens and 20a. land in Derby and Normanton. William and Elizabeth acknowledged these to be the right of Roland who, with Joan, had them of their gift. They remised and quitclaimed of, and warranted for, themselves and the heirs of Elizabeth to Roland, Joan and Roland's heirs. Roland and Joan gave £20. (6)

1292. Westminster. The morrow of Martinmas 1540. P: Nicholas Garlyke. D: John Eyre. Cconcerning 1 mess., 1 garden, 14a. land and 2a. pasture in Hardykwall in the parish of Tyddyswall. Nicholas had these of the gift of John who remised and quitclaimed of, and warranted for, himself and his heirs to Nicholas and his heirs. Nicholas gave £40. (7)

1293. Westminster. The morrow of All Souls 1540. P: Godfrey Foliambe, kt. D: John Staveley, esq. Concerning a fourth part of the manor of Northege Hall and 10 mess., 12 cottages, 1 dovecot, 300a. land, 100a. meadow, 300a. pasture, 300a. woodland, 500a. gorse and heath and 10s rent in Northege Hall, Assheover and Wyngreworth. Godfrey had these of the gift of John who remised and quitclaimed of, and warranted for, himself and his heirs to Godfrey and his heirs. Godfrey gave £46. (8)

1294. Westminster. The morrow of All Souls 1540. P: Godfrey Foliambe, kt. D: Richard Gardhowse and Agnes h.w. Concerning a moiety of 1 mess. in Chesterfeld. Godfrey had the moiety of the gift of Richard and Agnes who remised and quitclaimed of, and warranted for, themselves and the heirs of Agnes to Godfrey and his heirs. Godfrey gave 20 marks of silver. (9)

1295. Westminster. Quindene of Easter 1541. P: Hugh Holyngshed. D: Christopher Savage, esq. Concerning 1 mess., 3 tofts, 2 gardens, 100a. land,

10a. meadow, 20a. pasture and 6a. woodland in Bodon. Hugh had these of the gift of Christopher who remised and quitclaimed of himself and his heirs to Hugh and his heirs. He also warranted for himself and his heirs against himself and his heirs. Hugh gave £40. (10)

1296. Westminster. Quindene of Easter 1541. P: Robert Revell. D: Thomas Revell. Concerning the manor of Ogeston and 6 mess., 1 cottage, 300a. land, 40a. meadow, 100a. pasture, 100a. woodland and 200a. moorland in Ogeston, Holmegate, Wheytcroft and Brakyntwhat. Robert had these of the gift of Thomas who remised and quitclaimed of, and warranted for, himself and his heirs to Robert and his heirs. Robert gave £300. (11)

1297. Westminster. The morrow of the Purification 1541. Quindene of Easter 1541. P: John Porte, esq. D: John Beamonnt, esq. and Elizabeth h.w. Concerning 2 mess., 7 cottages, 8a. land, 20a. meadow, 20a. pasture and 20a. woodland in Melborne and Kyngys Newton. John Porte had these of the gift of John and Elizabeth who remised and quitclaimed of, and warranted for, themselves and the heirs of Elizabeth to John Porte and his heirs. John Porte gave £100. (12)

1298. Westminster. Easter three weeks 1541. P: Richard Blakwall. D: Robert Stubbyng. Concerning 1 mess., 20a. land, 6a. meadow, 10a. pasture and 10a. woodland in Northeyge in the parish of Assheover. Richard had these of the gift of Robert who remised and quitclaimed of, and warranted for, himself and his heirs to Richard and his heirs. Richard gave £40. (13)

1299. Westminster. The morrow of Trinity 1541. P: Nicholas Burwey, John Beamond and William Hurt. D: Henry Bothe. Concerning 5 mess., 10 tofts, 1 mill, 1 dovecot, 2 gardens, 50a. land, 100a. meadow, 200a. pasture, 20a. woodland, 100a. gorse and heath and £10 rent in Erlaston. Henry acknowledged these to be the right of William who, with the other plaintiffs, had them of his gift. He remised and quitclaimed of, and warranted for, himself and his heirs to the plaintiffs and the heirs of William. The plaintiffs gave £100. (14)

1300. Westminster. Octave of Michaelmas 1541. P: William Hollys, kt. D: Brian Rye, gent. Concerning 3 mess., 1 water mill, 4 gardens, 60a. land, 20a. meadow and 40a. pasture in Wytwell. William had these of the gift of Brian who remised and quitclaimed of, and warranted for, himself and his heirs to William and his heirs. William gave £60. (15)

1301. Westminster. The morrow of All Souls 1541. P: Nicholas Garlike. D: John Eyr. Concerning 1 mess., 14a. meadow and 14a. pasture in Sterndall and Chelmerdon in the parish of Bakewell. Nicholas had these of the gift of John who remised and quitclaimed of, and warranted for, himself and his heirs to Nicholas and his heirs. Nicholas gave £40. (16)

1302. Westminster. Octave of Michaelmas 1541. P: Thomas Calton, citizen and goldsmith of London, and Margaret h.w. D: Humphrey Quarmebye and Elizabeth h.w. Concerning 4 mess., 1 cottage, 130a. land, 30a. meadow, 40a. pasture, 10a. woodland and 4s rent in Chaddesden and Derby. Humphrey and Elizabeth acknowledged these to be the right of Thomas who, with Margaret, had them of their gift. They remised and quitclaimed of themselves and the heirs of Humphrey to Thomas, Margaret and the heirs of their bodies to hold of the chief lord etc forever. Remainder to the right heirs of Thomas. Humphrey warranted for himself and his heirs. Thomas and Margaret gave £124. (17)

1303. Westminster. Octave of Hilary 1542. P: Thomas Pope, kt. D: Henry Bothe, esq. Nicholas Burwey, John Beamond, junior, and William Hurt. Concerning the manors of Arleston, Egyngton and Hylton and 50 mess., 10 tofts, 1 mill, 1 dovecot, 2 gardens, 1000a. land, 200a. meadow, 60a. pasture, 100a. woodland, 100a. gorse and heath and £10 rent in Arleston, Egyngton, Hylton, Barrowe, Normanton, Syndefen alias Synfen, Steynson and Asshe together with the advowson of the church of Egyngton. Thomas had these of the gift of the defendants who remised and quitclaimed of themselves and their heirs to Thomas and his heirs. They warranted for themselves and the heirs of Henry against Henry and his heirs. Thomas gave £800. (18)

1304. Westminster. Easter one month 1542. P: John Holland son of Guy Holland. D: The same Guy Holland. Concerning 5 mess., 1 cottage, 6 gardens, 200a. land, 20a. meadow, 100a. pasture and 60a. woodland in le Lees alias Leighous. John had these of the gift of Guy who remised and quitclaimed of, and warranted for, himself and his heirs to John and his heirs. John gave 140 marks of silver. (19)

1305. Westminster. Octave of Hilary 1542. Quindene of Easter 1542. P: Thomas Pope, kt. D: John Beamont, senior. Concerning the manor of Arleston and 20 mess., 10 tofts, 1 mill, 1 dovecot, 2 gardens, 200a. land, 100a. meadow, 500a. pasture, 40a. woodland, 100a. gorse and heath and £10 rent in Arleston. Thomas had these of the gift of John who remised and quitclaimed of himself and his heirs to Thomas and his heirs. John also warranted for himself and his heirs against himself and his heirs. Thomas gave £800. (20)

1306. Westminster. Easter three weeks 1542. The morrow of Trinity 1542. P: The King. *[Henry VIII]* D: Richard Wakerley, esq. and Joan h.w., Thomas Pope, kt, and Edward Beamonnt, gent. Concerning 3 mess., 3 tofts, 1 garden, 1 orchard, 100a. land, 50a. meadow, 200a. pasture and 10s rent in Arleston. The king had these of the gift of the defendants who remised and quitclaimed of themselves and their heirs to the king and his heirs. They warranted for themselves and the heirs of Thomas against Thomas, bishop of Westminster and his successors. The king gave £60. (21)

1307. Westminster. The morrow of Trinity 1542. P: William Toples. D: Roger Warde and Elizabeth h.w. and William Ley. Concerning 2 mess., 1 cottage and 30a. land in Perwyche. William had these of the gift of the defendants who remised and quitclaimed of, and warranted for, themselves and the heirs of Elizabeth to William and his heirs. William gave 40 marks of silver. (22)

1308. Westminster. Quindene of Easter 1542. The morrow of Trinity 1542. P: Richard Randoll, gent.. D: William Crewker. Concerning 22a. pasture and 5a. swamp *(terra aqua cooperta)* in Twyford and Stenston. Richard had these of the gift of William who remised and quitclaimed of, and warranted for, himself and his heirs to Richard and his heirs. Richard then granted and rendered the pasture and swamp to William to hold for one month. Remainder to William Monnslowe for 49 years. Remainder to the right heirs of William Crewker to hold of the chief lord etc forever. (23)

1309. Westminster. Quindene of Easter 1542. The morrow of Trinity 1542. P: William Hollys, kt. D: James Strylley, gent., and Rachel h.w. Concerning the manor of Brough and 7 mess., 7 gardens, 7 orchards, 500a. land, 50a. meadow, 100a. pasture, 40a. woodland, 40a. gorse and heath and 20s rent in Brough, Hope, Castelton and Thorneley. William had these of the gift of James and Rachel who remised and quitclaimed of, and warranted for, themselves and the heirs of James to William and his heirs. William gave £170. (24)

1310. Westminster. Octave of Michaelmas 1542. P: Thomas Calton, citizen and goldsmith of London. D: Henry Anngers and Margaret h.w. Concerning 2 cottages, 14a. land, 3a. meadow and 6a. pasture in Chaddysden. Thomas had these of the gift of Henry and Margaret who remised and quitclaimed of, and warranted for, themselves and the heirs of Henry to Thomas and his heirs. Thomas gave 40 marks of silver. (25)

1311. Westminster. Octave of Michaelmas 1542. P: John Porte, esq. D: Vincent Mundy and Gillian h.w. Concerning 1 mess., 200a. land, 40a. meadow, 200a. pasture, 40a. gorse and heath and 2 separate fisheries in the waters of the Trent in Potlox and Fyndern. John had these of the gift of Vincent and Gillian who remised and quitclaimed of themselves and the heirs of Vincent to John and his heirs and warranted for themselves and the heirs of Vincent against Vincent and his heirs. John gave £200. (26)

1312. Westminster. Quindene of Trinity 1541. Octave of Hilary 1542. P: Nicholas Powtrell, gent. D: Roland Babyngton, esq. Concerning 19 mess., 200a. land, 90a. meadow, 110a. pasture, 40a. woodland, 40a. marsh, 100a.

gorse and heath and common pasture for 100 head of cattle in Derby, Somercotys, Swanwyk, Codnor and Beurepper. Nicholas had these of the gift of Roland who remised and quitclaimed of, and warranted for, himself and his heirs to Nicholas and his heirs. Nicholas then granted and rendered the tenements to Roland to hold of the chief lord etc for life, without impeachment of waste. Successive remainders to Joan, Roland's wife, for her life; to Augustus, to Michael and to Henry, sons of Roland, and the male heirs of their bodies; to Humphrey and to William, brothers of Roland, and the male heirs of their bodies; and to the right heirs of Thomas Babyngton, Roland's father. (27)

1313. Westminster. Easter three weeks 1542. P: Stephen Coldewell, gent., and Edward Rydge, gent. D: German Pole, esq. and Joan h.w. Concerning 2 mess., 300a. land, 40a. meadow, 100a. pasture, 140a. woodland and 35s rent in Wakebridge and Matlocke. German and Joan acknowledged these to be the right of Stephen who, with Edward, had them of their gift. They remised and quitclaimed of themselves and their heirs to Stephen, Edward and Stephen's heirs. Stephen and Edward then granted and rendered the tenements to German and Joan to hold to themselves and the heirs of their bodies of the chief lord etc forever. Remainder to the right heirs of German. (28)

1314. Westminster. Quindene of Easter 1542. P: Stephen Holme. D: John Shalcrosse. Concerning 3 mess., 100a. land, 12a. meadow, 20a. pasture and 10a. woodland in Wormhill and Bowdon. Stephen had these of the gift of John who remised and quitclaimed of himself and his heirs to Stephen and his heirs. Stephen then granted and rendered the tenements to John to hold of the chief lord etc for life. Successive remainders to Nicholas Wright and Ellen h.w. and the heirs of their bodies and to the right heirs of John. (29)

1315. Westminster. The morrow of Ascension 1543. The morrow of Trinity 1543. P: Thomas Pope, kt, and Elizabeth h.w. D: George Coton, kt, and Mary h.w. Concerning 2 mess., 2 cottages, 2 gardens, 200a. land, 100a. meadow, 600a. pasture and 400a. moorland in Alsopp in le Dale, Tysyngton, Asheborne, Perwyche and Thorp. George and Mary acknowledged these to be the right of Thomas who, with Elizabeth, had them of their gift. They remised and quitclaimed of themselves and the heirs of George to Thomas, Elizabeth and the heirs of Thomas. They warranted for themselves and the heirs of George against George and his heirs. Thomas and Elizabeth gave £120. (30)

1316. Westminster. The morrow of Trinity 1543. P: John Wylkynson and Edward Drable. D: John Selyok. Concerning 2 mess., 40a. land, 10a. meadow, 40a. pasture, 6a. woodland and 200a. gorse and heath in Dranfeld, Lymhall and Jurdenthorp. John Selyok acknowledged these to be the right of John Wylkynson who, with Edward, had them of his gift. He remised and quitclaimed of, and warranted for, himself and his heirs to John, Edward and John's heirs. John and Edward then granted and rendered the tenements to John Selyok to hold of the chief lord etc for life without impeachment of waste. Remainder to George Selyok, son and heir apparent of John Selyok, and his heirs. (31)

1317. Westminster. Easter one month 1543. The morrow of Trinity 1543. P: William Bradsha. D: Richard Bradsha. Concerning 2 mess., 2 gardens, 100a. land, 40a. meadow, 20a. pasture and 20a. woodland in Bawden. William had these of the gift of Richard who remised and quitclaimed of, and warranted for, himself and his heirs to William and his heirs. William gave 200 marks of silver. (32)

1318. St Albans. The morrow of Martinmas 1543. P: William Blythman. D: Brian Rye, gent., son and heir apparent of Ranulf Rye. Concerning the manor of Whytewell and 100a. land, 100a. meadow, 200a. pasture, 200a. woodland and 400a. common in Whytewell together with the advowson of the church of Whytewell. Brian acknowledged these to be the right of William and he granted that the manor, tenements and advowson which Ranulf held for life of the inheritance of Brian and which ought to revert to Brian and his heirs on the death of Ranulf should remain instead to William and his heirs to hold of the chief lord etc forever. Brian and his heirs warranted. William gave £160. (33)

1319. Westminster. Octave of Hilary 1544. P: William Smyth. D: Thurstan Townend, clerk. Concerning 1 mess., 1 cottage, 1 garden, 17a. land, and 10a. meadow in Bradwall, Hope and Aston. William had these of the gift of Thurstan who remised and quitclaimed of, and warranted for, himself and his heirs to William and his heirs. William gave £40. (34)

1320. Westminster. The morrow of the Purification 1544. P: Francis Leek, esq. D: Ralph Denman, gent. Concerning 1 mess., 200a. land, 40a. meadow, 100a. pasture, 20a. woodland and 100a. gorse and heath in Sutton in le Dale. Francis had these of the gift of Ralph who remised and quitclaimed of, and warranted for, himself and his heirs to Francis and his heirs. Francis gave 50 marks of silver. (35)

1321. Westminster. Octave of Hilary 1544. P: John Morley, junior. D: John Flynte. Concerning 1 mess., 1 cottage, 1 garden, 1 orchard, 40a. land, 10a. meadow, 100a. pasture, 6a. woodland and 100a. gorse and heath in Alfreton. John Morley had these of the gift of John Flynte who remised and quitclaimed of, and warranted for, himself and his heirs to John Morley and his heirs. John Morley gave £30. (36)

1322. Westminster. Easter one month 1544. P: The King *[Henry VIII]*. D: John Howe and Alice h.w. Concerning 1 mess., 1 cottage, 2 gardens,

100a. land, 20a. meadow, 100a. pasture, 20a. woodland and 100a. gorse and heath together with tithes of corn and hay in Dale, Stanley and Spondon. The king had these of the gift of John and Alice who remised and quitclaimed of, and warranted for, themselves and the heirs of Alice to the king and his heirs. The king gave £40. (37)

1323. Westminster. Quindene of Easter 1544. P: Peter Frechevill, esq. D: Ankertil Carter, chaplain, son and heir of John Carter. Concerning 1 mess., 20a. land, 12a. meadow, 6a. pasture, 2a. woodland and 20a. gorse and heath in Staveley and Staveley Netherthorpe. Peter had these of the gift of Ankertil who remised and quitclaimed of, and warranted for, himself and his heirs to Peter and his heirs. Peter gave 40 marks of silver. (38)

1324. Westminster. Quindene of Easter 1544. P: James Browster and John Potte. D: Stephen Crosseley and Edward Crosseley. Concerning 2 mess., 100a. land, 60a. meadow, 40a. pasture, 10a. woodland and 100a. gorse and heath in Chapell, Coumbes and Bowdon. Stephen and Edward acknowledged these to be the right of James who, with John, had them of their gift. They remised and quitclaimed of, and warranted for, themselves and the heirs of Edward to James, John and the heirs of James. James and John gave £80. (39)

1325. Westminster. Quindene of Easter 1544. P: John Porte, esq. D: Francis Pole and Catherine h.w. Concerning the manor of Dale and 20 mess., 30 tofts, 1 water mill, 1 dovecot, 1 barn, 1 garden, 4000a. land, 3000a. meadow, 6000a. pasture, 3000a. woodland, 8000a. gorse and heath and 40s rent in Dale, Spondon, Ilkeston, Elbaston and Sandyacre together with the advowson of the church of Dale. John had these of the gift of Francis and Catherine who remised and quitclaimed of themselves and their heirs to John and his heirs. They also warranted for themselves and the heirs of Catherine against Francis and his heirs. John gave £340. (40)

1326. Westminster. Octave of the Purification 1544. Quindene of Easter 1544. P: Richard Harper. D: Thomas Fyndern, esq. and John Porte, esq. Concerning (i) the manor of Swartelyngcote and 20 mess., 15 tofts, 300a. land, 250a. meadow, 300a. pasture, 15a. woodland, 500a. gorse and heath and 20s rent in Swartelyngcote, Chylcote, Tyknall, Eggynton, Staynston and Twyford; and (ii) the manor of Wyllyngton and 20 mess., 15 tofts 300a. land, 150a. *[sic; recte 250a.]* meadow, 300a. pasture, 15a. woodland, 500a. gorse and heath and 20s rent in Wyllyngton. Richard had all these tenements of the gift of Thomas and John who remised and quitclaimed of, and warranted for, themselves and the heirs of Thomas to Richard and his heirs. Richard then granted and rendered the tenements to John to hold for a term of 7 years from the feast of the Annunciation of the Blessed Virgin Mary next following. The tenements in (i) are to remain to Thomas and his heirs to hold of the chief lord etc forever while the tenements in (ii) are to remain first to Joan Fyndern, sister of Thomas, to hold of the chief lord etc for her life and then to Thomas and his heirs. (41)

1327. Westminster. Quindene of Trinity 1544. P: Thomas Rolleston. D: Thomas Babyngton, esq. Concerning 2 mess., 2 cottages, 40a. land, 20a. meadow, 40a. pasture, 20a. woodland and 20a. gorse and heath in Alfreton, Lutchurche, Normanton and Derby. Thomas Rolleston had these of the gift of Thomas Babyngton who remised and quitclaimed of, and warranted for, himself and his heirs to Thomas Rolleston and his heirs. Thomas Rolleston gave £40. (42)

1328. Westminster. The morrow of Trinity 1544. P: William Bradshawe of Derbie, butcher. D: Robert Smyth of Derbie, glover, and Alice h.w. Concerning 1 mess., 1 cottage and 2 gardens in Derby. William had these of the gift of Robert and Alice who remised and quitclaimed of, and warranted for, themselves and the heirs of Robert to William and his heirs. William gave £40. (43)

1329. Westminster. The morrow of Ascension 1544. The morrow of Trinity 1544. P: Stephen Cobbe. D: John Selick, gent. Concerning the manor of Drawnfeild and 10 mess., 8 tofts, 1 water mill, 4 gardens, 1000a. land, 500a. meadow, 800a. pasture, 300a. woodland, 2000a. gorse and heath and £12 rent in Drawnfeild, Stubley, Colley, Woodhowse, Chestefeild, Tapton, Caloe, Hasylland, Boythorpe and Newbold. Stephen had these of the gift of John who remised and quitclaimed of, and warranted for, himself and his heirs to Stephen and his heirs. Stephen gave £300. (44)

1330. Westminster. Octave of Michaelmas 1544. P: Thomas Sheldon. D: William Meyre and Henry Meyre. Concerning 2 mess., 30a. land, 20a. pasture and 4a. woodland in Monyashe, Flagge and Baukewell. Thomas had these of the gift of William and Henry who remised and quitclaimed of themselves and their heirs and warranted for themselves and the heirs of William, to Thomas and his heirs. Thomas gave £40. (45)

1331. Westminster. The morrow of Martinmas 1544. P: Francis Leke, esq. D: Ralph Asche. Concerning 3 mess., 3 barns, 3 gardens, 100a. land, 30a. meadow, 100a. pasture, 20a. woodland, 100a. gorse and heath and 2s rent in Sutton in le Dale. Francis had these of the gift of Ralph who remised and quitclaimed of, and warranted for, himself and his heirs to Francis and his heirs. Francis gave 80 marks of silver. (46)

1332. Westminster. Michaelmas three weeks 1544. P: Nicholas Powtrell and Adam Eyre, gent. D: John Chaworth, kt, and Thomas Babyngton, esq. Concerning a moiety of the manors of Wyllyamthorp and Hynkersell alias Inkersell and 20 mess., 500a. land, 500a. meadow, 500a. pasture, 300a.

woodland, 200a. gorse and heath and 100s rent in Wyllyamthorp, Hynkersell, Heth, Staley and Normanton. John and Thomas acknowledged these to be the right of Nicholas who, with Adam, had them of their gift. They remised and quitclaimed of themselves and the heirs of Thomas to Nicholas, Adam and the heirs of Nicholas, and warranted for themselves and the heirs of Thomas against Thomas and his heirs. Nicholas and Adam then granted and rendered the moiety to John to hold of the chief lord etc for life without impeachment of waste. Successive remainders to the male heirs of the body of Thomas Chaworth, kt, ancestor of Thomas Chaworth, esq. ancestor of John, to Thomas Babyngton and the heirs of his body, to the heirs of the body of Elizabeth Babyngton, Thomas's wife, and to the right heirs of Elizabeth. (47)

1333. Westminster. Michaelmas one month 1544. P: Thomas Eyre. D: Hugh Eyre. Concerning three-fourths of 2 mess., 50a. land, 10a. meadow, 4a. pasture and 3a. woodland in Shatton and Brounsyde. Thomas had the three parts of the gift of Hugh and remised and quitclaimed of, and warranted for, himself and his heirs to Thomas and his heirs. Thomas gave £30. (48)

1334. Westminster. Quindene of Trinity 1544. Octave of Michaelmas 1544. P: Henry Maly[v]erer, clerk, and Robert Rydyall, clerk. *[This is the only reference to Robert: in the remainder of the fine the name is given as Richard.]* D: William Malyverer, kt, and Joan h.w. Edmund Malyverer, Thomas Malyverer, Ralph Bygod, junior, and Ralph Bygod, senior. Concerning the manor of Egkyngton and 60 mess., 2 dovecots, 800a. land, 100a. meadow, 700a. pasture, 400a. woodland, 500a. gorse and heath and £24 rent in Egkyngton, Stalay, Burlandys, Reynaldshawe, Estmosborugh, Westmosborugh, Plumley, Regwey alias Regwell, Barleburgh, Kynwal-demaysshe, Beyghton, Wallarthorpe, Dogmanton, Troway, Spynkhyll and Bramley together with the advowson of the church of Egkyngton. The defendants acknowledged these to be the right of Henry who, with Richard, had them of their gift. They remised and quitclaimed of themselves and the heirs of Joan to Henry, Richard and Henry's heirs. William, Joan and Ralph Bygod, senior, warranted for themselves and the heirs of Joan. Henry and Richard then granted and rendered the advowson to William and Joan to hold for life. Successive remainders to Edmund and the male heirs of his body, to Thomas and the male heirs of his body and to Ralph Bygod, senior, and his heirs, each to hold of the chief lord etc forever. Henry and Richard also granted and rendered an annuity of 20 marks issuing from the manor and tenements to Edmund and the male heirs of his body to receive in equal portions at the feasts of the Annunciation of the Blessed Virgin Mary and St Michael, archangel, the first payment to be on the first feast immediately after the deaths of William and Joan. *[Distraint clause as in*

869.] Remainder to Thomas. They granted a similar annuity of 20 marks to Ralph Bygod, junior, and the male heirs of his body to receive as for Edmund. *[Remainder not stated.]* Finally, Henry and Richard granted and rendered the manor, tenements and rent to William and Joan to hold of the chief lord etc without impeachment of waste for their lives and the longer of the two. Remainder to Ralph Bygod, senior, and his heirs. (49)

1335. Westminster. Octave of the Purification 1545. Quindene of Easter 1545. P: Edward Aston, kt. D: William Paget, kt, and Ann h.w. Concerning the manor of Edleston alias Edilueston and 20 mess., 6 tofts, 300a. land, 200a. meadow, 300a. pasture, 250a. woodland, 100a. heath, 100a. marsh and 40s rent in Edleston together with the advowson of, and the free disposal and right to the prebend of the benefice of rector of, the church of Edleston. Edward had these of the gift of William and Ann who remised and quitclaimed of themselves and the heirs of William to Edward and his heirs and warranted for themselves and the heirs of William against themselves and the heirs of William. Edward gave £229. (50)

1336. Westminster. Quindene of Easter 1545. P: Robert Swane. D: John Swane. Concerning 1 mess. and 7½a. land in Fayrefeld. Robert had the messuage and the land of the gift of John who remised and quitclaimed of, and warranted for, himself and his heirs to Robert and his heirs. Robert gave £40. (51)

1337. Westminster. Quindene of Easter 1545. P: Peter Frechevyle, kt, and Elizabeth h.w. D: Francis Leeke, kt. Concerning the manor of Staveley and 10 mess., 10 tofts, 10 cottages, 2 dovecots, 10 gardens, 200a. land, 40a. meadow, 100a. pasture, 10a. woodland, 100a. moorland, 100a. marsh and 40s rent in Staveley, Staveley Netherthorpe and Barle together with a moiety of the benefice of rector of the church of Staveley. Francis acknowledged these to be the right of Peter who, with Elizabeth, had them of his gift. He remised and quitclaimed of, and warranted for, himself and his heirs to Peter, Elizabeth and Peter's heirs. Peter and Elizabeth gave £200. (52)

1338. Westminster. Quindene of Easter 1545. P: William Fletcher. D: Edmund Walker and Elizabeth h.w. Concerning 1 mess., 2 gardens and a horse mill in Derby. William had these of the gift of Edmund and Elizabeth who remised and quitclaimed of, and warranted for, themselves and the heirs of Edmund to William and his heirs. William gave 40 marks of silver. (53)

1339. Westminster. Quindene of Easter 1545. P: Thurstan Townend, clerk, and John Savage. D: John Thornell. Concerning 1 mess., 1 garden, 40a. land, 10a. meadow and 10a. pasture in Thornell and Hoope. John Thornell acknowledged these to be the right of Thurstan who, with John

Savage, had them of his gift. He remised and quitclaimed of, and warranted for, himself and his heirs to Thurstan, John and John's heirs. Thurstan and John then granted and rendered the tenements to John Thornell to hold for life of the chief lord etc. Successive remainders to Nicholas Thornell, son of John, to John Thornell, junior, and to Thomas Thornell, and the heirs of their bodies; and to the right heirs of John Thornell, the father. (54)

1340. Westminster. Quindene of Easter 1545. P: Mark Draycot, gent. D: William Glosopp and Margery h.w. Concerning a moiety of 2 mess., 40a. land, 20a. meadow, 10a. pasture and 10a. woodland in Burnaston, Codnor, Holbroke and Kylburn. Mark had the moiety of the gift of William and Margery who remised and quitclaimed of, and warranted for, themselves and the heirs of Margery to Mark and his heirs. Mark gave 40 marks of silver. (55)

1341. Westminster. Quindene of Easter 1545. P: Richard Warde. D: Edmund Walker and Elizabeth h.w. Concerning 1 mess. in Derby. Richard had the messuage of the gift of Edmund and Elizabeth who remised and quitclaimed of, and warranted for, themselves and the heirs of Edmund to Richard and his heirs. Richard gave 40 marks of silver. (56)

1342. Westminster. Octave of Michaelmas 1545. P: John Beamonnt, esq. George Stephynson. Concerning a moiety of 2 mess., 10a. land, and 40a. pasture in Workysworth. John had the moiety of the gift of George who remised and quitclaimed of, and warranted for, himself and his heirs to John and his heirs. John gave £30. (57)

1343. Westminster. Octave of Michaelmas 1545. P: William Symondys, gent., Henry Warde, clerk, and Edward Colbarne. D: George Greysley, kt, and Catherine h.w. Concerning the manors of Draklowe and Caldwall and 4 mess., 1 water mill, 100a. land, 500a. meadow, 1000a. pasture, 60a. woodland, 1000a. gorse and heath and 20s rent in Draklowe, Caldwall, Stapynhyll and Walton together with the right of fishing in the waters of the Trent. George and Catherine acknowledged these to be the right of Henry who, with William and Edward, had them of their gift. They remised and quitclaimed of themselves and the heirs of George to the plaintiffs and the heirs of Henry. They also warranted for themselves and the heirs of George against George and his heirs. (58)

1344. Westminster. Octave of Martinmas 1545. P: James Leveson, esq. D: Thomas Pope, kt, and Elizabeth h.w. Concerning 2 mess., 2 cottages, 2 gardens, 200a. land, 100a. meadow, 600a. pasture and 400a. moorland in Alsopp in le Dale, Tysyngton, Asheborne, Perwiche and Thorpe. James had these of the gift of Thomas and Elizabeth who remised and quitclaimed of themselves and the heirs of Thomas to James and his heirs. They warranted for themselves and the heirs of Thomas against Thomas and his heirs. James gave 200 marks of silver. (59)

1345. Westminster. Octave of Michaelmas 1545. P: Nicholas Garlycke. D: Francis Hopkynson and Mary h.w. Concerning 3 mess., 3 barns, 3 gardens, 20a. land, 20a. meadow and 4a. pasture in Tydeswall in Alto Pecco. Nicholas had these of the gift of Francis and Mary who remised and quitclaimed of themselves and their heirs and warranted for themselves and the heirs of Francis to Nicholas and his heirs. Nicholas gave 110 marks of silver. (60)

1346. Westminster. Quindene of Hilary 1546. P: William Paget, kt. D: Walter Horton, esq. Concerning the manor of Brysyngcote and 8 mess., 1 garden, 1 orchard, 200a. land, 100a. meadow, 500a. pasture, 100a. woodland and 4d rent in Brysyngcote and Bratby. William had these of the gift of Walter who remised and quitclaimed of, and warranted for, himself and his heirs to William and his heirs. William gave £200. (61)

1347. Westminster. Octave of Hilary 1546. P: John Rossyngton. D: John Yate. Concerning 2 mess., 2 barns, 2 gardens, 50a. land, 50a. meadow, 20a. pasture and 5a. woodland in Scropton and Foston. John Rossyngton had these of the gift of John Yate who remised and quitclaimed of, and warranted for, himself and his heirs to John Rossyngton and his heirs. John Rossyngton gave £40. (62)

1348. Westminster. Quindene of Easter 1546. P: James Ayssheton, gent. D: Richard Kynwolmershe, gent. Concerning 1 mess. and 1 smallholding *(croftum terre)* in Kynwolmershe. James had the messuage and smallholding of the gift of Richard who remised and quitclaimed of, and warranted for, himself and his heirs to James and his heirs. James gave £10. (63)

1349. Westminster. Quindene of Easter 1546. P: Clement Agard, esq. D: Ellen Markham, widow, and William Markham, gent., her son. Concerning 1 mess., 1 garden, 1 toft, 12a. land, and 2a. pasture in Foston. Clement had these of the gift of Ellen and William who remised and quitclaimed of, and warranted for, themselves and the heirs of Ellen to Clement and his heirs. Clement gave £20. (64)

1350. Westminster. Easter one month 1546. The morrow of Trinity 1546. P: William Lytton, gent. D: Robert Moseley and Lucy h.w. Concerning a fourth part of 3 mess., 3 barns, 3 gardens, 60a. land, 24a. meadow, and 8a. pasture in Tyddeswall and Lytton. Robert and Lucy acknowledged these to be the right of William and granted for themselves and the heirs of Lucy that this fourth part, which Ellen Redyman, widow, held for life of the inheritance of Lucy and which ought to revert to Lucy and her heirs on the death of Ellen, should remain instead to William and his heirs to hold of the chief lord etc forever. Robert and Lucy and Lucy's heirs warranted. William gave £40. (65)

1351. Westminster. Quindene of Easter 1546. The morrow of Trinity 1546. P: Thomas Babyngton, esq. D: Robert Glose and Agnes h.w., William Mylner and Alice h.w. and Joyce Redyman. Concerning 3 parts of 3 mess., 3 barns, 3 gardens, 60a. land, 24a. meadow and 8a. pasture in Tyddeswalle and Lytton. The defendants acknowledged these to be the right of Thomas and they granted for themselves and the heirs of Agnes, Alice and Joyce that the three parts which Ellen Rediman, widow, held for life of the inheritance of Agnes, Alice and Joyce and which ought to revert to them and their heirs on Ellen's death should remain instead to Thomas and his heirs to hold of the chief lord etc forever. The defendants warranted for themselves and the heirs of Agnes, Alice and Joyce to Thomas and his heirs. Thomas gave £80. (66)

1352. Westminster. The morrow of Trinity 1546. P: John Selyok, esq. D: Thomas Dynham, esq. Concerning a moiety of the manor of Norton and 15 mess., 3 cottages, 1000a. land, 300a. meadow, 800a. pasture, 700a. woodland, 200a. marsh and heath and £10 rent in Magna Norton, Parva Norton, Hymmysworth, Lees, Herdyng, Povey, Hasylbarowe, Lightwood, Cold Aston, Somerles and Jordynthorp. John had the moiety of the gift of Thomas who remised and quitclaimed of, and warranted for, himself and his heirs to John and his heirs. John gave £300. (67)

1353. Westminster. The morrow of Trinity 1546. P: Richard Crosse. D: Edmund Pylkyngton, esq. Concerning 1 mess., 35a. land, 4a. meadow and 70a. pasture in Sponedon. Richard had these of the gift of Edmund who remised and quitclaimed of, and warranted for, himself and his heirs to Richard and his heirs. Richard gave £40. (68)

1354. Westminster. Octave of Michaelmas 1546. P: John Beamont. D: Nicholas Hudson and Dorothy h.w. Concerning 2 mess., 20a. land, and 40a. pasture in Wyrkysworthe. John had these of the gift of Nicholas and Dorothy who remised and quitclaimed of, and warranted for, themselves and the heirs of Dorothy to John and his heirs. John gave £40. (69)

1355. Westminster. Octave of Michaelmas 1546. P: Thomas Babyngton, esq. D: Thomas Denham and George Denham. Concerning a moiety of the manor of Alfreton and 10 mess., 4 tofts, 200a. land, 100a. meadow, 120a. pasture and 40a. woodland in Alfreton, Swanwyke, Ryddynge and Somercott. Thomas Babyngton had these of the gift of Thomas and George who remised and quitclaimed of, and warranted for, themselves and the heirs of Thomas to Thomas Babyngton and his heirs. Thomas Babyngton gave £420. (70)

1356. Westminster. Octave of Michaelmas 1546. P: Henry Bucklowe. D: James Peerson and Ellen h.w. Concerning 1 mess. and 1 garden in Assheborne. Henry had the messuage and garden of the gift of James and Ellen who remised and quitclaimed of themselves and their heirs to Henry and his heirs. They also warranted for themselves and the heirs of Ellen against Ellen and her heirs. (71)

1357. Westminster. Octave of Michaelmas 1546. P: The king *[Henry VIII]*. D: John, viscount Lysle, knight of the most noble order of the Garter, the king's grand admiral, and the lady Joan, h.w. Concerning the manors of Spondon, Chaddesden, Boroughaysshe, Lokkowe and Over-lokkowe, the offices of rector of, and the churches of, Spondon and Chaddesden and 40 mess., 50 gardens, 1 water mill, 1000a. land, 200a. meadow, 600a. pasture, 200a. woodland, 1000a. gorse and heath and £20 rent in Spondon, Chaddesden, Boroughaysshe, Lokkowe and Overlokkowe together with the advowsons of Spondon and Chaddesden. The king had these of the gift of John and Joan who remised and quitclaimed of, and warranted for, themselves and the heirs of John to the king and his heirs. The king gave £700. (72)

1358. Westminster. Octave of Michaelmas 1546. P: William Nedham, gent., and William Alestre. D: William Garrett. Concerning 1 mess., 80a. land, 20a. meadow, 100a. pasture and 20a. woodland in Foosyde. William Garrett acknowledged these to be the right of William Nedham who, with William Alestre, had them of his gift. He remised and quitclaimed of, and warranted for, himself and his heirs to the plaintiffs and the heirs of William Nedham. The plaintiffs gave £80. (73)

1359. Westminster. Octave of Michaelmas 1546. P: Richard Johnson, otherwise called Richard Edmondson. D: John Pyckard and Alice h.w. Concerning 1 mess., 8a. land, and 8a. pasture in Newbold. Richard had these of the gift of John and Alice who remised and quitclaimed of, and warranted for, themselves and the heirs of Alice to Richard and his heirs. Richard gave £40. (74)

CHRONOLOGICAL TABLE OF JUSTICES

The following list gives the numbers of the first and last fines in this volume heard by each justice of the court of Common Pleas. A single number indicates that a justice appears only on that occasion; 'a' numbers denote the second of two hearings.

684	685	Friskeneye, Walter de	867	882	Knyvet, John
684	767	Bereford, William de	875	881	Delves, John
684	802	Bousser, John de	879	917	Fyncheden, William de
684	802	Herle, William de	879	932	Wichyngham, William de
684	802	Mutford, John de	908	911	Cavendissh, John de
686	850a	Stonore, John de	908	946	Kirketon, Roger de
697		Stanton, Hervey de	918	966	Bealknapp, Robert
698	802	Scrop, Henry le	920a	966	Fulthorp, Roger de
712	735	Travers, John	932a	943	Percehay, Henry de
712	861	Wylughby, Richard de	944	958	Asty (Hasty), Henry
717	756	Canterbrigg, John de	951	966	Burgh, William de
717	822	Inge, John	951	966	Holt, John
718	734	Scoreburgh, Robert de	967	1002	Cherlton, Robert de
718	734	Thorp, Robert de	967	1002	Sydenham, Richard
718	738	Malberthorp, Robert de	967	1002	Wadham, John
740	822	Aldeburgh, Richard de	967	1023	Rikhill (Rykhill), William
740	822	Shardelowe, John de	967	1041	Thirnyng, William
747a	845a	Shareshull, William de	989	1024	Markham, John
752a	765	Trevaignon (Trevaygnon),	997	1041	Hankeford, William
		John (de)	998a	1021a	Brenchesle, William
775a	822	Basset, William	1018	1074	Cokayn, John
775a	822	Scot, William	1022	1043	Colpepir, John
775a	858	Hillary, Roger	1025	1063a	Hill (Hull, Hulle), Robert
767		Bacoun, John	1042	1057a	Norton, Richard
767		Benstead, John de	1046	1053a	Lodyngton (Ludyngton),
767		Trikyngham, Lambert de			William
800		Parnyng, Robert	1046	1073a	Preston, John
800	821	Wodestok, James de	1054	1089	Babyngton, William
805		Heppescotes, Thomas de	1054	1089	Martyn, John
805	850a	Kelleshull, Richard de	1061a	1062	Hals, John
827a	863a	Stouford, John de	1061a	1090	Juyn, John
837	850a	Fencotes, Thomas de	1066	1099	Strangways, James
851	866	Grene, Henry	1075	1090	Cottesmore, John
853	863a	Seton, Thomas de	1075	1101	Paston, William
859	909	Thorp, Robert de, of Thorpe	1091	1108	Neuton, Richard
861a	880	Motelowe, Henry de	1091	1110a	Ayscogh, William
864	916	Moubray, John	1091	1110a	Fulthorp, Thomas
865	966	Skipwyth, William de	1099		Paston, Thomas

143

1100	1110a	Portyngton, John	1178	1202	Boteler (Botiller, Buteler), John
1102	1113	Ayssheton, Nicholas			
1108	1113	Ardern, Peter	1178	1204	Rede, Robert
1109	1112	Prysot, John	1182	1187	Grevyle, William
1109	1113	Danvers, Robert	1184	1191	Fairfax, William
1110	1117	Danby, Robert	1188	1213	Eliot (Eliott, Elyot), Richard
1111	1117	Moille, Walter	1192	1226	Pollard, Lewis
1111	1117	Nedeham, John	1203	1209	More, John
1113	1132	Chokke, Richard	1205	1209	Erneley (Ernele), John
1114	1128a	Littelton, Thomas	1210	1236	Broke, Richard
1115	1117	Yonge, Thomas	1210	1257	Brudenell, Robert
1118	1134	Neel, Richard	1214	1285	Fitzherbert, Anthony
1118	1157	Bryan, Thomas	1227	1276	Englefeld, Thomas
1130	1134	Catesby, John	1227	1359	Shelley, William
1130	1134	Starky, Humphrey	1243	1260	Norwiche (Norwyche), Robert
1133	1144	Touneshend, Roger			
1135	1138	Haugh, John	1261	1345	Baldwyn (Baldewyn), John
1137	1170	Danvers, William	1277	1341	Willughby, Thomas
1139	1177	Vavasour, John	1286	1312a	Jenney, Christopher
1144	1147	Fyneux, John	1313	1359	Browne (Broun), Humphrey
1148	1166	Wode, Thomas	1344	1359	Monntague (Monntagu), Edward
1162	1183	Fyssher, John			
1167	1177	Frowyk, Thomas	1346	1359	Hynde, John
1171	1181a	Kyngesmyll, John			

144

INDEX OF JUSTICES

This list gives the numbers of fines printed in this volume heard by each justice; 'a' numbers denote the second of two hearings.

146

INDEX OF PERSONS AND PLACES

Derbyshire place-names are arranged under civil parishes as given in K. Cameron, *The place-names of Derbyshire* (English Place-Name Society, XXVII-XXIX, 1959), but Ordnance Survey spellings are used where these differ from Cameron's. Pre-1974 county names are given for places outside the ancient county of Derbyshire, together with cross-references from county headings for all places outside present-day Derbyshire. Quotation marks indicate places which have not been definitely identified, whether within Derbyshire or not. A question mark preceding a figure means that it is uncertain whether or not the document in question does refer to the place concerned. Arabic numbers refer to documents, Roman to pages.

Allestry (Alastre, Alestre), Robert de, chap., 698
William, 1358
Alletson (Alotessone), Hugh, of Gresley, and Agnes h.w. and Robert their son, 710
Allorwas: see Alrewas
Allott (Alotte), John, 1084
Allport (Aldeport), Robert de, parson of Newton Regis, 849
Allsop (Alsop(p)), George, and John h.w., 1265
John, 1265
Thomas de, of Parwich, 780
William, of Ireton, 1101
Alotessone: see Alletson
Alotte: see Allott
Alport (Aldeport), in Youlgreave, q.v.
Alrewas (Allorwas), Staffs
Thomas Rider of, 928
Alred, Richard, esq., 1103
Alrewaslegh: see Alderwasley
Alsop(p): see Allsop; Alsop en le Dale
Alsop en le Dale (Alsop(e), Alsopp), 836, 1102, 1315, 1344
Alto Pecco: see High Peak
Altham, Edward, of London, clothworker, 1259
Alton, in Ashover, q.v.
Alvaston (Alwoston), 729
manor of, 687
see also Boulton
Alybon: see Albon
Ambaston, in Elvaston, q.v.
Amington (Amynton), Staffs
Nicholas de Caumnill of, 691
Andrew (Andreu, Andrewe), John, chap., 990, 1017, 1026, 1048, 1049
William, and Agnes h.w., 914
Angers (Anngers), Henry, and Margaret h.w., 1310
Annesley (Annesleye), John de, chiv. and Isabel h.w., 965; de, kt, 690
Annett (Anot), Maude widow of William, and Agnes her daughter, 973
Anston, Richard, 1241
Ansty, ?Warw
William del Hyll, alias William Parker, of, 985
Appleby (Appelby, Appulby), Edmund de, jun. and Agnes h.w., 841
George, 1264
Archer, Nicholas, and Ann h.w., 1253
Argent, Nicholas, and Maude h.w., 758
Arleston (Erlaston, Erleston), 1299, 1303, 1305, 1306
manor of, 1068, 1303, 1305
Armitage (Hermitage), Agnes del, 808

Arnfield (Arnefeld), Robert, 1285
Thomas, 1285
Arnold, John, gent., 1189
Arrowsmith (Arowesmyth), William, clerk, 998, 1015
Arundel, Eleanor d', daughter of Richard earl of, 839
Ash (Aisshe, Assh(e)), 1022, 1027, 1031, 1209, 1303
manor of, 953, 1022, 1209
Ash (Asche, Asshe(s)), George, 1223
John, 1223; del, 991
Ralph, 1331
Richard, 1264
Roger, clerk, 1223
Ashbourne (Asheborne, Asshborne, Asshburne, Asshebo(u)rne, Assheburn(e), xiv, 731, 735, 748, 773, 778, 803, 818, 819, 821, 822, 830, 1156, 1182, 1215, 1240, 1315, 1344, 1356
(Sir) John Co(c)kayn(e) of, viii, 803, 898, 958
Ashbourne (Asshborne, Asshebourne, Assheburn(e)), Henry de, clerk, 958, 961
John de, 752, 754; de, cit. and goldsmith of London, and Joan h.w., 936
Thomas de, 761
Ashby (Assheby), Ellis, 1213
John, 1147
William, esq. and Agnes h.w., 1173
Asheborne: see Ashbourne
Asheover: see Ashover
Ashford (Assheford), 844, 902
manor of, 859
Robert de Wardlowe of, 928
Ashleyhay (Asshelehey), 1238
Ashover (Asheover, Assheover, Assher, Asshover, Asshovre, Aysshover, Esshover, Esshovre), 1211, 1255, 1274, 1276, 1280, 1290, 1293
manor of, 775, 784, 1211
Alton in, 1211
Eddlestow (Edynstowe) in, 1211
Milltown (Mylnetown) in, 1211
Northedge (Northege, Northegehall, Northege Halle, Northeyge) in, 1211, 1274, 1276, 1280, 1290, 1293, 1298
manor of, 1274, 1276, 1280, 1290, 1293
Overton in, 1211
Ravensnest (Ravennest) in, 1211
Stubben Edge (Stubbyng) in, 1211
Robert del Grene of, 867
Robert de Wynfeld of, 775
Roger de Deynecourt, parson of, 731
Ashover (Asshover), William son of Hugh de, 988
Joan wife of, 988

148

Ashton (Assh(e)ton, Ayssheton), Benedict de, 1018
James, gent., 1348
John de, chap., 1075
Ashwell (Assewell), Robert de, parson of Mackworth, 904
Asshborne, Asshburne, Asshebo(u)rne, Assheburn(e): see Ashbourne
Asshe: see Ash
Assheby: see Ashby
Assheford: see Ashford
Asshelehey: see Ashleyhay
Assheover: see Ashover
Assher: see Ashover
Asshes: see Ash
Assheton: see Ashton
Asshover, Asshovre: see Ashover
Asshton: see Ashton
Aston, 1319
Aston, Edward, kt., 1335
Geoffrey son of Jordan de, 708
Alice wife of, 708
Henry de, and Maude h.w., 705
John de, 940, 958, 961; de, chap., 948; de, and Maude h.w., 842
William de, 787
Aston on Trent (Aston, Aston upon Trent next Weston), 979, 1000, 1188, 1275
Astwith (Estwayte), in Ault Hucknall, q.v.
Atherstone on Stour (Adreston), Warw
William de Herdewyk, parson of, 878
Audley (Audeley), John Tychet kt. lord, and Mary h.w., xi, 1216
Ault Hucknall
Astwith (Estwayte) in, Henry Howeland of, 989
Batley (Batele) in, 888
Hardwick (Hardewyk) in, William Hardewyk of, 1054
Rowthorn (Routhorn) in, 888
Stainsby (Steynesby) in, manor of, 702
Aust, Walter, and Mabel h.w., 826
Aylwaston: see Elvaston
Aynesworth(e): see Ainsworth
Ayssheton: see Ashton
Aysshover: see Ashover

Babington (Babyngton), Anthony, 1211; esq. 1242
Arnold, 1146
Henry, clerk, 1146, 1162
John, esq. 1120; of Dethick, esq. 1122; kt and Elizabeth h.w., 1133
Ralph, clerk, 1181
Roland, 1181, 1188, 1209
Roland, esq. 1291, 1312
Joan wife of, 1291, 1312

Augustus, Henry and Michael, sons of, 1312
Humphrey and William, brothers of, 1312
Thomas, father of, 1312
Thomas, 1054, 1153, 1162, 1181, 1238; esq. 1107, 1327, 1351, 1355; esq. and Elizabeth h.w., 1332; esq. and Isabel h.w., 1079; of Dethick, 1146
William, 1057; and Margery h.w., 1052; kt, 1079
Bache, Simon, clerk, 1010
Badsworth (Baddesworth), Yorks WR
William Vavasour, esq. of, 1144
Bagenald: see Bagnall
Baggaley (Baggeley), Thomas de, 782
Bagnall (Bagenald, Baugnell), Roger de, 991
Thomas, of Mackworth, 977
Bagot, Lodowick, kt, 1250
Bagshawe (Bagshagh), Thomas, 1194
Thomas son of William, 1049
William de, 999
Bailey (Ba(i)ly), Otwell, 1219
William, of Leek, and Emma h.w., 1067
Bakepuz (Bakepuiz), John de, and Margery h.w., 783
Ralph de, parson of Barton Bakepuiz, 783
William, chiv. and Joan h.w., 909
Baker, Edmund, 1172, 1210
Edward, 1202
John, 1214
William, of Swadlincote, and Catherine h.w., 1082
Bakewell (Baukewell(e), Baukwell, Bauquell), 713, 793, 834, 835, 844, 877, 902, 928, 1151, 1183, 1330
manor of, 743, 1151
Burton (Burton next Baukwell) in, 844
Holme (Hulm) in, 844
Potlock (Potlok) in, manor of, ?706, ?901, ?909
Henry Muryman of, 793
William Overlynton, vicar of, 850
Bakewell (Baucwell, Bauk(e)well, Bawekewell), Henry de, chap., 901, 909
Hugh, 1154
John, 1154; clerk, 1235
Nicholas, of Oakerthorpe, 1154; de, 924; and Joan h.w., 939, 942
Roger de, 686, 695, 936
William, 1154
see also Bekewell
Baldwin (Baldwyn), John, 1214
Balgy, Thomas, 1143
Ball (Balle), Agnes, 808
Ballidon (Balyden), 1284
manor of, 1284

Balsham, William de, 901, 909
Baly: see Bailey
Balyden: see Ballidon
Bancroft, Henry, 1109
  William, 1109
Banks, (Bank), Thomas del, of Alkmonton,
  and Joan h.w., 1058
Barber (Barbour), Richard, and Catherine
  h.w., 1195
  Thomas, and Catherine h.w., 1219
Barbry, Thomas, chap., 712
Barclay (Barkeley, Berkleye), Maurice, kt,
  1178
  Thomas de, of Cubley, chiv., 878
  John and Nicholas sons of, 878
  Thomas son of, and Gillian h.w., 878
  Walter son of, 878
Barewe: see Barrow
Barkeley: see Barclay
Barker (Barkere), Ralph, 944, 991; of Dore,
  1007
Barkston (Barkeston), Yorks WR, 1106
Barlay: see Barlow
Barlborough (Barleborowe, -broughe, -
  brugh, -burgh, Barlyborough), 686, 871,
  992, 1023, 1213, 1232, 1258, 1268, 1277,
  1334
  advowson of, 1277
  manor of, 1258, 1268, 1277
  Pebley (Publey) in, 1232
Barlborough (Barleburgh), John de, and
  Agnes h.w., 1006
Barlow (Barle(y)), 782, 1224, 1271, 1337
Barlow (Barlay, Barley), John, 1045; clerk,
  991
  Robert, esq., 1233; jun., 944; senior, 944;
  senior, esq., 1121
  Robert, of Chesterfield, son of John, 1134
  Alice wife of, 1134
Barlyborough: see Barlborough
Barnaby (Barneby), Emma widow of Robert
  de, and Margaret her daughter, 723
Barnes (Bernes), Joan widow of Roger del,
  1033
Baron: see Barron
Barr (Barre), Agnes widow of Roger atte, 991
  Margery widow of William atte, of Derby,
  781, 786
  Robert brother of, 786
  William son of William atte, of Derby, 781
Barrington (Baryngton), Philip de, 782
Barron (Baron), Roger, 1093
Barrow (Bar(e)we), Henry de, 761, 794
  Richard de, vicar of Duffield, 852
Barrow upon Trent (Barrowe), 1303
Barton, Oliver de, 869, 946, 953, 961, 964; de,
  and Alice h.w., 938, 939, 942, 955

Ralph de, 1031
Randolphe de, and Joan h.w., 1031
Richard de, chap., 1030
  Thomas, and Ellen h.w., 1196
Barton Blount (Barton Bakepuiz), 783
  Ralph de Bakepuiz, parson of, 783
Barwe: see Barrow
Baryngton: see Barrington
Basford (Baseford), Notts, Richard de
  Haloum, vicar of, 919
Basford: see Beresford
Basingwerk Abbey (Basyn(g)werk), Flintshire
  church of the Blessed Mary at, abbot of,
  914, 1056
Baslow (Bas(se)lowe), 886, 891, 954, 1049,
  1161
  manor of, 1072
  'Stonhallond' in, 954
  see also Bubnell
Bassett (Basset), Deonise, 747, 820
  John, of Cheadle, chiv. and Joan h.w., 941;
  esq., 1245; kt, and Joan h.w., 1004, 1006
  Maude, 747
  Ralph, of Nether Haddon, 747
  William, jun., esq., 1238
Bassingbourn (Bassyngbourn), Hugh de, 799
  Humphrey de, and Olive h.w., 799
Basyn(g)werk: see Basingwerk Abbey
Bate, Henry, 991
  Isabel wife of Thomas, viii
  John, 991; of Sawley, 973
  William, and Alice h.w., 1126; esq., and
  Alice h.w., 1115
Batele: see Ault Hucknall, Batley in
Bateleye:see Batley
Bateson, William son of William, of Little
  Hucklow, 779
Batley, in Ault Hucknall, q.v.
Batley (Bateleye), Robert de, and Agnes h.w.,
  837
Baucwell: see Bakewell
Baugness: see Bagnall
Baukwell(e), Baukwell, Bauquell: see
  Bakewell
Bawden: see Chapel en le Frith, Bowden in
Bawekewell: see Bakewell
Bawman, John, 1263
Baxter, Denis, clerk, 1220, 1222, 1235
Baynham (Beynham), Alexander, kt, 1189
  Christopher, esq., 1189
Bayresford: see Beresford
Beale (Bele), John, chap., 842, 843
Beamond, Beamonnt: see Beaumont
Beard (Berd(e)), in New Mills, q.v.
Beard (Berde), Nicholas, 1218
  Richard de, and Emma his daughter, 1028
Bearwardcote (Ber(e)ward(e)cote, Berwar-

150

decotes), 718, 980, 981, 985, 1096
manor of, xii, 1010
John Cokayn of, 980, 981, 985
Beauchamp, Thomas (de), and Joan h.w.,
854-856
Beauchief,church of St Thomas martyr at,
Robert abbot of, 1004
Beaumont (Beamond, Beamonnt), Edward,
gent., 1306
John, 1299, 1354; esq., 1342; esq. and
Elizabeth h.w., 1297; jun., 1303; sen.,
1305
John viscount, 1103
Thomas, 1175
Beaurepeire: see Belper
Beck (Beek(e), Bek), Henry de, 714
Nicholas, chiv., 840
Robert de, and Robert his son, 728
Bedfordshire: see Stotfold
Beek(e): see Beck
Beeley, Fallange (Phalange) in, 1197, 1198
Beeley (Beleye), John de, of Bramcote, and
Elizabeth h.w., 862
Beeston (Bieston), Roger, clerk, 1220, 1222,
1235, 1265
Beighton (Be(y)ghton), 762, 1237, 1334
Waterthorpe (Wallarthorpe) in, 1334
Bek: see Beck
Bekewell, Henry, 1252
see also Bakewell
Bele: see Beale
Beler, Roger, 690, 696
Roger and Thomas sons of, 696
Beleye: see Beeley
Bell, William, 1144
Belper (Beaurepeire, Beurepper), 965, 1312
Benet: see Bennett
Benge, William, of Repton, clerk, 1035
Bennett (Benet), William, clerk, 1109, 1114
Bentley (Benteleye): see Fenny Bentley;
Hungry Bentley
Bentley, Thomas, 1174
Berd(e): see Beard; New Mills, Beard in
Beresford (Basford, Bayresford, Beref(f)ord,
Berford), Edmund de, clerk, and
Baldwin and John his sons, 839
Elizabeth widow of Baldwin, chiv., 1057
James, 1201; clerk, 1167, 1203
Bereward(e)cote: see Bearwardcote
Berford: see Beresford
Berford Manor: see Measham, manor of
Berkleye: see Barclay
Bernes: see Barnes
Bernhull: see Burnhill
Bernreve, Richard le, 822
Roger le, 822
Berry (Bury), Christopher, chap., 1137, 1138

Berward(e)cote,   Berwardecotes: see
Bearwardcote
Besand, John, chap., 1042
Beurepper: see Belper
Beveridge (Beveregg(e)), Richard, of Chester-
field, 935, and Joan h.w., 962
William, 991
Beverley, Richard de, and Margery h.w., 825
Beyghton: see Beighton
Beynham: see Baynham
Bieston: see Beeston
Biggin (Byggyng), Adam, vicar of Har-
tington, 1036
Bilborough (Bilburgh), Robert de, chap., 741
Bildeswath: see Buildwas
Billups (Byllup), John, 1213
Bingham (Byngham), Richard, 1085; and
Anne h.w., 1181
William de, chiv., 833; de, kt, 800
Birchels: see Hassop, Birchells in
Birchewode: see Alfreton, Birchwood in;
Norbury, Birchwood in
Birchills (Birchells, Birchil(le)s, Birchulles,
Byrchelis), in Hassop, q.v.
Birchitt (Byrched), in Coal Aston, q.v.
Birchover (Birchovere), 849
Birchover (Birchovere), Thomas de, and
Cecily h.w., 849
Alice, Catherine and Elizabeth daugh-
ters of, 849
William, of Spondon, and Joan h.w., 977
Birchulles: see Hassop, Birchills in
Birchwood (Birchewode), in Alfreton, q.v.; in
Norbury, q.v.
Bird (Birde, Byrde), Ralph, 1172
Richard, 1256
Birmingham (Birmyngeham), John and Alice
h.w., 1098
Birnaston: see Burnaston
Birtton: see Burton
Blackwall (Blakwalle), George, son of
Robert, 1194
Ralph, 1188
Richard, 1125, 1140, 1188, 1298
Robert, 1111; and Mary h.w., 1148
William, and Emma h.w., 1075; del, of
Tissington, and Maude h.w., 906
Blackwell (Blacwell, Blakwall, Blakwell) (in
High Peak), 1194
manor of, ?684, ?801, ?1052
Blackwell (Blacwell, Blak(e)well) (in Scars-
dale), 1278
manor of, ?684, ?801, ?1052, 1278
Blagden, Ralph, and Margaret h.w., 1247
Blagg (Blagge), Robert, 1186; baron of the
king's exchequer, 1210
Blakewell: see Blackwell

Blakwall(e): see Blackwall; Blackwell
Blakwell: see Blackwell
Blount (Blound), family, lords Mountjoy, xii
Edward, kt, 1149, 1150
John, gent., 1215
Sanchia, 1037
Walter, 1215; gent., 1214; kt, 1119
William, and Emma h.w., 843; kt, of
Mountjoy, 1214; kt, lord Mountyoye,
1256; lord Mountjoy, and Elizabeth
h.w., 1171
Blythe (Blyth), Catherine, widow, and
William, her son, 1229
John, clerk, 1237; de, 991
William, gent., 1237
Blythman, William, 1318
Bobenhill, Bobenhull: see Bubnell
Boddington (Bodyngton or Bonyngton),
John, 1010
Bodon: see Chapel en le Frith, Bowden in
Bodyngton: see Boddington
Boilleston: see Boylestone
Bolere: see Bowler
Boleton: see Boulton
Bolingbroke (Bolyngbrok), Bertram de, and
Joan h.w., 851, 871
Henry of, son of John of Gaunt, xi
Bolland, Humphrey, 1224
Bolsover, Whaley (Walley) in, John de
Steynesby of, 801
Bolton: see Boulton
Bolyngbrok: see Bolingbroke
Bone (Bonne), Edward, 1289
John le, of Stapenhill, 745
William, son of, 745; Agnes h.w., 745
Bonnington (Bonyngton or Bodyngton),
John, 1010
Booth (Bothe), Charles, clerk, 1173
Henry, 1061, 1299; de, 1055; del, 1031; del,
and Elizabeth h.w., 1025; del, and Isabel
h.w., 1029, 1062; esq., 1303; of
Littleover, 1003
Humphrey, and Margaret h.w., 1249
John del, jun. and Joan h.w., 1060; esq.,
1114; of Henry, 1068
William, esq., 1172
Borrowash (Boroughaysshe), in Ockbrook,
q.v.
Bosson (Bosonn), John and Isabel h.w., 802
Boston (St Botho), Lincs, William de Spaigne
of, 955
Boteler: see Butler
Botelesford: see Bottlesford
Bothe: see Booth
Bothum: see Mellor, Bottom's Hall in
Botiller: see Butler
Bottlesford (Botelsford), ?Wilts, Henry de

Codyngton, parson of, 888
Bottom's Hall (Bothum), in Mellor, q.v.
Botyler: see Butler
Bou(e)don: see Chapel en le Frith, Bowden in
Boughton (Bughton), John (de), and Elizab-
eth h.w., 991, 1002
Boulton (Bol(e)ton, Bulton), 729, 831, 1205,
1238
manor of, 1050
Boure: see Bower
Bovey (Boveye), Ralph de, 912
Bowden (Bawden, Bo(u)don, Bouedon in the
Peak, Bow(e)don), in Chapel en le Frith,
q.v.; see also New Mills
Bowden (Bowdon), Otwell, 1249
Bowden Head (Bowdenhedde), in Chapel en
le Frith, q.v.
Bower (Boure, Bowere), John, of Derby, 949;
del, of Whitfield, 1013
Thurstan(n) atte, of Tideswell, 986; del,
1013; de la, and Margaret h.w., 933
Bowler (Bolere), William, of Bowden, 1066
Bown, Edward, and Alice h.w., 1169
Boyleston (Boilleston), 783, 1113
advowson of 1011, 1077
manor of, 1011; called Cotonmaner, 1077,
1113
Boythorpe (Boythorp), in Chesterfield, q.v.
Bra: see Bray
Brackenfield (Brakynthwayt, Brakyntwhat),
867, 1296
Ogston (Ogaston, Ogeston) in, 867, 1296
manor of, 1296
Bradbourne (Bradburn(e), Bradeborne,
Bradeburn), 770, 803, 818, 819, 822, 830
manor of, 735
Bradburn (Bradburne, Bradeborne,
Bradeb(o)urn), Humphrey, esq., 1149,
1164
John de, 830; de, senior, 735
Richard de, 830
Roger de, and Maude h.w., 735, 770
John son of, 735, 770
Richard and Thomas sons of, 735
William son of, 735, 770
William son of Roger de, jun., 830
Margaret wife of, 830
Bradbury (Bredbure), Hugh, and Ellen h.w.,
1083
Ralph, of Ollersett, 1218
Bradeborne, Bradeb(o)urn: see Bradbourne;
Bradburn
Bradeley(e): see Bradley
Bradeshawe: see Bradshaw
Bradewell: see Bradwell
Bradley (Bradeley(e)), 748, 778, 819, 941,
1149, 1176, 1233

152

Brokhey, John, parson of Radbourne, 1112
Brom(e): see Broome
Bromeley: see Bromley
'Bromeside', 1219
Bromhall (Bromhale, Brommale), John, and
Maude h.w., 993, 1002
Bromley (Bromeley), Thomas, esq., 1261
Brommale: see Bromhall
Brompton: see Brampton
Bromwich, Sir John, x
Bronaldeston: see Burnaston
Brook (Brok, Bythebrok), John son of Roger,
703
Thomas atte, 825
Broome (Brom(e)), Stephen del, of Hucklow,
and Ellen h.w., 967
William, chap., 1067; del, chap., 1075
Brotton, John de, 808
Brough, 1309
manor of, 1309
see also Shatton
Broun(e): see Brown
Brounsyde: see Chinley, Brownside in
Brown (Broun(e), Browne), Adam, 991
John, 991, 1081; esq. and Alice h.w., 1272;
of Matlock, 995
Richard, 1082; and Joan h.w., 808; of
Repton, xii, 1030, 1088
Thomas, 1226
Brownside (Brounsyde), in Chinley, q.v.
Browster: see Brewster
Brudenell, Robert, chief justice of common
pleas, 1216
Brugge: see Bridge
Brunaldeston: see Burnaston
Brushfield (Britterichefeld, Brusshefeld, Bryt-
rychefeld, Wrightrichefeld), 816, 885,
933, 1171
Brym(m)yngton: see Brimington
Brynaston: see Burnaston
Brysley: see Brisley
Brysyngcote: see Bretby, Brizlincote in
Brytrychefeld: see Brushfield
Bubnell (Bobenhill, Bobenhull, Bubenhull,
Bubynhill), 886, 891, 990, 1017, 1049,
1161
Robert Abbot of, 1049
Buckinghamshire: see Leckhampstead,
Shenley
Bucklow (Bucklowe), Henry, 1356
Bucstones: see Buxton
Buggesworth: see Buxworth
Bughton: see Boughton
Buildwas (Bildeswath), John son of Walter
de, 707
Alice wife of, 707
Bulclogh, William, 1038

Bulkeley, William, 1256
Bullock (Bullok(ke)), Henry, clerk, 1188
James, and Mary h.w., 1286
John, 1188
Bulneys, John, clerk, 844
Bulton: see Boulton
Burdett (Burdet), Hugh, 813
Robert, 795; and Elizabeth h.w., 693
Burgess (Burghes), Emma widow of Robert
del, 735
Thomas del, and Agnes h.w., 880
Burgulon, John, of Nether Weston, and
Maude h.w., 1046
'Burlandys', 1334
Burley (Burleye), in Duffield, q.v.
Burley (Burleye), Henry son of William de,
sen., 698
William de, chap., 898, 918
Burnaston (Birnaston, Bronaldeston, Brunal-
deston, Brynaston), 718, 980-982, 1003,
1096, 1340
William Cartere of, 1032
Burnaston (Brenlaston), William, 1002
Burham (Burneham), Thomas, 1231
Burnhill (Bernhull), Thomas de, and Isabel
h.w., 846, 858
Bursyngcote: see Bretby, Brizlincote in
'Burton' (Birtton)
Richard de Stafford, parson of, 753
Walter Draper of, 1062
see also Burton on Trent
Burton, in Abney, q.v.; in Bakewell, q.v.
Burton, William, and Catherine h.w., 1110;
and Margery h.w., 980
Burton on Trent (Burton), Staffs
abbot and convent of, 786
abbot of monastery of, 1279
Burwey, Nicholas, 1299, 1303
Bury: see Berry
Bussey (Buss(he)y), John, and Maude h.w.,
955; esq., 1255
Butler (Boteler, Botiller, Botyler), Roger le,
of Shustoke, 829
Thomas, esq., 1250, 1251
William le, 901, 909
Butterworth, Ewyn, and Joan h.w., 1137
Buxton (Bucstones, Buxston, Kyngesbuc-
stones), 778, 879, 1148, 1179
Buxton (Buxstones), Thomas, 1067
Buxworth (Buggesworth), 1282
Buyldyng, William, of Littleover, and Alice
h.w., 1003
Byggyng: see Biggin
Bygod, Ralph, jun., 1334; sen., 1334
Byllup: see Billups
Byngham: see Bingham
Bynham, Richard de, 834

Byrched: see Coal Aston, Birchitt in
Byrchelis: see Hassop, Birchills in
Byrde: see Bird
Bythebrok: see Brook
Bywater (Bythewater), John, 690
  William, 690

Cade, John, 1221; and Elizabeth h.w., 1200
  Elizabeth, widow, 1290
Calais Staple, John Stokkes, merchant of, xiii
Calale, Calall: see Calow
Calcraft (Calcrofte), Ralph, and Elizabeth
  h.w., 1223
Caldecote: see Caldicott
Caldelowe: see Callow; Hathersage, Callow
  in; Mapleton, Callow in
Caldewell: see Caldwell
Caldicott (Caldecote), John de, parson of
  Letchworth, 797
Caldlowe: see Hathersage, Callow in;
  Mapleton, Callow in
Caldon, John de, 780, 812
Caldwell (Caldewell, Caldwall), 761, 827,
  1251, 1343
  manor of, 761, 800, 1251, 1343
  John Child of, 827
Caldwell (Caldewell, Caldwall), Ralph, 1244;
  de, and Cecily h.w., 800
Callale: see Calow
Callow (Caldelowe), ?753, ?1070
  manor of, ?vii, 716, ?925, ?963, ?1095
  Hasker in, 1169
  John le Porter of, ?753
  Richard Foljambe, jun. of, ?807
  see also Hathersage, Callow in; Mapleton,
  Callow in
Calow (Calall, Cal(l)ale, Calo(w)e), 851,
  1054, 1224, 1265, 1329
Calow (Calall), William de, 991
Calton, Thomas, cit. and goldsmith of
  London, 1310; and Margaret h.w., 1302
Calton, in Edensor, q.v.
Camden, Robert, gent., 1250, 1251
Campana (le Chaumpeyn(e) (in alto pecco))
  office of forester in, 1009, 1108
Cantrell, Ralph, clerk, 1205, 1215
Capella de le Fryth: see Chapel en le Frith
Car Colston (Kyrcolston), Notts
  Roger Lanne of, 1035
'Cardellesfeld', in Chaddesden, q.v.
Cardoyle, William de, of Spondon, chap., 738
Carnfield (Carlyngthawyte, Carlyngwayt), in
  South Normanton, q.v.
Carr, John, 1180
Carrington (Caryngton), John, esq., 1282
Carsington (Kersinton, Kersyngton), 695,
  1008, 1046, 1101

John Haghton of, 1101
John del Stone of, 1046
Carter (Cartere), Ankertil, chap., son of
  John, 1323
  William, of Burnaston, 1032
Cartwright (Cartwryght), John, of Stretton,
  sen., 1024
Carwardine (Carwardon), Robert, 1250
Caryngton: see Carrington
Castell: see Castle
Castellan (Castlyn, Chasteleyn), John, gent.,
  1287
  Roger, 792
  William, merchant, 1287
Castell Greysley: see Gresley, Castle; Gresley,
  Castle, or Church
Castelton: see Castleton
Castle (Castell), John, 1194
Castle Gresley: see Gresley, Castle; Gresley,
  Castle, or Church
Castleton (Castelton (in pecco)), 778, 803,
  819, 845, 1132, 1243, 1263, 1309
  John del Halle of, 845
Castleton (Castelton), John son of Gervase
  de, 721
  Thomas de, vicar of Wirksworth, 921
Castlyn: see Castellan
Cater (Catour), John le, of Smalley, 691
Caumbes, Henry de, and Agnes h.w., 715
Caumnill, Nicholas de, of of Amington, and
  Sarah h.w., 691
Caunt, John, and Joan h.w., 991; chap., 1184
Cawardon: see Carwardine
Caym, Walter, of Derby, 697
Cestrefeld: see Chesterfield
Chaddesden (Chaddesdene, Chaddysden,
  Chaddysdon, Chadesden), 727, 729,
  738, 740, 781, 853, 918, 974, 1118, 1154,
  1234, 1238, 1241, 1266, 1302, 1310, 1357
  advowson of, 1357
  manor of, 889, 895, 913, 1241, 1357
  office of rector of, 1357
  'Brawdewode' in, 1118
  'Cardellesfeld' in, 1118
  William le Herberiour of, chiv., 740
Chaddesden (Chaddesdene), Geoffrey de,
  parson of Long Whatton, 853, 912
  Joan widow of William de, 889
  master Nicholas de, 957; clerk, 853
Chalencheswod, Henry and John sons of
  Richard de, 827
Challoner (Chaloner), Robert, of Sheffield,
  and Richard his son, 1051
Chamberlain (Chamberleyn), Thomas, 1059
Chandos (Channdos, Chaundos), John, chiv.,
  862
  Robert de, parson of Radbourne, 731

157

159

Robert, 1087; Groos, William, 974; Gybon, William, 870; Haukeswelle, John, 984; Hilton, William, 987; Hulland, John de, 929; Hulton, William de, 964; Leche, William, 929; Leggealden, John, 1005; Longeford, Richard de, 759; Marche, William del, 856; Milner, Thomas, 1062; Pakemon, William, 875; Pryker, William le, 810; Shypen, Robert del, 854; Sivekere, Peter le, 781, 785; Sklater, William, 987; Smith, Robert, 1328; Spondon, William de, 832; Stokke, Ellis del, 1053; Thomas del, 1029; Tapley, Thomas de, 966; Throstyll, William, 1087; Thurleston, Henry de, 789; Trowelle, John de, 899

Derby, Robert de, 885, 933
    Isabel wife of, and Catherine and Margaret her sisters, 885
    Thomas de, draper, 1042
    William, 860; de, 855
Derlaston: see Darlaston
Derley(e): see Darley; Darley Abbey
Derleye in le Peek: see Darley
Derton: see Darton
Derwent, 1180
Dethick (Dethek, Dethykke)
    advowson of the chapel of St John Baptist in, 1079
    manor of, 1079
    John Babyngton, esq. of, 1122
    Thomas Babyngton of, 1146
    see also Lea
Dethick (Dethek, Dethik), Geoffrey de, 690
    William, 1264; de, 892, 922
Deyn(e)court: see Deincourt
Dexter, Thomas, of Stretton en le Field, and Margaret h.w., 1024
Dicker (Dicher, Dyker), Richard son of Thomas le, 882
    Joan wife of, 882
    Thomas, of Abney, and Agnes h.w., 951
Dingley (Dyngley), John, esq., 1261
Dixon (Dykson, Dyxson), Arthur, 1226
    Nicholas, clerk, 1090
    Robert, and Anne h.w. daughter of Fulk Sutton, 1269
Dobbin (Dobbyn), Thomas, parson of Westbury, 815
Dogmanton: see Duckmanton
Doidsawt, Robert, 982
Doile: see Doyle
Dokemonton: see Duckmanton
Donisthorpe (Donasthorp, Donesthorpe), 1250, 1283
Dore (Dore next Norton), 840
    Limb Hill (Lymhall) in, 1316

Ralph Barkere of, 1007
Richard Hikson of, 951
Dounville: see Dunville
Doveridge (Dovvebrugge), 894, 940
    Eaton Dovedale (Eyton in Dovedale) in, manor of, 908
    see also queried entries under Coldeaton
    West Broughton (Westbrocton) in, 1215
    manor of, 714
Dow (Dowe), John, and Cecily h.w., 1001
Doyle (Doile), Edward, and Anne h.w., 1162
Drabble (Drable), Edward, 1316
Draicote: see Draycott
Drakelow Drak(e)lowe), 826, 1251, 1343
    manor of, 1251, 1343
Dranfeld: see Dronfield
Draper, Hugh, of Chesterfield, and Cecily h.w., 991
    Payne le, of Derby, and Avis h.w., 774
    Walter, of Burton, 1062
Drawnfeild: see Dronfield
Draycott (Draicote, Draycot, Draycot(t)e), John de, chiv. and Alice h.w., 840
    Mark, gent., 1340
    Philip, esq., 1245; esq., and Elizabeth h.w., 1246
    Richard de, 760; de, of Eaton, and Gillian h.w., 730
Drew (Drewe), William, of Matlock, tailor, and Alice h.w., 873
Dronfield (Dranfeld, Drawnfeild, Dronfeld), 782, 922, 991, 1134, 1153, 1155, 1224, 1229, 1316, 1329
    advowson of, 782, 1007
    manor of, 983, 1224, 1329
    Thomas Gonnifray, parson of, 944
Dronfield (Dronfeld), John de, chap., 836
Dronfield Woodhouse (Woodhowse), 1224, 1329
    Cowley (Colley) in, 1224, 1329
    Stubley in, 1224, 1329
Dubber, Robert, of Coventry, and Emma h.w., 949
Duckmanton (Dogmanton, Dokemonton, Dukmanton), 776, 777, 1006, 1334
Duckmanton (Duckemanton), Thomas, gent., 1189
Dudley, John, kt, and Joan h.w., 1241
    John Sutton, lord, 1103
Duerham: see Durham
Duffield (Duffeld), 852, 927, 965, 1012, 1147, 1150, 1189
    Burley (Burleye) in, ?698
    Richard de Barwe, vicar of, 852
    Thomas Stanley of, 1042
    William de Moneassh/Monyassh, vicar of, 957, 958

Duffield (Duffeld), Robert, chap., 1049
William de, clerk, 853
Duffield Frith (Duffeld Frith, — Fryth), 805, 814
Dukmanton: see Duckmanton
Duncalf, John, vicar of Prestbury, 1080
Dunstan (Dunston), Thomas de, and Emma h.w., 752
Dunston, 851, 922, 962, 991
Dunville (Dounville), John, and Maude h.w., 830
Durham (Duerham)
Richard bishop of, 1163
Richard de Sutton of, 784
Durrant (Durannt), Thomas, 991; and Agnes h.w., 1159; of Chesterfield, 959
Dyker: see Dicker
Dykson: see Dixon
Dyngley: see Dingley
Dynham: see Denham
Dyxson: see Dixon

Earley (Erle), John, chap., 725
East Bridgford, (Estbriggeford), Notts
John Walker parson of, 1054
East Retford (Retford), Notts
John Roulay of, 1051
Eaton (Eyton): see Coldeaton; Doveridge, Eaton Dovedale in; Little Eaton; Long Eaton
see also Alsop en le Dale
Eaton (Eton), William, 1090
Eaton Dovedale (Eyton in Dovedale), in Doveridge, q.v.
Eccles (Ekkels), William de, and Ellen h.w., 1018
Eckington (Egkyngton, Eckyn(g)ton, Hekyngton), 809, 965, 1023, 1155, 1200, 1334
advowson of, 965, 1334
manor of, 1334
Bramley in, 1334
Lightwood (Lyghtwood) in, ?1286, ?1352
Litfield (Letfeld) in, 1155
Mosborough (Estmosborugh, Mosburghe) in, 1237, 1334
Plumbley (Plumley) in, 1334
Renishaw (Reynaldshawe) in, 1334
Ridgeway (Regwell, Regwey) in, 1334
Spinkhill (Spynkhill) in, 1334
Troway in, 1334
West Mosborough (Westmosborugh) in, 1334
Eddlestow (Edynstowe), in Ashover, q.v.
Edenesoure: see Edensor; Ensor
Edensour (Eden(e)soure, Edneso(u)re, Ednesouere), 834, 844

manor of, 802, 946
Calton in, 812
William Leche of, 1026
Edilueston: see Edlaston
Edingale (Ednynghale), 692, 771, 772
'The middlefeld' in, 771
Nicholas le Mareys of, 772
Edlaston (Edilueston, Edleston)
advowson of, 1335
manor of, 1335
see also Wyaston
Edmondson, Richard, alias Richard Johnson, 1359
Edneso(u)re, Ednesouere: see Edensor
Ednynghale: see Edingale
Edynstowe: see Ashover, Eddlestow in
Egginton (Egenton, Eg(g)ynton, Egyn(g)ton on le Heth), 739, 767, 1031, 1060, 1093, 1168, 1303, 1326
advowson of, 862, 1303
manor of, 1303
Roger Netham, rector of, 1211
Egginton (Egynton), Maude widow of William de, 767
William son of William de, 767
Eggnestowe: see Egstow
Egkyngton: see Eckington
Egstow (Eggnestowe), 1222
Egyn(g)ton: see Egginton
Ekkels: see Eccles
Ekyn(g)ton: see Eckington
Eland, Thomas, 955
Elbaston: see Elvaston
Elford, Staffs
Henry de Tymmore, parson of, 911
Elkesley, Joan, 1107
Ellington (Elynton), Roger de, 739
Ellot, Henry, 1208
Richard, 1208
Elme: see Elms
Elmeton: see Elmton
Elms (Elme), John, 966
Elmton (Elmeton), 993, 1002
Creswell (Crossewell) in, 1278
manor of, 1278
Elmton (Elmeton), Walter de, and Joan h.w., 851
Elton, manor of, 1047
Elvaston (Ailwaston, Aylwaston, Elbaston), 900, 950, 1002, 1184, 1227, 1238, 1325
manor of, 806, 960, 1119
Ambaston in, 897
Richard le Sower of, 897
Thulston (Thurlaston, Thurleston) in, 900, 1184, 1227, 1238
Thomas Robardson of, 900
William de Braylesford of, 897

161

Humphrey, 1246; esq., 1207
Joan, widow, 1209
John, 1181; clerk, 1207, 1231; esq., 1156, 1207, 1228; of Norbury esq., 1209; of Somersal Herbert, and Alice h.w., 884
Nicholas, 1011, 1116; and Alice h.w., 808; esq., 1119
Ralph, 1116, 1124
Thomas, 1011; clerk, 1162, 1181; doctor of decretals, 1228; esq., 1238
William, gent. and Ann h.w., 1282
Fitzwilliam, Edward, esq., 1059
Flagg (Flagge), 1148, 1330
Fleccher: see Fletcher
Flegh, John, and Margery h.w., 925
Fletcher (Fleccher), William, 1338; of Tunstead, 1039
Flint (Flynte), John, 1321
Flintshire: see Basingwerk Abbey
Foljambe (Fol(e)iaumbe, Foliam(m)be, Folyamb, Fuliambe), family, xii
Edward, esq., 1047
Godfrey, 1197; and Avina h.w. and Richard their son, 868; chiv. and Avina h.w., 913; esq., 1196, 1198; jun., 902; kt, 889, 895, 907, 1212, 1220, 1222, 1235, 1265, 1274, 1276, 1280, 1290, 1293, 1294; sir, the younger, xi
Henry, 1159; esq., 1132; senior, esq., 1165
James, esq., 1236
John, of Longstone, and his daughters, Catherine, Isabel, wife of Robert de Derby, and Margaret, 885; son of Richard, of Longstone, 816
Richard, 836; of Callow, jun., 807; parson of Normanton, 850; son of Richard, 716
Elizabeth wife of, 716, 807, 836
Robert de, clerk, 998
Roger, of Little Longstone, 816
Thomas, 971
Folow: see Foolow
Folvyll, Walter de, 842, 843
Folyamb: see Foljambe
Foolow (Folow, Fowelowe), 883, 1243
Foosyde: see Hayfield, Phoside in
Forbour(e): see Furber
Forche, Thomas de la, 696
Ford (Forde), Robert de la, 756
Foston, 1214, 1347, 1349
see also Scropton
Foucher, John, 909; and Isabel h.w., 994; le, 901
Robert de, of Osmaston, 741
Fouler: see Fowler
Foun: see Fownes
Fowelowe: see Foolow
Fowler (Fouler), John, 1126

Fownes (Foun), Richard son of Richard le, 766
Fox, John, chap., 1069
Thomas, and Ellen h.w., 1155
William, chap., 1072
Francis (Francess, Frannce(y)s), Henry, and Agnes h.w., 918; gent., and Agnes h.w., 1239
John 1215
Richard, esq., 1193
Robert, chiv. and Isabel h.w., 1050
Thomas, esq., 1050
Franklin (Fraunkeleyn), William, 808
Frannce(y)s: see Francis
Fraunkeleyn: see Franklin
Frecheville (Frecchevylle, Frechevill, -evyle, -ewell, Fre(s)chev(v)ill), Anker, 950; and Agnes h.w., 960
Nicholas, gent., 1248
Peter, esq., 1323; kt, and Elizabeth h.w., 1337
Ralph de, and Margaret h.w., 687, 689; de, and Ralph his son, 690; kt, 956
Freeman (Fremon), Ralph, of Rowsley, and Elizabeth h.w., 921
Freschev(v)ill: see Frecheville
Frith, The (Urlesfryth), in Hartington Upper Quarter, q.v.
Frormanby, Richard de, of Harpham, and Isabel h.w., 956
Fuliambe: see Foljambe
Fullwood (Fulwode), in Hulland, q.v.
Furber (Forbour(e)), Robert, 1074; of Derby, 1087
Fyndern(e): see Findern
Fyssher: see Fisher
Fyton: see Fitton

Gansell, Robert, parson of Cromwell, 1090
Gardhowse, Richard, and Agnes h.w., 1294
Garlick (Garleke, Garlike, Garly(c)ke), John, and Margaret h.w. and Nicholas their son, 1257
Nicholas, 1279, 1292, 1301, 1345
Garnham (Gernonn), John, 743
John son of, and Alice h.w., 743
Garrett, William, 1358
Garton, Henry de, 822
Gaunt, John of: see Lancaster
Gell, John, 1194
Geneson: see Jeneson
Gernonn: see Garnham
Gibbons (Gybon), William, of Derby, and Aline h.w., 870
Gifford (Gyfford), Thomas, esq., 1266
Gilbert (Gylbert), John, 1177
Robert, 1155; and Joan h.w., 1129

guardian, 811
Richard de, of Alkmonton, chap., 892
Hallam (Haloum), Richard de, vicar of Basford, 919
Thomas de, chap., 919
Hallam, Kirk (?Halom, Kirkhalum, Kyrkehalum), 729, 912
manor of, ?813
Hallam, Little (?Halom, Parva Halum), in Ilkeston, q.v.
Hallam, West (?Halom, West Halom), 1124
advowson of, ix, 1124
manor of, ix, ?813, 1124
Hallewynnefeld: see Wingfield, North
Halley, Ralph, 1037
Halo(u)m: see Hallam
Hambury: see Hanbury
Hammond (Hamond), William, 690
Hampton, Robert de, of Chesterfield, and Ellen h.w., 793
Thomas, of Leicester, 1127
William de, of Thulston, and Maude h.w., 935
Hamstall Ridware (Ridewarehampstall, Rydware), Staffs
John Coton, sen. of, 1113
William de Coton of, 1011
Hanbury (Hambury), Henry de, and Isabel h.w., 720, 733; de, chiv., 807
Hanson (Hanneson), John, of Repton, barker, and Agnes h.w., 1030
Harboro' (Herbarowe), in Brassington, q.v.
Harcourt (Harecourt), Roger, 965; and Margaret h.w., 924
Hardwick (Hardewyk), in Ault Hucknall, q.v.
Hardwick (Hardewyk, Herd(e)wyk), Thomas, clerk, 1010
William, of Hardwick, 1054; de, parson of Atherstone on Stour, 878
Hardyk(e)wall: see Wormhill, Hargatewall in
Harecourt: see Harcourt
Hargatewall (Hardyk(e)wall, Herdwykwall), in Wormhill, q.v.
Harlesthorpe (Tharlesthorp(e)), in Clowne, q.v.
Harper, Richard, 1326
Harpham (Harpeham), Yorks E.R.
Richard de Frormanby of, 956
Harthill (Herthull), 1284
manor of, viii, 958, 961, 1085, 1284
Hartington (Hertindon, Hertyn(g)don), 857, 879
soc of, 'Roglymedewe' in, 1036
Adam Byggyng, vicar of, 1036
Henry de la Pole of, 820, 857
John de la Pole of, xi, 879
Nicholas del Hull of, 747

Richard de la Pole of, 778, 818, 819, 821, 822, 845
Hartington Middle Quarter
Crowdecote (Croudecote) in
bailiwick of forester of, 879
forester of free chase at, xi
Fernydale in, 1036
Hartington Upper Quarter
The Frith (Urlesfrith) in, bailiwick of, 1036
Hartshorne (Hartyshorne, Herteshorn), 787, 1175
Nether Hall in, manor of, 1175
Overhall in, manor of, 1175
Harvey (Hervy), Robert, and Cecily h.w., 903
Haseland: see Hasland
Haselbache: see Hazlebadge
Haselwode: see Hazelwood
Hasilbache: see Hazlebadge
Hasker, in Callow, q.v.
Hasland (Haseland, Haslond, Hasylland), 851, 1153, 1212, 1224, 1329
Hassop, 835, 1183
Birchills (Birchels, Birchil(le)s, Birchulles, Byrchelis), in, 835, 850, 887, 944, 1183
manor of, 1183
Hastings (Hastingys, Hastynges), Edward, kt lord Hastynges, 1152
George, kt lord Hastynges, 1224
William, esq., 1171, 1252
see also Huntingdon
Hasylbarowe: see Norton, Hazlebarrow in
Hasylland: see Hasland
Hasylwode: see Hazelwood
Hatfeld: see Glossop, Hadfield in; Hadfield
Hatherfeld, Richard, chap., 1087
Hathersage (Hathersedge, -segge, Hathursege, Haverse(g)ge, Hetherseche), 1254, 1268, 1277
manor of, 722, 1180, 1268, 1277
Callow (Cald(e)lowe) in: see queried entries under Callow, above
Robert de Neubold of, chap., 722
Hatton, 718, 980, 981, 1231
Hauberk, Laurence, 888
William, and Christian h.w., 888
Haukesoke, William de, and Margery h.w., 952
Haukeswelle: see Hawkswell
Haversegge: see Hathersage
Hawkswell (Haukeswelle), John, of Derby, and Margaret h.w., 984
William son of, and Agnes h.w., 984
Hayes (Heye), Henry del, and Deonise h.w., 1026
William del, and Avis h.w., 832; del, of Stanton by Bridge, and Alice h.w., 1042
Hayfield (Hayfeld), 1080

165

Kinder (Kynder) in, 1018, 1195, 1249
Phoside (Fooside) in, 1358
Hayward (Heyward), Richard le, 690
Hazelwood (Haselwode, Hasylwode), 1150, 1171, 1189
manor of, 1171
Hazlebadge (Haselbache, Hasilbache)
manor of, 1072
John de Strelley of, kt, 1045
Hazlebadge (Haselbache), Adam, 988
Hazlebarrow (Hasylbarowe), in Norton, q.v.
Heage (Heghegge), 805, 814
Heale (Hele), Thomas de, of Stanton by Dale, and Agnes h.w., 912
Heanor (Hen(n)ore), 965, 1040, 1163
manor of, 1163
Langley (Langeleye next Henovere) in, 729, 991, 1163
manor of, 1163
Heath (Heth), 1332
Heathcote (Heth(e)cote), James, sen., 1127
Richard, 1127, 1179
Robert de, and Emma h.w., 863
Thomas, 1271
Heather (He(y)ther), John, sen., 1244; jun., 1256
Thomas, 1256; and Mudwina h.w., 1262
Heath Houses (Hethehouses), in Church Broughton, q.v.
Hedricheshay: see Idridgehay
Heghegge: see Heage
Hekyngton: see Eckington
Hele: see Heale
Helowe: see Highlow
Helpringham (Helpryngham), William de, 916
Hemsworth (Hymmesworth, Hym(m)ysworth), in Norton, q.v.
Hen(n)ore: see Heanor
Henry, Cecily widow of Roger son of, 991
Gilbert, of Yoxall, and Maude his daughter, 771
Robert son of, 690
Simon son of, 690
Henry VIII, king, 1306, 1322, 1357
Heppals, Hugh, and Isabel h.w., 1178
Herbarowe: see Brassington, Harboro' in
Herberio(ur), Isabel widow of William, chiv., 889
William le, of Chaddesden, chiv., and Isabel h.w., 740
Chad, Edmund, Henry, Thomas, William sons of, 740
Herdeby, John de, chap., 687
Herdewyk: see Hardwick
Herdings (Herdyng), in Norton, q.v.
Herdwyk: see Hardwick

Herdwykwall: see Wormhill, Hargatewall in
Herdyng: see Norton, Herdings in
Herez (Her(i)tz), John de, 696; de, kt, 690; kt, 1059
Herleston, John de, chap., 891
Herley: see Hurley
Hermitage: see Armitage
Hert: see Hurt
Herteshorn: see Hartshorne
Hertfordshire: see Letchworth
Herthull: see Harthill
Hertindon, Hertyn(g)don: see Hartington
Hertz: see Herez
Hervy: see Harvey
Heth: see Heath
Heth(e)cote: see Heathcote
Hethehouses: see Church Broughton, Heath Houses in
Hether: see Heather
Hetherseche: see Hathersage
Hewitt (Hewet), John, 1259; and Joan h.w., 1208
Nicholas, 1259; and Joan h.w., 1237
Richard, and Alice h.w., 1259
Heye: see Hayes
Heyr: see Eyre
Heyther: see Heather
Heyward: see Hayward
Hibbert (Hilberd), John, parson of 'Thornford', 871
Hickson (Hikson), Richard, of Dore, and Joan h.w., 951
Highlow (Helowe)
manor of, 986
Nicholas Pycworth of, 986
High Peak (Alto Pecco), 1143, 1345
serjeanties in the forest of, 1019
Highton (Hiton), Ralph de, of Sudbury, and Isabel h.w., 996
Hikson: see Hickson
Hilberd: see Hibbert
Hill (Hyll), William del, of Ansty, alias William Parker, and Ellen h.w., 985
Hillary, Edward son of Henry, 813, 817
Alice wife of, 813, 817
Robert, parson of Sutton Coldfield, 813, 817
Hilton (Hylton), 1031, 1303
manor of, 1303
Hilton (Hylton), John, and Margaret h.w., 1092
Thomas, 1202
William, of Derby, and Margaret h.w., 987
Hints (Hyntes), William son of William de, 831
Hiton: see Highton

166

Hobbis (Hobbys), Thomas, clerk, 1173
Hobert: see Hubberd
Hockerston (Hokeneston), John de, and
  Isabel h.w., 913
Hoddinott (Hodinet, Hodynet), Eudes de,
  and Margery h.w., 861
  Margery widow of Eudes de, 876; wife of
  Ede de, 815
Hodegray, Robert, and Margery h.w., 1073
Hodgson (Hoggeson), William, vicar of
  Youlgreave, 1036
Hodinet, Hodynet: see Hoddinott
Hoggeson: see Hodgson
Hogh, Richard, 1192
Hokelowe: see Hucklow
Hokelowe Magna: see Hucklow, Great
Hokenale: see Hucknall
Hokeneston: see Hockerston
Holand: see Hulland
Holborn, Nicholas, 1230
Holbrook (Holbroke), 1340
Holland, Guy, and John his son, 1304
Hollington (Hollyngton, Holynton), 735, 769,
  860, 1228
Hollingworth (Holynworth), Isabel, widow,
  1218
Hollinshead (Holyngshed), Hugh, 1295
Hollis (Hollys), William, gent., 1278; kt,
  1268, 1277, 1300, 1309
Hollyngton: see Hollington
Hollys: see Hollis
Hollywood End (Holywodehede), in
  Ludworth, q.v.
Holme (Hulm(e)), in Bakewell, q.v.; in
  Newbold, q.v.
Holme (Hulm(e)), Geoffrey de, 1031, 1068
  John son of Nicholas de, 797
  Stephen, 1314
Holmesfield (Holmesfeld), William, vicar of
  Tideswell, 1048, 1049
Holmgate (Holmegate), in Clay Lane, q.v.
Holonde: see Hulland
Holt, Thomas de, of Mapperley, and
  Constance h.w., 919
Holyngshed: see Hollinshead
Holynton: see Hollington
Holynworth: see Hollingworth
Holywodehede: see Ludworth, Hollywood
  End in
Home, William, 1252
Honbel, William, of Sudbury, 831
Hone: see Hoon
Honford, John de, and Emma h.w., 879
Hoon (Ho(w)ne, Howen(e)), 720, 792, 795,
  1214, 1231
  manor of, 693
Hope (Hoope, Hope in alto Pecco), 803, 818,

819, 997, 1105, 1132, 1243, 1309, 1319,
  1339
  bailiwick of forester in, 1143
  manor of, 1243
  parish of, 1180
  Richard Walkeden, vicar of, 1084, 1098,
  1105
  William Wodderove of, 1019
Hopkinson (Hopkynson), Francis, 1279; and
  Mary h.w., 1345
Hopowell: see Hopwell
Hopton, 695
Hopton, William de, jun., and Joan h.w., 695
Hopwell (Hopowell), 905, 1238
  manor of, 1238
  Robert de Strelleye of, 905
Horbury (Horbere, Horbyri), William, clerk,
  991; de, and Beatrice h.w., 1040
Hord: see Hurd
Hornby, Henry, clerk, 1173
Horsknave, William le, and Agnes h.w., 703
Horsley (Horseleye), 853
  Roger Normanton of, 1041
Horsley, Adam, clerk, 922
  Thomas, chap., 1013
Horspool (Horspole), John, clerk, 1057
Horton, Walter, esq., 1346
Horwich End (Horwych), in Fernilee, q.v.
Horwood (Horwode), John, and Maude h.w.,
  946
Horwych: see Fernilee, Horwich End in
Hosewyf: see Hussey
Hotost, John, and Margaret h.w., 1106
Houghton: see Pleasley, Stony Houghton in
Howe, John, and Alice h.w., 1322
Howeland: see Howland
Howen(e): see Hoon
Howland (Howeland), Henry, of Astwith,
  989
Howne: see Hoon
Hubbard (Hobert), James, 1163
Hucklow (Hokelowe, Hukelowe), John de,
  915
  William de, 866
Hucklow, Great (Hokelow Magna), 1243
  manor of, 1243
Hucklow (Huk(e)lowe), Great or Little, 1084
  Stephen del Brome of, 967
Hucklow, Little (Parva Hokelowe, Parva
  Huklowe), 1098
  William Bateson of, 779
Hucknall (Hokenale)
  Agnes widow of Richard de, of Ilkeston,
  and John her son, 952
Hudson (Hudeson), Nicholas, and Dorothy
  h.w., 1354
  Thomas son of William, 936

167

Ellen wife of, 937
Huggerford, Robert de, and Margery h.w.,
920
Huk(e)lowe: see Hucklow
Hull, Richard del, parson of Wolverton, 820
Richard son of Nicholas del, of Har-
tington, 747
William del, 808
Hulland (Holand, Holonde), 731, 735, 1149
Fullwood (Fulwode) in, 1149
Hulland (Holand), John de, of Derby, chap.,
929
Otes de, chiv., 859
Thomas de, chiv. and Joan h.w., 859
Hulm(e): see Bakewell, Holme in; Holme;
Newbold, Holme in
Hulton, William de, of Derby, and Margaret
h.w., 964
Huncyndon, Agnes widow of Robert de, 803
Margery widow of Robert de, 818, 819,
821, 822
Hungry Bentley (Benteleye, Bentley), ?895,
1116
manor of, 1116
Hunt (Hunte), John, 1188, 1194, 1222
Richard le, 775
Robert le, of Uttoxeter, and Felise h.w.,
823
Thomas, 965, 1148
William, parson of Gotham, 922
Huntingdon (Huntyngdon), George earl of,
1251
see also Hastings, George
Hurd (Hord), Alan, gent., 1255
Hurley (Herley), Humphrey, and Margaret
h.w., 1203
'Hurst', manor of, 739
Hurst, The (Whitffeld Hurst), in Glossop,
q.v.
Hurt (Hert), Henry, chap., 1192
William, 1299, 1303; of Nether Haddon,
and Margery h.w., 812
Hussey (Hosewyf, Huse), Giles, kt, 1217
John, kt, 1217
Robert, esq., 1217
Roger, 1057
'Hyde'
Richard Lane of, 1041
Hyll: see Hill; Tupton, Hagg Hill in
Hylton: see Hilton
Hymmesworth, Hym(m)ysworth: see Norton,
Hemsworth in
Hynkersell: see Inkersall; Staveley, Inkersall
in
Hyntes: see Hints

Ible (Ibull next Werkysworth), 1185

Idridgehay (Hedricheshay, Idrichehay), 716,
836
Ilkeston, 729, 1001, 1325
Little Hallam (?Halom, Parva Halum) in,
729
manor of, ?813
Richard de Hokenale of, 952
William de Lynton, parson of, 864
Ingewardby: see Ingwardby
Ingmanthorpe (Yngmanthorpe), in Bramp-
ton, q.v.
Ingram, Robert, chiv., 741, 742
Margery daughter of, 741, 742
Orframina wife of, 741
Ingwardby (Ing(e)wardeby)
Nicholas de, 822, 829
Aubrey daughter of, Isabel wife of,
Philip and Thomas sons of, 829
Reginald de, 695
Richard de, parson of Stanton by Bridge,
829
Robert de, 688
William de, 688, 712
Nicholas son of, and John, Nicholas,
Philip, Thomas and William his sons,
712
Inkersall (Hynkersell, Inkersall), in Staveley,
q.v.
Inkersall (Hynkersell), John de, chap., 922
Ireby, Anthony, gent., 1217
Ireland (Irlaunde, Irlond), John, 1157; and
Elizabeth h.w., 1160
Robert de, 734, 757; kt, 904
Isote wife of, 734, 757
John son of, 734, 757; Hawis h.w. and
Robert his brother, 757
Robert son of, 734, 904
Ireton: see Kirk Ireton; Weston Underwood,
Ireton in
Ireton (Irton), John de, 1068
Richard de, 746
Irlaunde, Irlond: see Ireland
Irton: see Ireton

Jacks (Jakes), Thomas, 1155
Jackson (Jakson), John, of Etwall, 982
Jakes: see Jacks
Jakson: see Jackson
James, John, 924
Jeneson (Geneson), Walter, and Margery
h.w., 808
Jewell (Jouell), Robert, and Agnes h.w., 1146
Jeykynson, Robert, clerk, 1202
Johnson, Richard, alias Richard Edmondson,
1359
Roger, 1163
Jolliffe (Jolyf), John, of Tutbury, 894

Jordanthorpe (Jordynthorp, Jurdenthorp), in Norton, q.v.
Jouell: see Jewell
Jow (Jowe), John, clerk, 1078
Jurdenthorp: see Norton, Jordanthorpe in

Kebble: see Keeble
Kedleston (Ketel(e)ston), Ketilston), 919
    manor of, 699
    John Curson of, 1116
    William, parson of, 699
Keeble (Kebble), John, 690
Kelham, Thomas, gent., 1217
Kendal (Kendale), Bartholomew, 1126
    John, 1126
    William, 1126
Kersinton, Kersyngton: see Carsington
Ketel(e)ston: see Kedleston
Keterich, Keterych: see Kittridge
Keteryng: see Kettering
Ketilston: see Kedleston
Kettering (Keteryng), Northants
    John de Outeby, parson of, 970
Kew (Ku), Henry le, and Alice h.w., 763
Kibble, Robert, 690
Kilburn (Kylborne, Kylburne), 1135, 1238, 1340
Killamarsh (Kynewaltmersshe, Kynnolmarsshe, Kynwaldemaysshe, Kynwaldmarshe, Kynwaldmersshe, Kynwalmarsh(e), Kynwelmarsshe, Kynwoldmersshe, Kynwolmarshe, Kynwolmershe), 923, 1023, 1208, 1259, 1268, 1277, 1334, 1348
    manor of, 1268, 1277
    'an iren smythe' in, 1208
    John atte Kirke of, 923
Killamarsh (Kynwaldmersh, Kynwolmarshe, -mershe), Richard, gent., 1348
    Thomas, and Cecily h.w., 1201
    William son of John de, 686
    Maud wife of, 686
Kilvington (Kylvyngton), Richard de, and Margery h.w., 991
Kime (Kyme), William, clerk, 1142
Kinder (Kynder), in Hayfield, q.v.
King's Newton (Kynges Neweton, Kyngys Newton, Neweton), in Melbourne, q.v.
Kingsterndale (Stern(e)dall), 1125, 1301
    Cowdale (Coudale, Cowedale) in, 879, 1111, 1125, 1140, 1148
    Staden (Sta(ve)don, Stadun) in, 1037, 1111, 1125, 1148
    William Ragge of, 999
Kirk (Kirke, Kyrke), John atte, of Killamarsh, 923
    Ralph, 1083; de, and Christian h.w., 1111

Kirk Hallam, Kirkhalum: see Hallam, Kirk
Kirk Ireton, ?1189
    William Alsop of, ?1101
Kirk Langley (Churchelangele, Kirkelongley, Kyrkelangeleye, -long(e)ley, -longeleye, Longeley(e)), 705, 715, 735, 749, 824, 848, 1112, 1170, 1174
    Henry de Meignill of, 705
    William Cursonn, parson of, 848
    William le clerk of, 749
Kittridge (Keterich, Keterych), William, and Deonise h.w., 1064, 1078
Kneton: see Kniveton
Kneveton, Knevyton: see Kniveton
Knifesmith (Knyffesmyth), Alice, 991
Knight (Knyght), Henry, 1241
Knightley (Knyghtley), Richard, and Alice h.w., 1081
Kniveton (Kneton, Kneveton, Knyveton), 695, 735, 803, 818, 819, 821, 822, 830, 1129, 1189
    manor of, 700
    Henry Moyse of, chap., 749
Kniveton (Knevyton, Knyfton, Knyveton), Edmund de, 731
    Eleanor de, 731
    Henry de, kt, 1041
    Henry son of William de, 731
    Isabel wife of, 731
    Humphrey, 1177
    Isabel widow of William de, 731
    John, 1157, 1170, 1176, 1189; de, 731; esq., 1156; son of John de, sen., 961; of Sturston, gent., 1240; of Underwood, gent., 1240; and Anne h.w., xiv
    Margery de, 731
    Matthew, esq., 1240
    Nicholas, 1129; de, 957; esq., 1150; jun. esq., 1147
    Richard, 1153, 1155, 1157, 1161, 1176; esq., 1156, 1171, 1177
    Thomas, and Margaret h.w. and John, Nicholas, Robert and Thomas their sons, 1097
    William son of Henry de, 700
Knowles (Knolles), John, and Constance h.w., 884
Knyffesmyth: see Knifesmith
Knyfton: see Kniveton
Knyght: see Knight
Knyghtley: see Knightley
Knyveton: see Kniveton
Ku: see Kew
Kylborne, Kylburne: see Kilburn
Kylvyngton: see Kilvington
Kyme: see Kime
Kynder: see Hayfield, Kinder in

169

of Harlesthorpe, and Joan h.w., 833
John de, 736
Leicestershire: see Chilcote, Donisthorpe, Groby, Lockington, Long Whatton, Measham, Oakthorpe, Packington, Stretton en le Field, Willesley
Leke: see Leake
Lemmings (Lemyng), William, and Nichola h.w., 915
Lemyngton: see Leamington
Letchworth (Lecheworth), Herts
John de Caldecote, parson of, 797
Letfeld: see Eckington, Litfield in
Leventhorp(e), John, xii; de, 1010
Lever, John, of London, saddler, 1041
Leversage, Leversuche: see Liversidge
'Leverton', Robert Pigot of, 951
Leveson: see Lowson
Levines, Alan de, of Leckhampstead, and Cecily h.w., 954
Ley, William, 1307
see also Lee
Leycamstede: see Leckhampstead
Leycestre: see Leicester
Leynton, John, 1103
Lichefeld: see Litchfield
Lichfield: see Coventry & Lichfield
Lightwood (Lyghtwood), in Eckington or Norton, qq.v.
Limb Hill (Lymhall), in Dore, q.v.
Linacre (Lynacre), in Brampton, q.v.
Linacre (Lynakre), George, esq., 1212
Lincoln, William bishop of, 1103
Lincolnshire: see Boston, Nettleham
Lindale (Lyndale), William de, 690
Linnett (Lynet), William, and Elizabeth h.w., 1014
Linton (Lynton), 1250
Linton (Lynton), William de, parson of Ilkeston, 864
Lisle (Lysle), John viscount, K.G., grand admiral, and lady Joan h.w., 1357
Lister (Lyster), Richard, esq., 1216
Litchurch (Lutchirch, Lutchurch(e), Lytchurche), in Derby, q.v.
Litchfield (Lichefeld), Aymer de, and Margery h.w., 911
Nicholas de, parson of Chesterton, 911
Litfield (Letfeld), in Eckington, q.v.
Little Chester (Parva Chester), in Derby, q.v.
Littlechester (Parva Cestre), Simon de, 727
Little Eaton: see queried entries under Coldeaton
Little Hallam: see Ilkeston, Little Hallam in
Little Hucklow: see Hucklow, Little
Little Longstone: see Longstone, Little

Little Norton (Parva Norton), in Norton, q.v.
Littleover (Parva Over), 1003
Henry Bothe of, 1003
William Buyldyng of, 1003
Litton (Luton, Lytton), 882, 917, 1014, 1047, 1350, 1351
Henry atte Touneshende of, 882
Innocent Trotte of, 917
Litton (Luton, Lytton), John, chap. and Robert his brother, 1136; de, 740; de, and Christian h.w., 931, 945
Thomas, 1260
William, 1148, 1260; gent., 1350
Liversidge (Leversage, Leversuche, Lyversage, Lyversegge), Laurence, and Margaret h.w.,1165
Richard, 1021, 1060
Robert, 1206; and Alice h.w., 1227
Lochagh, Lochawe: see Spondon, Locko in
Lockington (Lokynton), Leics
John de Spondon, vicar of, 787
Lockington (Lokynton), William son of Henry de, of Breaston, and William his son, 726
Locko (Lochagh, Lochawe, Lokhagh, Lokhawe, Lokhaye, Lokkowe, Overlokkowe), in Spondon, q.v.
Locko (Lokkaie), Henry son of John de, chap., 885
Lokynton: see Lockington
London
St Gregory in, John parson of, 743
citizens of: Altham, Edward, 1259; Lever, John, 1041; Metcalf, Jacob, 1259; Palmere, Gratian le, 778, 818; Pygot, William, 819; Sonnyng, Robert, 1259
citizen and clothworker of: Rogers, Richard, 1259
citizens and goldsmiths of: Asshborne, John de, 936; Calton, Thomas, 1310
citizens and mercers of: Aleyn, Christopher, 1255, John, jun., 1255
Long Eaton (Longa Eyton, Longayton, Longeyton), 729, 760, 973, 1262
Henry Randulf of, 760
see also queried entries under Coldeaton
Longedon: see Longstone
Longeley(e): see Kirk Langley; Langley
Longesdon: see Longstone
Longeyton: see Long Eaton
Longford (Langford, Longeford, Longforth), 831, 1205, 1215, 1228
Longford (Langeford, Longeford, Longforth(e)), family, xii, xiii
Nicholas, chiv. and Margery h.w., 971, 972; de, chiv., 737; de, kt, 690; sir, ix

Ralph, 1238; kt, 1250, 1268; kt, and Dorothy h.w., 1277, 1278
Richard de and Joan h.w., 808; de, of Derby, and Sarah h.w., 759
Longstaff (Longstaffe), William, chap., 991
Longstone (Longe(s)don), John de, clerk, 881
John son of Walter de, 745
Longstone, Great (Magna Longuisdon), 835, 1013
Longstone, Great, or Little (Languisdon, Longesdon), 1171
John Foliaumbe of, 885
Richard Foleiaumbe of, 816
Longstone, Little (Parva Longesdon, Parva Longusdon), 816, 835, 885, 887, 944, 1013
manor of, 1013
Monsal Dale (Menesale, Moensall, Mornesale) in, 816, 885, 933, 1013
Roger Foleiaumbe of, 816
Long Whatton (Longa Whatton), Leics
Geoffrey de Chaddesden(e), parson of, 853, 912
Lorimer, John le, of Eaton, 730
William, 991
Lorwenche, John, and Margery h.w., 889
Loscoe (Lasco, Loscowe), 1163, 1181, 1247
manor of, 1163
Lother, Geoffrey, 1023
Loundres, Thomas, and Joan h.w., 1057
Lovell, Thomas, kt, 1163
Lowe, Denis, 1233
Humphrey, and Margaret h.w., 1135, 1158
John, clerk, 1109
Laurence, 1135
George and Thomas brothers of, 1135
Robert, 1233
William, 991; del, 965
Lowson (Leveson), James, esq., 1344
Lucas, Thomas, 1163
Ludworth, Hollywood End (Holywodehede) in, 1080
Lullington (Lullyngton), 1081
Lutchirch, Lutchurch(e): see Derby, Litchurch in
Luton: see Litton
Lyeth, John, 1210
Lyghtwood: see Eckington, Lightwood in; Norton, Lightwood in
Lymestre, John de, 754
Lymhall: see Dore, Limb Hill in
Lynacre: see Brampton, Linacre in
Lynakre: see Linacre
Lyndale: see Lindale
Lynese, Robert, 1266
Lynet: see Linnett
Lynton: see Linton

Lysle: see Lisle
Lyster: see Lister
Lytchurche: see Derby, Litchurch in
Lyteson (Leteson), Robert, 1250
Lyttel Weston: see Weston Underwood, Nether Weston in
Lytton: see Litton
Lyversage, Lyversegge: see Liversidge

Mackley (Mackeleye, Makeley), in Sudbury, q.v.
Mackley (Mackeleye, Makleye), Alice daughter of Ralph de, 895
Thomas de, and Emma h.w., 701
Mackworth (Macworth, Mak(e)worth), 804, 842, 843, 969, 977, 978, 998, 1015, 1216
advowson of, 1216
manor of, 1216
Robert de Assewell, parson of, 904
Thomas Bagenald of, 977
Thomas Tochet, parson of, 966, 1002
William Fairlet of, 969
Mackworth (Macworth, Mak(e)worth), George, and Ann h.w., 1206
John, clerk, 1015, 1022, 1027; de, clerk, 1029
Robert de, 698, 738, 802
Thomas, and Alice h.w., 1022
William de, parson of Shenley, 875
Magna Longesdon: see Longstone, Great
Magna Norton: see Norton
Magna Overe: see Mickleover
Magna Roulesley: see Rowsley
Magna Stretton in Scaruesdale: see Stretton
Magna Tapton: see Tapton
Mainwaring (Maynwaryng), Richard, esq., 1245
Makeley: see Sudbury, Mackley in
Mak(e)worth: see Mackworth
Makleye: see Mackley
Malyverer: see Maleverer
Manchester (Manchastre), John, 1079, 1085
Manger, John, 991
Roger, 991
Mansfield (Maunsfeld), Henry de, 991
Mapelton: see Mapleton
Maperley, Mapirley: see Mapperley
Mapleton (Mapelton)
Callow (Cald(e)lowe) in: see queried entries under Callow, above
Richard Pikard of, 754
Mapelton (Mapulton), Henry son of Geoffrey de, 773
Mapperley (Maperley, Mapirley, Mapurley), 919, 1124, 1152
manor of, 1152
John Pewetrell of, 1008

172

Thomas de Holt of, 919
William Morton of, gent., 1112
Mapulton: see Mapleton
Mapurley: see Mapperley
March (Marche), John, and Agnes h.w., 1081
William del, of Derby, and Alice h.w., 856
Marchington (Marchynton, Marchynton
Mountgomery, Marchyngton sub
Nedwood), Staffs, 884
manor of, 825
Henry Smyth of, 996
Marchington (Marchinton), Ralph de, and
Elizabeth h.w., 724
Reginald de, and Catherine h.w., 724
Mareschal: see Marshall
Mareys: see Marris
Margerrison (Margerieson), Thomas, and
Thomas his son, 808
Markeaton (Mar(ke)ton), 804, 978, 998,
1015, 1216
manor of, 1216
Henry Phelipot of, 978
Markham (Markeham), Ellen, widow, and
William, gent. her son, 1349
Robert, and Ellen h.w., 1214; gent. and
Ellen h.w., 1231
Marmion (Marmyon), Thomas, and Agnes
h.w., 1102
Marris (Mar(r)eys), John, clerk, 692
Nicholas, 692, 771; le, of Edingale, 772
Joan wife of, 692, 771, 772
Richard son of, 771
Marsh (Mersshe), John del, chap., 991
Marshall (Mareschal, Marsshall), William,
991, 1144; le, 808
Marston Montgomery (Merston), ?996, ?1186
Marston on Dove (Merston next Tutbury),
?996, 1168, ?1186
Martell, Robert, 936
Martin (Marten, Martyn), John, and Emma
h.w., 721, 732
Nicholas, chap., 943
Ralph, and Maude h.w. and Ranulf their
son, 1210
William, clerk, 1228
Marton: see Markeaton
Martyn: see Martin
Masey: see Massey
Mason, William, clerk, 1224
Massey (Masey), Robert de, and Maude h.w.,
724
Mather, Edward, 1169
Matheu: see Matthews
Matlock (Matlocke, Mat(te)lok), 873, 892,
1169, 1267, 1281, 1313
Willersley (Willardesleye) in, 769
John Broun of, 995

William Drewe of, tailor, 873
Matlock (Matlok), William son of Richard
de, 873
Matthews (Matheu), Henry, and Lettice h.w.
and Henry their son, 808
Maubank, Philip, and Joan h.w., 992
Mauleverer (Malyverer), Edmund, 1334
Henry, clerk, 1334
Thomas, 1334
William, kt and Joan h.w., 1334
Maunsfeld: see Mansfield
Mawdeley, John, gent., 1215
Maynwaryng: see Mainwaring
Measham (Meysham), manor of, Berford
Maner, 1057
Measham (Meysham), Henry son of William
son of Roger de, 865
Maude, wife of, 865
Medilton: see Middleton; Stoney Middleton
Meignill, Meignyll: see Meynell
Melbourne (Melbourne, Melbourn,
Melburne), 1126, 1128, 1190, 1225, 1297
church of St Michael of, honour of St
Catherine in, 1191
advowson, precentorship and prebend
of, 1191
King's Newton (Kynges Neweton, Kyngys
Newton, Neweton) in, 1126, 1128, 1297
Mellor, Bottom's Hall (Bothum) in, 1080
Menesale: see Longstone, Little, Monsal Dale
in
Mercaston (Murcaston, Myrkaston), 719
manor of, 1097
Mercaston (Merkaston, Murcaston), Robert
de, and Maude h.w., 994
Roger de, 825
Merlege, William, 1117
Merriman (Muryman), Ralph son of Henry,
of Bakewell, 793
Margery wife of, 793
Mersshe: see Marsh
Merston: see Marston
Metcalf, Jacob, of London, clothworker,
1259
Meter, William (le), chap., 885, 887
Meverell, Humphrey, gent., 1189
Mewer, John, chap., 1184
Meyer (Meyre), Henry, 1330
William, 1330
Meygnyll: see Meynell
Meyneley, John, clerk, 1114
Meynell (Meignill, Meignyll, Meygnyll,
Meynill), Giles de, chiv. and John and
Robert his brothers, 824
Henry de, 735; de, of Kirk Langley, 705
Hugh de, chiv., 786, 838, 860
Alice wife of, and John, Robert and

Thomas sons of, 838
Ralph, and Elizabeth his daughter, x
Meyre: see Meyer
Meysham: see Measham
Michel: see Mitchell
Mickleover (Magna Overe)
  Robert vicar of, 740
Middleton (Middelton, Myddelton), John,
  gent., 1210
  Robert, 1108
  Thomas, 1205; gent., 1186
Middleton by Wirksworth (Midylton), ?1177,
  1202
Middleton by Youlgreave (Middelton next
  Yolgreve), ?1177
  manor of, viii, 1085
Middleton: see also Stoney Middleton
Midilton Clyff: see Eyam, The Cliff in
Midylton: see Middleton by Wirksworth
Milltown (Mylnetown), in Ashover, q.v.
Milner (Mylner), Thomas, of Derby, hewer,
  1062
  William, and Alice h.w., 1351
Milton (Mylton), in Repton, q.v.
Milton, John de, chap., 901, 909
  Roger de, 701
Miners: see Mynors
Mitchell (Michel), John, of Coventry, and
  Eleanor h.w., 953
Moensall: see Longstone, Little, Monsal Dale
  in
Mogyn(g)ton: see Weston Underwood, Mug-
  ginton in
Mold (Molde), Robert, clerk, 918; of
  Twyford, 740; parson of Breadsall, 890;
  vicar of Spondon, 864
Mollett (Molet), Thomas, 1175
Moneassh: see Monyash
'Monffreth', 1180
Moniash, Moniasshe: see Monyash
Monnslowe: see Munslow
Monntgomery: see Montgomery
Monnyng, William, clerk, 1168
Monsal Dale (Menesale, Moensall, Mor-
  nesale), in Longstone, Little, q.v.
Montgomery (Monntgomery, Monte
  Gomeri, Monte Gomery, Moungomery,
  Mountgomery), family, xii
  Catherine wife of Walter son of Walter de,
  901, 909
  Edward de, and Catherine h.w., 808, 825,
  831
  John, Thomas and Walter sons of,
  831
  John de, 808; kt, 1160
  Maude widow of Walter de, chiv., 920
  Nicholas, kt, and Joan h.w., 1086

Sir Nicholas, and Anne h.w., x
  Sir Nicholas, son of, xi
  Walter de, chiv., 808, 825
  Alice wife of, 808
  William son of, 825
  Walter de, kt, and Maude h.w., 874
  Nicholas son of, and Ann h.w., 874
  Walter son of Walter de, and Margaret
  h.w., 808
Monyash (Moniash, Moniasshe,
  Monyassh(e), 709, 844, 1148, 1260, 1330
  manor of, 844, 902
Monyash (Moneassh, Monyassh(e)), John
  son of Henry de, 886
  Thomas, clerk, 1114
  William de, vicar of Duffield, 957, 958
Mordaunt, John, 1163
More, Christopher, 1224
  Robert, 1200; clerk, 1240
  Roger, 1202
Morhall: see Morrall
Morley, 919, 1238
  manor of, 864
  Henry Stathum of, 1118
  John Stathum of, 1070
Morley (Morleye), John, jun., 1321
  Lucy de, 836
Mornesale: see Longstone, Little, Monsal
  Dale in
Morrall (Morhall), Thomas de, clerk, 924
Morton, 1255
  John parson of, 834
Morton (Morten), John, and Margery h.w.,
  1152
  Robert, and Alice h.w., 1152
  William, of Mapperley, gent., and Alice
  h.w., 1112
Mosborough (Estmosborugh, Mosburghe), in
  Eckington, q.v.
Moseley, Robert, and Lucy h.w., 1350
Moston, William de, and Lucy h.w., 807
Moton: see Mutton
Moumford: see Mumford
Moungomery: see Montgomery
Mounson, John, esq., 1217
Mountgomery: see Montgomery
Mountjoye (Mountyoye, Munioye), lord: see
  Blount, William
  lords, xii
  Margery widow of Serle de, 734
  William Blount of, kt, 1214
Mourten, William, 1233
Mower, Thomas le, 690
Moyse, Henry, of Kniveton, chap., 749
Mugginton (Mogyn(g)ton), in Weston
  Underwood, q.v.
Mugginton (Mogynton), Robert de, and

176

Over Offerton: see Offerton
Overseal: see Seal
Overton, in Ashover, q.v.
  see also Offerton
Oxeley: see Oxley
Oxenbrig, Thomas, 991
Oxley (Oxeley), James, 1203
Oxton, John de, 922, 993

Packington (Pakynton next Wyvellesleye),
  712
Packman (Pakemon), William, of Derby, and
  Margery h.w., 875
Padley (Padelay), Roger de, 815
  Thomas, and Rose h.w., 1105
Page, Richard, 1133, 1166
  William, and Alice h.w., 1166
Paget, William, kt, 1346; kt and Ann h.w.,
  1335
Paistonhirst: see Peasunhurst
Pakemon: see Packman
Pakynton next Wyvellesleye: see Packington
Palliser (Palisser), William, and Agnes h.w.,
  1184
Palmer (Palmere), Gratian le, of London, and
  Gillian h.w., 778, 818
  Thomas, 1103
Panely, Robert de, Agnes h.w., 728
Pare, John de, parson of Rolleston, 904
Parke, Edward del, and Isabel h.w., 1015
  John, 916, 963
Parkehall: see Pilsley, Park Hall in
Parker, John, 1258; le, and Margery h.w., 808
  William, alias William del Hyll, of Ansty,
  and Ellen h.w., 985
Park Hall (Parkehall in Northwynfeld), in
  Pilsley, q.v.
Parva Cestre/Chester: see Derby, Little
  Chester in
Parva Halum: see Ilkeston, Little Hallam in
Parva Hokelowe, Parva Huklowe: see
  Hucklow, Little
Parva Ireton: see Weston Underwood, Ireton
  in
Parva Longesdon, Parva Longusdon: see
  Longstone, Little
Parva Norton: see Norton, Little Norton in
Parva Over: see Littleover
Parva Tapton: see Tapton
Parva Weston: see Weston Underwood,
  Nether Weston in
Parwich (Parwiche, Parwyche, Perwiche,
  Perwyche, Peverwiche, Peverwych(e)),
  735, 778, 780, 803, 818, 819, 821, 822,
  829, 830, 872, 1102, 1164, 1202, 1284,
  1307, 1315, 1344
  Robert de la Dale of, 822

Thomas de Alsop of, 780
Parwich (Peverwiche), Margery widow of
  Ralph de, 822
  Roger son of Nicholas de, 822
Pattishall (Patteshull), William de, and Joan
  h.w., 857
Payne, John, 1241
Paynell, Richard, and Isabel h.w., 1233
Pearson (Peerson), James, and Ellen h.w.,
  1356
Peasunhurst (Paistonhurst), John de, 922
Pebley, in Barlborough, q.v.
Peerson: see Pearson
Pembridge (Penbrug(g)e), Fulk de, chiv. and
  Margaret h.w., 908
  Isabel widow of Fulk de, kt, 1072
Penkeston: see Pinxton
Penistone (Penystone(e)), John (de), and
  Felise h.w., 881, 891, 990, 1017
Pennant (Pennannt), Edward, 1202
  John, clerk, 1203
Pentrie (Pentrye), John, and Elizabeth h.w.,
  894; del, and Alice h.w., 940
Penyston(e): see Penistone
Percy, Ralph de, chiv., 983
Perkin/Perkinson (Perkyn alias Perkynson),
  John, and Elizabeth h.w., 1227
Perponnte: see Pierrepont
?Pershore (Pershovere), Worcs
  Thomas le Porter of, 798
Perwiche, Perwyche: see Parwich
Peryent, Humphrey, and Joan h.w., 1197
Peveril, honour of, 696
Peverwiche, Peverwych(e): see Parwich
Pewetrell: see Powtrell
Peyt, Richard, son of Thomas and Agnes
  Peyt and brother of Elizabeth Randall,
  1291
Phalange: see Beeley, Fallange in
Phelipot: see Philpott
Philips, John, parson of Cubley, 878
Philpott (Phelipot), Henry, of Markeaton,
  and Maude h.w., 978
Phoside (Fooside), in Hayfield, q.v.
Pickard (Pikard, Pyckard), John, and Alice
  h.w., 1359
  Richard, of Mapleton, and Riquera h.w.,
  754
Pickworth (Pycworth), Nicholas, of Highlow,
  and Margaret h.w., 986
Pierrepont (Perponnte, Pyerponnt), George,
  esq., 1270
  Henry, kt, 1086
  William, kt, 1211
Piggott (Pigot, Pygot), Hugh, of Nettleham,
  and Agnes h.w., 959
  Richard, parson of Pinxton, 815

Humphrey, 1234; and Elizabeth h.w., 1302
Thomas, and Elizabeth h.w., 1234
Quarndon (Quer(u)ndon), Peter de, 694, 753;
de, of Steeple, 711
Quarneby, Querneby: see Quarmby
Quer(u)ndon: see Quarndon
Qwitfeld: see Glossop, Whitfield in
Quarmby (Quarmebye, Quarneby, Quer-
neby), Elizabeth, widow, and Humphrey
her son, 1275
Humphrey, 1234; and Elizabeth h.w., 1302
Thomas, and Elizabeth h.w., 1234
Quarndon (Quer(u)ndon), Peter de, 694, 753;
de, of Steeple, 711
Quarneby, Querneby: see Quarmby
Quer(u)ndon: see Quarndon
Qwitfeld: see Glossop, Whitfield in

Rabb (Rabbe), Walter, and Henry his son,
847
Radbourne (Rodbourn, Rod(e)burne,
Roddeburne, Rodebowrne), 862, 1210
advowson of, 965
manor of, 862, 965
John Brewode, parson of, 978
John Brokhey, parson of, 1112
Robert de Channdos, parson of, 731
Radcliff: see Ratcliffe
Ragg (Ragge), William, and Maude h.w.,
883; of Staden, and Maude h.w., 999
Randall (Randoll), Richard, gent., 1308
William, and Elizbabeth h.w. sister of
Richard Peyt, 1291
Randolph (Randolf, Randulf), Henry, of
Long Eaton, and Alice h.w., 760
Thomas son of Henry, 760
Ratcliffe (Radcliff, Ratclyff), Geoffrey, and
Cecily h.w., 1112
Robert, and Joan h.w. kinswoman and
heir of Ralph Cromwell of Cromwell,
kt, 1124
Raueson: see Rawson
Raulyn: see Rawlings
Ravensnest (Ravennest), in Ashover,
q.v.
Rawlings (Raulyn), Henry, of Wheatcroft,
982
Rawlinson (Rawlynson), Guy, 1218
Rawson (Raueson), Roger, and Joan h.w.,
1036-1038
Reasby, Lionel, 1254
Thomas, 1254
Redman (Rediman, Redyman), Ellen, widow,
1350, 1351
Joyce, 1351
Redser, John, clerk, 986
Redyman: see Redman

Regwell, Regwey: see Eckington, Ridgeway
in
Rempston, Sir Thomas, xii
Thomas, chiv., 1010
Renishaw (Reynaldshawe), in Eckington, q.v.
Repton (Repyn(g)don, Repyngton), 728,
1030, 1035, 1055, 1071, 1082, 1261
manor of, 1261; called 'Strauleyespart',
1041
Milton (Mylton) in, 1261
St Trinity in, John Yong prior of, 1283
John Hanneson of, 1030
Richard Brown (Broun) of, xii, 1030, 1088
Repton (Repyngton), William, 1010
Reresby, Adam de, kt, 690
Ralph de, 690, 775
Retford: see East Retford
Retherby, Peter de, chap., 689
Revell, Hugh, 1166
Robert, 1296
Thomas, 1115, 1296
Reynaldshawe: see Eckington, Renishaw in
Reynold, Richard, 1126
Riboef, Richard son of Richard de, 741, 742
Walter son of, 741, 742
Richmond (Richemund), Yorks N.R.
Henry de Walter, archdeacon of, 844
Riddings (Ryddynge(s)), in Alfreton, q.v.
Rider, Thomas, of Alrewas, and Joan h.w.,
928
Ridware (Rideware, Ryd(e)ware), Bernard,
clerk, 1073
Thomas de, and Agnes h.w., 898
Walter de, chiv. and Joan h.w., 803
Ridewarehampstall: see Hamstall Ridware
Ridge (Rydge), Edward, gent., 1313
Ridgeway (Regwell, Regwey), in Eckington,
q.v.
Ridgeway (Riggeway), John, clerk, 1109
Rigby, Hugh, and Isabel h.w., 1128
Robert, 1128
Riggeway: see Ridgeway
Ripley (Rippleye)
Richard Saundressone of, 927
Riselegh: see Risley
Riseley, Roger son of Richard le, 932
Risley (Riselegh, Ryseleye, Rysley), 717, 729
manor of, 1034
Herbert Wyn of, 697
Hugh Ponger, 717
Rivers (Ryvere), Richard de la, kt, and
Margaret sen. and Margaret jun. his
daughters, 696
Robert, Thomas, brasyer, and Emma h.w.,
1109
Robertson (Robardson), Thomas, of Thul-
ston, 900

179

Ralph de, and Alice h.w., 718
Richard, and Emma h.w., 1044
Roger de, 751
Sherburn (Shirburn), Roger de, 702
Shert: see Shirt
Sherwood (Shirwode), John de, 741
Shethesby, William de, of Coventry, and
  Margery h.w., 899
Shipley, 952
Shipley (Shyppley), Robert, and Eleanor
  h.w., 981
Shippen (Shypen), Robert del, of Derby, and
  Lettice h.w., 854
Shirbrok: see Shirebrook
Shirburn: see Sherburn
Shirebrook (Shirbrok), 896
Shirland
  Reginald Graye of, 991
Shirley (Sherley, Shirleye), Alice, viii
  Ralph de, and Margaret h.w., 822; gent.,
    1225; kt, 1143, 1191
  Roger de, 877
Shirt (Shert), Hugh, and Catherine h.w., 1141
Shirwode: see Sherwood
Shore, Isabel widow of Ralph, 1094
  John, 1094
  Richard de, 1080
Shottle (Shothyll), 1171
  park of, 1171
Shrewsbury, George earl of, 1152, 1153, 1155,
  1245, 1251
Shuckstonefield (Shukthorn(e)), in Crich, q.v.
Shustoke (Shurstoke), Warw.
  Roger le Botyler of, 829
Shydyord: see New Mills, Shedyard in
Shypen: see Shippen
Shyppley: see Shipley
Sidenfen: see Sinfin
Silkstone (Silkestone), John de, 991
Simmonds (Symond(ys)), Humphrey, 1251
  William, gent., 1343
Sinfin (Sidenfen, Syndefen, Synfen), 1303
  manor of, 746
  see also Arleston
Sivekere, Syvekere, Peter le, of Derby, chap.,
  781, 785
Skarysdale: see Scarsdale
Skidmore (Skydemore), John, gent., 1189
Sklater: see Slater
Skorer: see Scorah
Skydemore: see Skidmore
Slack (Sclak), Robert son of Robert del, and
  Thomas his son, 763
Slater (Sclatier, Sklater), Robert, 1081
  William, of Derby, and Lucy h.w., 987
Smalley (Smalleye), 691
  John le Catour of, 691

Smalley (Smalleye), Bartholomew, 1184
  Richard de, and Alice h.w., 900
  Robert, and Lucy h.w., 1145, 1154
Smeton, Robert, chap., 1030
Smisby (Smythesby), 1175
  manor of, 704, 751
Smisby (Smythisby), Thomas de, chap., 826
Smith (Smyth), Henry, of Marchington, and
  Maude h.w., 996
  John, 1200; chap., 948; esq., 1255; le, 808;
    le, of Tideswell, chap., 943
  Ralph the, of Bradwell, 708
  Robert, and Emma h.w. and John their
    son, 1060; of Derby, glover, and Alice
    h.w., 1328
  Thomas, and Joan h.w., 1168
  William, 1014, 1017, 1319
Smythesby, Smythisby: see Smisby
Snaith (Sneyth), John de, and Alice h.w., 810
Snelston (Snelleston), 733, 807, 1207, 1246
  manor of, 874
Sneyth: see Snaith
Solney (Sulny), Alfred son of Alfred de, 841;
  de, chiv., 861, 876
  Sir John, and Alice and Margery his
    sisters, ix
Somerby, Gilbert de, and Maude h.w., and
  Roger his son, 762
Somercotes   (Somercotis,   Somercott,
  Somercotys), in Alfreton, q.v.
Somercotes, Thomas, 1010
Somerles: see Unstone, Summerley in
Somersal (Somersale), John de, chap., 940
Somersal   Herbert   (Churchesomursale,
  Somersale, Somursale), 884
  John FitzHerbert of, 884
  John Shagh of, 976
Somerville (Somervill), Roger de, and
  Margery h.w., 684, 801
Somursale: see Somersal Herbert
Sonnyng, Robert, of London, draper, 1259
Sothyll, Elizabeth, widow, 1167
Souter, John le, of Whitehough, and Alice
  h.w., 968
  Robert le, and Agnes h.w., 808
  Thomas le, and Avis h.w., 808
Southewell: see Southwell
South Normanton (Normanton, Normanton
  next Blacwell, Normonton), ?759, 1332
  advowson of, ix, 815, 861, 876, 972
  manor of, ix, 815, 861, 876, 971
  Carnfield (Carlyngthawyte, Carlyngwayt)
    in, 1133, 1166
  Richard Foliaumbe, parson of, 850
Southwell(Southewell), Richard de, chap.,
  922
South Wingfield: see Wingfield, South

182

benefice of rector of, 1337
manor of, 689, 1337
Inkersall (Hynkersell, Inkersell) in, 1332
  manor of, 1332
Netherthorpe (Staveley Netherthorpe) in,
  1323, 1337
John Thomasson of, 910
Robert de Norton of, 910
Staveley, John, and Agnes h.w., 1056; esq.,
  1293
Staveley Romley: see Clowne, Romeley in
Stayn(e)ston: see Stenson
Staynton, William de, and Agnes h.w., 809
Steeple (Stephull), in Wirksworth, q.v.
Steeple (Stepell), Peter de, of Wirksworth,
  and Margery h.w., 838
Stenson   (Stayn(e)ston,   Stenston,
  Steyn(es)ton, Steynson), 994, 1060,
  1303, 1308, 1326
John Warde of, 1088
Stepell: see Steeple
Stephenson (Stephynson), George, 1342
Richard, and Alice h.w., 1142
Stephull: see Wirksworth, Steeple in
Steppyngstones, John, clerk, 1114
Sternedall: see Kingsterndale
Steynesby: see Ault Hucknall, Stainsby in;
  Stainsby
Steynson (Steyn(es)ton): see Stenson
Stocks (Stok, Stokke(s), Stok(k)ys), Ellis de,
  1029, 1055; del, 1069, 1078
Ellis del, of Derby, and Cecily h.w., 1053
Thomas son of, and Agnes h.w., 1053
John, merchant of the Calais Staple, xiii
Robert del, 1068
Thomas del, of Derby, 1029; del, and
  Agnes h.w., 1068; sen. and Elizabeth
  h.w., 1091
Stoke (Stooke in le Peke), 1121
  manor of, 1121
Stokes, Thomas, of Stotfeld, sen., 1024
Stokke(s), Stok(k)ys: see Stocks
Stone (Ston(es)), Geoffrey del, 822
John del, of Carsington, 1046
Ralph, 1101
Stoney Middleton (Medilton), ?1177
'Stonhallond', in Baslow, q.v.
Stony Houghton (Houghton), in Pleasley,
  q.v.
Stonystan(n)ton: see Stanton by Bridge
Stooke in le Peke: see Stoke
Stotfold (Stotfeld), Beds
Thomas Stokes, sen. of, 1024
Strauley, Hugh de, esq., 1061
John de, kt, and Joan h.w., 1041
Strauleyspart: see Repton, manor
Strecton in Scarvesdale: see Stretton

Stredleye (Stredeleye), Hugh de, 812
Philip son of Philip de, 835
Alice wife of, 835
Street (Strete), William, and Maude h.w.,
  1122
Strelley (Strelleye, Strylley), James, gent. and
  Rachel h.w., 1309
Joan, 1276
John de, of Hazlebadge, kt, 1045
Philip de, and Nichola h.w., 728
Robert de, of Hopwell, and Agnes h.w.,
  905
Strete: see Street
Stretton (Magna Stretton in Scaruesdale,
  Strecton in Scarvesdale), 735
  manor of, 742, 858, ?911
John Cartwright of, ?1024
Stretton en le Field (Stretton, Stretton next
  Appulby), 1024
  manor of, ?911
John Cartwright of, ?1024
Thomas Dexter of, 1024
Strygil, Adam, of Denby, 788
Strylley: see Strelley
Stubben Edge (Stubbyng), in Ashover, q.v.
Stubbyng, Robert, 1298
Stubley, in Dronfield Woodhouse, q.v.
Sturston, 1233
John Knyveton, gent. of, 1240
Styrley, Nicholas, 1247
Sudbury, 920, 1215
  manor of, 808
Mackley (Mackeleye, Makeley) in, 701,
  1214
Ralph de Hiton of, 996
Thomas del Lee of, 996
William Honbel of, 831
Sudbury (Sudbiry), William de, 912
Sudeley, Henry, esq., 1283
Sudell (Sewdell), Richard, chap., 1211; clerk,
  1232, 1242
Sulney: see Newton Solney
Sulny: see Solney
Summerley (Somerles), in Unstone, q.v.
Sutton, Ann Dyxson, daughter of Fulk, 1269
John, and Elizabeth h.w., 1218
John, lord Dudley, 1103
John son of Richard de, of Durham, 784
Joan wife of, 784
Richard de, and Alice h.w., 950; esq., 1199;
  gent., 1178
Robert, esq., 1217
Thomas, gent., 1269
Sutton Coldfield (Sutton in Col(e)feld),
  Warw.
Robert Hillary, parson of, 813, 817
Sutton on the Hill

184

manor of, ?839
Sutton Scarsdale (Sutton en le Dale, Sutton in Dal), 1320, 1331
advowson of, 813
manor of, 813, ?839
Richard de Grey (Gray) of Sandiacre, parson of, 813, 817
see also Duckmanton
Suward: see Seward
Swadlincote (Swart(e)lyngcote), 1326
manor of, 1326
William Baker of, 1082
Swain (Swane), John, 1336
Robert, 1336
Swallow (Swalowe), John, 1258
Swane: see Swain
Swanland (Swanlond), Thomas de, and Elizabeth h.w., 821
Swanwick (Swanwyk(e)), in Alfreton, q.v.
Swart(e)lyngcote: see Swadlincote
Swathwick (Thwathewayte), in Wingerworth, q.v.
Swathwick (Thwathweyt), Richard son of Nicholas de, 791
Edusa wife of, 791
Swift (Swifte, Swyft), Alexander, 1254
John, 1208
Robert, jun. and Ellen h.w. daughter of Nicholas Wykersley, esq., 1254
Swillington (Swyllyngton), Robert de, chiv., 945
Swyft: see Swift
Swyllyngton: see Swillington
Swynnerton (Swynarton), Robert de, chiv. and Joan h.w., 938
Symond(ys): see Simmonds
Syn(de)fen: see Sinfin
Syvekere: see Sivekere

Taberer, William, and Douce h.w., 1156
Taddington (Tadyngton), 1194
Priestcliffe (Presclyff) in, 1194
Taddington (Tadinton), John son of Ives de, 709
Agnes wife of, 709
Tagg (Tagge), William, 1281; and Alice his mother, 1267
Tailboys: see Tallboys
Taillard, Walter, 1057
Taillour: see Taylor
Talbot, Thomas, 1155
see also Shrewsbury
Tallboys (Tailboys), John, esq., 1103; sen., 1090
Tansley (Tannesley), 988
Tapley, Thomas de, of Derby, and Margaret h.w., 966

Tapton (Magna Tapton, Parva Tapton, Tappeton), 851, 922, 959, 962, 991, 1002, 1115, 1127, 1134, 1153, 1155, 1224, 1235, 1329
Tapton, John de, 991; de, and Agnes h.w., 998
Mary de, 991
Robert de, 991
Taylor (Taillour, Tayllour), Adam le, of Harlesthorpe, and Alice h.w., 736
Cuthbert, 1272
John, chap., 1066
Richard, of Trusley, 978
Robert le, of Tideswell, and Margery h.w., 796
William, and Alice h.w., 1093
Temple, Richard, jun., 1264; sen. and Elizabeth h.w., 1264
Tenerey, John, of Eaton, and Margaret h.w., 973
Terry (Tirry, Tyrry), Richard, 808
William, of Cubley, 1005
Thacker, Alan le, 690
Tharlesthorp(e): see Clowne, Harlesthorpe in
Thomas, John son of, 825
Thomasson, John, of Staveley, 910
Thomason, William, and Joan h.w., 825
Thorley, Thomas, chap., 1153; clerk, 1171
Thorneley, Thornell: see Thornhill
Thornesete: see New Mills, Thornsett in
'Thornford'
John Hilberd, parson of, 871
Thornhill (Thorneley, Thornell, Thornhyll), 1236, 1309, 1339
Thornhill (Thornell, Thornhull), John, and Nicholas his son, 1339; jun., 1339
Nicholas, 1223; de, 811
Thomas, 1339
Thornsett (Thornesete), in New Mills, q.v.
Thorpe (Thorp), 773, 1315, 1344
Thorpe (Thorp), Stephen de, jun. and Joan h.w., 1089; de, sen., 1089
Throssell (Throstell, Throstyll), Robert, 1074
William, of Derby, 1087
Thulston (Thurlaston, Thurleston), in Elvaston, q.v.
Thulston (Thurleston), Henry de, of Derby, and Joan h.w., 789
Thurgarton, Notts
Edmund Cooke of, 993
Thurlaston, Thurleston: see Elvaston, Thulston in; Thulston
Thurmundeleye, Richard de, chap., 918
Thurvaston, 831, 1215
Thwathewayte: see Wingerworth, Swathwick in
Thwathweyt: see Swathwick

Wensley (Weddenesleye, Wendesley, Wenneslay, Wen(n)esley), Sir Thomas, xi
Thomas de, 957, 958, 961; de, chiv. 986; de, kt, 965
Thomas son of Roger, 902
Wentworth, Roger, kt and Anne h.w., 1151
Werkesworth: see Wirksworth
Wermynton: see Wormington
'Werrington' (Weryngton)
William del Lee of, 870
Wessington (Wyssyngton), 867
West Broughton (Westbrocton), in Doveridge, q.v.
'Westbury'
Thomas Dobyn, parson of, 815
West Hallam, West Halom: see Hallam, West
Westminster
abbots of monastery of St Peter of: Edmund, 1106; John, 1139, 1142, 1163, 1171, 1180, 1191, 1201, 1216, 1246; Thomas, 1120; William, 1277, 1278, 1280
Thomas bishop of, 1306
West Mosborough (Westmosborugh), in Eckington, q.v.
Weston, Robert de, chap., 929
Thomas son of Thomas de, 779
Isabel wife of, 779
Weston on Trent, 1192
Weston Underwood (Weston Underwodd), 1029
Corkley (Cortelay next Duffeld, Corteley) in, 889, 895
Ireton (Parva Ireton) in, 735, ?1189
William Alsop of, ?1101
Mugginton (Mogyn(g)ton) in, 719, 965, 1097, 1147, 1189
advowson of, 862, 965
Nether Weston (Lyttel Weston, Parva Weston) in, 699
John Burgulon of, 1046
Whaley (Walley), in Bolsover, q.v.
Wheatcroft (Whetecroft, Wheytcroft), in Crich, q.v.
Wheston, 915, 951, 1014, 1139, 1288
Whetecroft, Wheytcroft: see Crich, Wheatcroft in
Whitall: see Whitehall
White, Robert, clerk, 1232
Whitehall (Whitall), William, gent., 1236
Whitehals: see Whitehouse
Whitehough (Whithal(u)gh), in Chapel en le Frith, q.v.
Whitehouse (Whit(e)hals), John, chap., 1099
Nicholas, and Emma h.w., 1130
Richard, 1099
William, of Chesterfield, 1130

Whitewell: see Whitwell
Whitffeld Hurst: see Glossop, The Hurst in
Whitfield (Qwitfeld, Whitffeld), in Glossop, q.v.
Whithalgh: see Chapel en le Frith, Whitehough in
Whitals: see Whitehouse
Whithalugh: see Chapel en le Frith, Whitehough in
Whittle (Whitill), in New Mills, q.v.
Whittington (Whityngton, Whyttyngton), 851, 922, 991, 1079, 1115, 1235
Whittington (Wityngton), Robert de, 991
Whitwell (Whitewell, Whyt(e)well, Wytwell), 871, 992, 1213, 1258, 1278, 1300, 1318
advowson of, 737, 1278, 1318
manor of, 1278, 1318
Whitwell (Whitewell), Robert de, 687, 689
Whorwood, William, gent., 1255
Whyston: see Wheston
Whytewell: see Whitwell
Whyttyngton: see Whittington
Wickersley (Wykersley), Ellen Swyft daughter of Nicholas, esq., 1254
Widdowson (Wydoson), Margaret, widow, 1262
Widmerpool (Wydmerpol), master Robert de, 684
Wigley (Wiggeleye, Wygley), in Brampton, q.v.
Wigley (Wiggeleye, Wygg(e)ley, Wygley), John, 1267; de, 707; de, and Robert his son, 791
Richard, 1267, 1281
William, of Wirksworth, and Agnes h.w., 1070
Wild (Wilde, Wylde), John, of Abney, 1058, 1063
Wildgoose (Wildegos), John, 808
Wilford, Gervase de, 806
Wilkinson (Wylkynson), John, 1316
Willersley (Willardesleye), in Matlock, q.v.
Willesley (Wyllesley, Wyvel(l)esleye), 1264, 1272
manor of, 688, 712
Williamson (Willyamson), Henry, of Cossall, and Margaret h.w., 1118
Williamthorpe (Williamthorp, Wyllyamthorp), in Wingfield, North, q.v.
Willington (Welynton, Wyllyngton, Wylugton), 744, 1088, 1168, 1326
manor of, xii, 1326
Simon Cundi of, 744
Willoughby (Wyll(o)ughby, Wylughby), Henry, kt, 1158, 1163, 1182
Sir Henry, xiv
Hugh de, son of Edward de, 1034

Hugh de, son of Hugh de, 1034
  Joan wife of, 1034
  Richard de, and Isabel h.w., 717
  Robert, esq. and Margaret h.w., 1119; de
    Broke, kt, 1163
Willyamson: see Williamson
Wilne (Wylne), 934, 1188
Wilne (Wylne), John (deceased), and
  Margaret his widow and Thomas his
  son, 1225
John (sen.), and Margaret h.w., 1190, 1191
  Thomas son of, 1190
Wilson, Ralph, and Agnes h.w., 1263
  Richard, 1241
Wiltshire: see Bottlesford
Wimbush (Wymbyssh), Nicholas, clerk, 1057
Windley (Wyndley, Wyn(d)eley, Wynle),
  1147, 1150, 1189, 1238
  manor of, 799
Windleyhill (Wyndeley Hill, Wyndleyhill)
  in, 1150, 1189
  manor of, 1189
'Wyndeley Riche', 'Wyndeleyryche' ?in,
  1147, 1189
Windsor (Wyndesore), Andrew, 1216
Wingerworth (Wyngerworth, Wyngirworth,
  Wyngreworth), 962, 1274, 1276, 1280,
  1290, 1293
  manor of, 782, 924, 1020
  Swathwick (Thwathewayte) in, 1115
Wingerworth (Wyngreworth), Roger de, 1020
Wingfield (Wynfeld), Roger son of Robert
  de, of Ashover, 775
Wingfield, North (Hallewynnefeld, North-
  wynfeld), 1255
  Williamthorpe (Williamthorp, Wyllyamth-
    orp) in, 942, 1332
  manor of, 938, 939, 1332
  Walter parson of, 834
Wingfield, North or South (Wyn(e)feld),
  manor of, 696, 1059
Wingfield, South
  Oakerthorpe (Ulkerthorp, Ulgarthorp) in,
    1252
  Nicholas Bawekewell of, 1154
  William Ulkerthorp of, 1090; esq., 1079
  Ufton in, 888
  manor of, 945, 1090
Winster (Wynster, Wynst(o)re, Wynstur),
  695, 849, 1136, 1201, 1215, 1238
  manor of, 1215
Winster (Wynstre), Roger de, and Annabel
  h.w., 877
Winter (Wynter), Robert, 1192
Wirksworth (Werkesworth, Wircusworthe,
  Wirkesworth, Workesworth, Workys-
  werth, Workysworth, Wyrkesworth,

Wyrkysworth(e)), 711, 735, 830, 838,
  995, 1182, 1202, 1203, 1342, 1354
  Steeple (Stephull) in
  Peter de Querundon of, 711
  Peter de Stepell of, 838
  Thomas de Castelton, vicar of, 921
  William Wygley of, 1070
Wirksworth (Wirkesworth), Robert de, chap.,
  849
'Witton', 831
Witty, Thomas, parson of Breadsall, 963
Wityngton: see Whittington
'Wlrychecroft', in 'Lee', q.v.
Wodderove: see Woodroffe
Wode: see Wood
Wodeford: see Woodford
Wodehous(e): see Woodhouse
Wodeward: see Woodward
Wodroffe: see Woodroffe
Woley(e): see Woolley
Wolseley, John, esq., 1264
Wolverton (Wolvardynton), Warw.
  Richard del Hull, parson of, 820
Wombwell (Wombewell), Thomas de, 941
Wood (Wode), John atte, Deonise h.w., 891;
  del, 991
  William atte, serjeant at arms, 868; del.
    chap., 1013
Woodford (Wodeford), Richard de, and Joan
  h.w., 715, 848
Woodhouse (Wodehous(e)), John, and
  Margery h.w., 1098
  William de, 954
Woodhowse: see Dronfield Woodhouse
Woodroffe (Wodderove, Wodroffe), George,
  1243
  Robert, 1019
  William, of Hope, 1019
Woodward (Wodeward), Robert le, 808
Woolley (Woley(e)), Richard de, and Joan
  h.w., 914
  William, and Emma h.w., 1100
Worcestershire: see Pershore
Workesworth, Workyswerth, Workysworth:
  see Wirksworth
Wormhill (Wormehill, Wormehull,
  Wormhull(e)), 778, 1009, 1019, 1039,
  1047, 1066, 1108, 1131, 1139, 1314
  Hargatewall (Hardyk(e)wall, Herdwy-
    kwall) in, 1075, 1257, 1279, 1292
  see also Fairfield, Green, Pig Tor in
Wormehill (Worm(e)hull), Thomas de, and
  Joan h.w., 721
  Thomas son of Alan de, 732
    Joan wife of, 732
Wormington (Wermynton), Robert, of
  Harboro', and Alice h.w., 1074

189

Wright (Wryght), John le, of Eyam, and Joan h.w., 943
Nicholas, and Ellen h.w., 1314
Richard, 1087
Wrightrichefeld: see Brushfield
Wrottesley, Walter, 1251
Wryght: see Wright
Wyaston (Wyardeston), 735
Wyatt (Wyot), John, 1135
Wychard, John son of Henry of 'Osbaston', 727
John son of John, 727
Alice wife of, 727
Wydmerpol: see Widmerpool
Wydoson: see Widdowson
Wygg(e)ley, Wygley: see Wigley
Wykersley: see Wickersley
Wylde: see Wild
'Wyleston', advowson of, 1113
Wylkynson: see Wilkinson
Wyllesley: see Willesley
Wyll(o)ughby: see Willoughby
Wyllyamson: see Williamson
Wyllyamthorp: see Wingfield, North, Williamthorpe in
Wyllyngton: see Willington
Wylne: see Wilne
Wylughby: see Willoughby
Wylugton: see Willington
Wymbyssh: see Wimbush
Wymeswold (Wymondeswold, Wymondsold), John, 1147
William, 1184
Wyn: see Wynn
Wyndeley: see Windley
Wyndeley Hill: see Windley, Windleyhill in
'Wyndeley Riche', ?in Windley, q.v.
Wyndesore: see Windsor
Wyndley: see Windley
Wyne, John le, chiv., 815
Elizabeth wife of, and Roger de Padelay, her guardian, 815
Wynefeld: see Wingfield
Wyneley: see Windley
Wynfeld: see Wingfield
Wyngerworth, Wyngirworth, Wyngreworth: see Wingerworth
Wynle: see Windley
Wynn (Wyn), Herbert, of Risley, and Maude h.w., 697
William le, chiv., 861
Wynster, Wynst(o)re, Wynstur: see Winster

Wynter: see Winter
Wyot: see Wyatt
Wyrkesworth, Wyrkysworth(e): see Wirksworth
Wyrthorp, William son of Richard de, 806
Agnes wife of, 806
Wyssyngton: see Wessington
Wytwell: see Whitwell
Wyvel(l)esleye: see Willesley

Yardley (Yerdeley(e)), Hugh, 1250, 1251
Walter de, and Hawis h.w., 808
Yates (Yate), John, 1347
Roger atte, and Avis h.w., 808
Yeaveley (Yeveleye), 735, 766
Yeldersley (Yildersley, Yildresleye), 1157, 1160
manor of, 734, 1160
Fenton in, 1233
Yeldersley (Yildreslegh), Robert, de, chap., 757
Yelgreve: see Youlgreave
Yerdeley(e): see Yardley
Yeveleye: see Yeaveley
Yildersley, Yildreslegh, Yildresleye: see Yeldersley
Yngmanthorpe: see Brampton, Ingmanthorpe in
Yolgreve: see Youlgreave
Yong(e): see Young
York, Henry duke of, xiv
Yorkshire E.R.: see Harpham
Yorkshire N.R.: see Richmond
Yorkshire W.R.: see Badsworth, Barkston, Beauchief, Dore, Norton, Saxton, Sheffield, Totley
Youlgreave (Yelgreve, Yolgreve), 790, 834, 887, 944
manor of, 835
Alport (Aldeport) in, 944
mill in, 958, 961, 1085
William Hoggeson, vicar of, 1036
Young (Yong(e)), John, prior of the monastery of St Trinity, Repton, 1283
Robert, 1106
Yoxall (Yoxhale), Staffs
Gilbert Henry of, 771

Zouche, Sir John, xiv
Philip la, 765
William la, Oakthorpe, 765